JOY

IS AN INSIDE JOB!

And it's FREE!

12 Timeless Secrets for
Abundance, Radiant Health and
Lifelong Happiness

Amanda Gore and Lenore Lewis

JOY IS AN INSIDE JOB

0 ——————————————————————————— -10
Death.   Bursting with energy
                                         and vitality and joy of life.

AMANDA GORE AND LENORE LEWIS

Published by Head2Heart Pty Ltd

ABN 73 088 184 810

Buderim. QLD 4556 Australia

Australia

61 414 282218

email: amanda@amandagore.com

Distributed by Head2Heart Pty Ltd.

For ordering information or special discounts for bulk purchases, please contact Amanda Gore on

amanda@amandagore.com

ISBN 978-0-9818794-7-5

Second edition. February 2015.

First published as The Gospel of Joy in 2009.

www.amandagore.com
www.thejoyproject.com
www.joyisaninsidejob.com

CONTENTS:

Note

The Real Authors Of This Book!

Writing this book changed my life! It taught me the vast difference between happiness and JOY!

This note is to share some of my experiences with you. I trust that you too will find the process of reading this book a blessing; and that it helps you discover your own path to joy, as writing it has done for me.

This whole book is dedicated to eradicating fear, eliminating un-happiness, giving you more control over your moods and helping you soar through the clouds to the Divine sunshine above.

25 years ago, I was a physiotherapist in Australia, working in sports medicine, ergonomics and occupational health. I had coauthored a book called The Office Athlete, which prompted a meeting planner to invite me to a conference.

Noted inspirational speaker Ron Tacchi was the emcee at the conference, and at the end of my session, he said, *"You should be a speaker!"* I answered, *"What's a speaker?"*

Ron then mentored me into the business, which in itself was a huge blessing. I have been speaking, consulting and writing since then about joy, emotional intelligence, leadership, connection, the human spirit, communication and relationships.

I lived in the United States for eight years from 2000 and was blessed from the moment my feet hit the ground there! The journey through writing this book has led me to a whole new dimension and understanding of life.

I had the knowledge in my head of all the principles and ideas I elaborate on here prior to writing the book, but I did not truly know all of them; I didn't have them embedded in my heart. I didn't operate from those principles, although I tried to.

For example, I understood forgiveness as an intellectual concept that I knew was important, but I now know about it in my heart, comprehend it better, and have experienced forgiveness - and being forgiven, although I am still working on both!

Instead of struggling with just writing about equanimity or inner peace, I have had some blinding flashes of the obvious and can see many aspects of my life from a completely different level and am behaving differently - with more peace and calm!

I did not create this book! I wrote it, of course, but really my Mum, who passed away in 2006, and her "spiritual writing team", (which included Miss Steve, my English teacher for all my years in primary school) created it. I was just a scribe!

Many people may find this hard to believe or imagine, but it's my belief system, and my experiences since then have shown me just how alive and constantly present my Mum's spirit is!

Have you ever woken up with a crystal clear thought or idea, seemingly out of nowhere?

Well, one morning, almost a year after Mum passed, after months of struggling with how to write this book, I woke up and I knew it was to be about joy; and I knew that the format it followed would be 12 secrets and weeks to joy, and I knew Mum and her team would help me, and I knew I had to meditate! So I did!

And each morning an idea would come to me and I would sit in silence with it, and then go and write. It only took about two days for each chapter as the words flowed easily out onto the pages.

I could feel Mum, Gracie and Miss Steve and a host of others helping me in this process. It was an amazing experience!

I want to thank them for patiently teaching me such spectacular lessons which have made my life much more joyful, and hopefully will allow you to see the astonishing light you truly are.

Disclaimer

This publication is for information purposes only, and is designed as a general reference and catalyst to seeking further information about some aspects of self-care. The authors and editors are not responsible for the results of any actions taken on the basis of any information neither in this publication, nor for any error in or omission from this publication.

Neither the publisher, nor online publisher, is engaged in giving medical or other advice or services. The publisher, online publisher, authors and editors, expressly disclaim all and any liability and responsibility to any person, whether a reader of this publication or not, in respect of anything, and of the consequences of anything done or omitted to be done by any such person in reliance, whether wholly or partially, upon the whole or any part of the content of this publication.

People should exercise their own independent skill or judgment or seek professional advice before relying on the information contained in this publication.

No legal liability or responsibility for any injury, loss or damage incurred by the use of, or reliance on, or interpretation of, the information contained in this publication is accepted.

Important Note:

My faith is in a spiritual not religious God, so I write about it here. My God is a Universal source of love, energy and power and based on years of reading, courses and experiences; a blend of beliefs from Quantum physics, Rudolf Steiner philosophies, Florence Shinn, the Bible and ancient wisdom philosophies!

If this is not appropriate or comfortable for you, please replace it with The Divine, Spirit, Universe, Source, Buddha, Allah, Love, Your Heart, Higher Wisdom, your higher self, your true self, your inside GOD or whatever it is that you believe in and can relate and connect to.

I truly believe we are all one and there is no separation - so we all have an 'inner God' that is a hologram of the larger "God" or force, energy, power etc.

I believe it's important to avoid judgment and allow everyone to have the freedom to have faith in whatever we wish, even if it is just ourselves. (Although if your faith is just in yourself – you may wish to consider something a little bit bigger!)

The fundamental secret to JOY is to

1. Connect to GOD (see above!)

and

2. Serve others in some way

THANKS MUM! LOVE YOU!

Acknowledgements

There are a lot people to thank for their contribution to, and influence on, this book. Just some of them are listed here.

I am blessed to know them all and grateful for their amazing contributions to my life.

God

Mum – Lenore Lewis

Miss Steve

Ken Wright

Mary Forte

Somer McCormick

Clelia Simart

Denise Rizzo

Michael Grinder

Keith Harrell

Jennifer Griffin

Sheryl Martin

My Lord

Gracie

The Committee

Robert and Cheryl Sardello

Kathy Warner, Bob Simmonds

Thomas Simart

Simon Gore

Dianne Hermans

Julianna Millar

Brenda Bailey

The Poscentes

Mel Davis

SPECIAL ACKNOWLEDGEMENTS

Robert and Cheryl Sardello from the School of Spiritual Psychology deserve a special mention for their contribution in developing my heart capacities, which are now clearly reflected in all I do. Through their writings and courses, many lives have changed or been transformed, including mine.

Without their work, this book would have been very different. Thank you both with my whole heart. The website for the classes is www. spiritualschool.org.

Mary Forte's inspired guidance made the final book possible. Bless you and thank you Mary.

JOY IS AN INSIDE JOB

Unlock the Secrets for Creating Abundance, Radiant Health and Lifelong Happiness!

"Jubilation is the motto for future times. In joy lies the greatest force." [1]

Prologue

MY JOURNEY!

When I began writing this book, I had no idea how to do it! Joy is not something we talk or think about much. Where would I start? What do I know about joy? How do you define it? How do you teach it? I had a million other questions.

My time frame was originally to write this book in February 2006, but destiny stepped in and my precious mother, Lenore Joan Lewis, a remarkable, courageous and beautiful woman, crossed the threshold that month.

36 months later, my mother was with me still - helping me write this book! I had worked inwardly a great deal since she passed and I had come to realize that joy is both complex and simple at the same time.

In a nutshell, joy comes from a relationship with God and/or the Divine.

It is so simple to do the little things that accumulate and create a soul bursting with joy. It may not always be easy, but it is simple!

And not much of what I write is new - but there may be new ways for you to look at things, We all know what needs to be done, but it's the doing it that is often the challenge!

And that's the aim of this book—to help you do those things! It gives you small steps that you can take, each one of which shares with you a different aspect of joy; all of which leads you towards living joyfully.

Follow the ideas and JOY- ercises, and keep a journal.

Review your joy level along the way. You might be amazed at how dramatically – and quickly - you change! This book is for everyone. It relates to both single and married people; to people with children or not; to ALL humans. We need to learn these secrets as it is part of our purpose in life. I have mentioned children as the bulk of people have children of their own; or are aunts of uncles. We can all be great role models for children to learn these sacred secrets!

This book is a gift from my mother, both to you and to me.

Another gift in this process was the little farmhouse my husband and I found in Vermont. The peace, silence and beauty I experienced there was perfect for writing. I knew that my mother helped us to find this haven, where I have been able to experience my own journey to joy. Bless you and thank you Mama!

Love and giving thanks is the essence of this book:

Love and gratitude.

From gratitude comes joy.

From reverence, comes gratitude.

From service, comes reverence.

From compassion, comes service.

From love, comes compassion.

In fact, everything good comes from love!

THE JOY PROJECT
FINDING JOY IN EVERYDAY LIFE

The most important thing in life is how you feel about yourself. The mission of the JOY project is to help people live from their hearts, eradicate fear and feel great.

It has been a fascinating journey returning to Australia and launching The Joy Project, which emerged from the book!

We have to date sold thousands of copies of this book and people have written amazing comments about their experiences, as they played through the daily joy-ercises.

This book is the "gateway" into your awareness. You will learn to live from the wisdom of your heart, not being controlled by your old habits, patterns, fears or emotions. *You will learn to feel great (or even better!) about yourself – which changes everything else around you.*

I was given an image one day of the earth as a beautiful globe with millions of tiny windows opening up all over it. As the windows opened, sparkling light would shine out.

I realized those windows represented the book and that as people opened the book and read it, they would see what glorious creatures of light they really were! They could see their true, astonishing nature!

MOST PEOPLE THINK THEY WANT TO BE HAPPY!

But happiness is just the beginning!

When asked, the number one thing people say they want is happiness. But *really* what they want is JOY!

The way I describe the difference is to imagine yourself running in an endless, pitch black corridor. It's black because it's full of your fears. You are desperately trying to find a light switch or window so you can see the light! And finally you do – the light comes on - you can breathe again. The fears are gone. You are happy at last.

But, very soon, the light bulb blows or worse, someone turns the light switch off and your happiness is plunged into dark fears again. Happiness is usually dependent on something external from you.

If you stood still in the dark long enough, and breathed, you would notice a faint light shining. The more you focused on it, the brighter and more beautiful it becomes. You would notice that the light is coming from inside you!

That is your JOY! The inner light that is always with you. Nothing can take it away from you.

True JOY is an inside job! It's that feeling you have when a two year old who adores you runs towards you with their arms outstretched yelling out your name!

Or the profound contentment and peace that comes when you are able to enjoy nature and her magnificence – watching a gorgeous sunset or sunrise.

It's that sense of fulfillment when you have genuinely helped someone else; the enthusiasm that comes from focusing on gratitude and not misery; the ability to love yourself and others and be compassionate and generous; to laugh, live through inspiration and not fear; to listen carefully and just generally have a deep sense of "all is well in my world" – even when it does not look like that!

This book teaches you how to discover your joy, share it with others – and help them to find their own joy!

Please share it with as many as you can (many buy copies for all their family and friends after they read it!)

Remember the parable "give a man a fish and he eats for a day. Teach him to fish and he eats for a lifetime"? In the same way, *giving someone this book teaches them how to live joyfully every day for the rest of their lives.*

FORM A JOY TRIBE – IT'S *FREE* AND FUN!

Gather together a group of like hearted, not just like-minded people, to support each other and share experiences as you travel through this book together. This is your "joy tribe"!

A joy tribe is like a book club but more fun! You all *play* your way through the daily JOY-ercises and practices. Do this with your children, life partner, best friend, colleagues at work, team mates – anyone else who is interested in being all they can joyfully be, and finding their own light!

It's a lot of fun when a few of you do it together! And *really* powerful when you do it as a family together.

YOUR TRIBE'S MISSION

As your tribe progresses through the secrets to joy, you can identify a mission – a way to serve others in any creative way.

Find lonely old people or children and do something to bring them joy; volunteer as a group somewhere; send packages to the military or poverty stricken nations; help children feel loved, worthy of love and that they are special; raise money for a worthy cause; create your own joy bookers scrapbook club; or just start with helping everyone in your tribe feel great about themselves!

The ideas are infinite. In this way you create your own "mini joy movement"! And contribute to our global joy movement.

And visit us at www.thejoyproject.com to learn more about creating "joy spots" and all aspects of joy – and connect to the global joy movement!

Isn't it exciting to be part of something so amazing? You will be part of an organization dedicated to helping everyone eradicate fear and find joy in everyday life.

I am full of awe and gratitude for you buying this book, hopefully creating your tribe, starting a mini joy movement and connecting and contributing to this significant global shift!

PS. We have an ***Online Joy School*** based on this book with expanded JOY-ercises, videos and activities! Visit us to find out more or join our membership at www.thejoyproject.com.

Introduction

> *"This is the day the Lord has made and*
> *I will rejoice and be glad in it."*
> *Psalm 118:24*

Joy is a gift for those who have a pure heart.

WHAT'S A PURE HEART?

A pure heart is one that wants only good for everybody; sees good in everyone and everything; and seeks opportunities to bring into the world. It means we can *truly* feel joy. *Fear stops us from feeling joy.*

Joy is like a hologram. No matter how many pieces the hologram image breaks into, the whole is always within the piece. *Remembering we are whole, and staying connected to our spiritual nature,* is fundamental for us to feel joy!

Our life journey is to *reconnect* to our wholeness – to that joy. It takes effort, awareness and waking up!

WE NEED TO WAKE UP!

We need to *wake up to and become conscious of* the importance of connecting to the *field of love* (or Divine realms if you prefer), connecting to *ourselves* and connecting to and *serving others* – this is the recipe for a joy filled life. It's a powerful habit to practice!

Our life quest is to manifest the whole. To develop the sacred capacity to "see" with a pure heart, and experience the wholeness in all the other hologram pieces called humans!

That is, to realize *we are one* with everyone and everything. That's the condition where true joy lives.

HOW TO USE THIS BOOK

You can read it all the way through, and simply focus on the secrets that resonate with you. Or skim through it and just pick out areas that you would like to work on.

You can open it at random, asking your higher self to show you what you need to learn right now. Focus on what you find on that page. It's fascinating how often that page has particular meaning for you at that moment.

Or, you can just dive in and make this a planned journey to joy. Do this by yourself, or with your tribe, family or friends. Working through the book and doing the joy-ercises alone or together, can lead to amazing insights - because we are actually practicing new habits and ways of thinking, even if we don't think the practice will help.

Doing anything for 66 days (*not* 21!) can make it a new habit. Most of us practice all our bad habits and patterns repeatedly for years!

This book is full of ways to practice new, joy creating habits and patterns! They work for you as an individual or a tribe.

It's like a parents manual for raising joyful, conscious, emotionally secure adults!

NOTES ON THINKING, CHANGE AND CHOICES!

"True thinking" happens in your heart – it's a "knowing" or sometimes a gut feeling.

Put your attention in your heart. Ask the questions *from* your heart. Then listen *to* your heart.

We *seem* to do all our thinking and self-talk in our heads, but our hearts really need to be in charge of our thinking and behavior.

Do you remember the old cartoons that had a character with a little devil sitting on one shoulder and an angel on the other, each competing to influence the person? This is how I imagine thinking with our heart operates. We have an imaginary "strategy box" sitting above our left shoulder and a "conscience box" on our right, and both of them are connected to our heart.

The heart "thinks" by receiving input from each box, and then it makes a choice as to what our right action or behavior will be.

Our hearts need to choose to follow Divine *inspiration*, which comes through the "conscience box". It's wise to *mindfully* filter all our decisions through the "conscience box".

The heart seeks information on *ways to behave* from the "strategy box" and if a faulty program, belief or fear is installed in the "strategy box", our hearts continue to make unwise decisions and our behaviors remain the same.

We need to *wake up to and recognize the faulty habits, programs, fears, beliefs and self talk* and act on the pure inspiration of the "conscience box".

Fear Rules Many of Us!

We are living lives of habits and patterns ruled unconsciously by fear.

We need to wake up to the fears embedded in the strategy box. Our environment is one of the many factors unconsciously influencing our choices. Others are genes, beliefs, family patterns and stories and what we saw our parents do.

We *must* learn to make the right choices, *inspired* choices. If we ask for help, and listen to the wisdom we are given, we will always be guided wisely. It's through our hearts and bodies that we feel and experience everything. When our hearts make wise choices, we feel calm and peaceful. *A churning stomach is often a sign of a poor decision or choice of strategy!*

We rarely understand the significance of our *physical* heart—until it stops working. What happens then? We die! Remember, we can be brain-dead and still alive, but since the physical body needs oxygen, once our heart stops, we can't survive.

Our spiritual heart is the portal for Divine love and pumps its life forces through our beings. The spiritual body needs to *give love* and to *have love*.

DROP TO YOUR HEART!

A great habit to develop that I mention throughout this book is learning how to "drop" to your heart to receive guidance.

I have done this unconsciously in the past, but learned so much more about the technique and its impact from Robert and Cheryl Sardello. I'll talk more about this later, but at its simplest, this is how it works:

To "think" with your heart and hear the heart's guidance, find a quiet spot (if needed), and become aware of the area around your heart. Focus on that area and see if you can "drop" your attention down to that part.

Then imagine that you are breathing through your heart; that the breath flows in and out through your heart.

As you continue to do that for a few minutes, a sense of peace and calm may flow through you. You may feel safe and secure, and after a time, there will be a sense of "knowing" what you need to do in a particular situation. Especially if you asked a question first!

You may also find that words flow into your consciousness. Or perhaps an image will float through that gives you an answer you needed, or some insight that solves a difficulty for you.

You may even feel a sense of compassion that helps you understand why another person is acting the way they are, and that will help you resolve a problem. A brilliant idea may even "pop" into your thinking! That's the way the heart works—it is *subtle, kind and very wise.*

Take a little time now to practice this exercise. You only need a couple of minutes. Once you are used to this, it becomes a joy creating habit and takes only a few seconds to have heart consciousness and access to that wisdom and love.

Go Via The Chute!

Another way you may be able to enter into your heart is by imagining a chute—like a laundry chute—going from the top of your head down through your body to the center of your heart.

Imagine a miniature you sliding down the chute, and landing gently in the interior space of your heart. Just allow yourself to be in there; stay and rest a while in the silence, beauty and peace.

YOU *CAN* CHANGE!

Neuroscience is showing us that we *can* change! A leopard *can* change its spots, and you *can* teach an old dog new tricks! *What we have learned is just what we have learned* and hardwired into our brains!

It then becomes a *habit or a pattern* of behavior or thinking. It's not absolute truth! It can be *un*-hardwired and *re*-hardwired differently which means *we can learn new behaviors and new ways to think and perceive the world.*

Try this. Cross your arms. Look at which hand or arm is on top. Exactly reverse them. Could you do it easily – or did you have to think about it? Did it confuse you? Did it feel uncomfortable? There is no reason for this other than you are used to the original way! Neither is "normal"! It's a learned habit.

As toddlers, we don't cross our arms until we copy our parents and adults to look cool! Or "kewl" as they teach me to say! Its not natural for us to cross our arms but we persevere and learn to feel comfortable one way!

We *really can* re-hardwire our brains and change our behaviors, but it feels strange until the "new" way has become the new habit.

WHY CHANGE APPEARS DIFFICULT

A critical life and joy skill is to learn, unlearn and relearn all our lives! Unlearn old habits and learn new ones! When we are asked to do something new, or we practice something new, the prefrontal cortex at the very front of our brains works really hard and sucks up tons of oxygen making us feel tired, and sometimes drained!

Remember when you were learning to drive? How challenging, scary and hard that was because there were so many new things we had to pay attention to? It was probably even more scary for our parents!

Well, what happens now? Sometimes I bet you arrive home and you can't remember one thing about the driving there!

After you have mastered a new skill or behavior, it is relegated to, and stored in, the basal ganglia - another part of your brain that is like the archive of every habit or pattern you have learned!

I started learning how to play the harp when I was 50 and it was enormously difficult, as I didn't even know how to read music! To coordinate my hands to do separate things, have them in the correct position, remember where the strings were *and* read the music was way too much initially!

But I persevered with my saint of a teacher and eventually it became easier. And we all know that practice makes perfect! In my case, it was practice meant at least I could identify the strings!

When you practice new JOYful habits for sixty six days *continuously*, you might be amazed at the changes you experience! Hey, that's only 2 months!

THE REAL "F" WORD - FEAR!

Change is often something that makes us all feel the "F" word! Fear! Fear is the real "F" word!

There is a little section in the oldest part of the brain (the limbic system) that lies right next to the prefrontal cortex. It's called the amygdala - I call it AMMY for short! AMMY tells us when to be fearful.

It's easy to trigger AMMY when we are doing new things because of its proximity to the prefrontal cortex, and AMMY'S life is dedicated to our survival not our success. It tells us to keep things as they are; to avoid anything that seems difficult, strange or new. It sees risk in anything that will bring about change.

And that was really useful in the days where doing something different could mean we could be attacked by a sabre tooth tiger and die! In scientific terms, this triggering of AMMY is called the "amygdala hijack" (found in Daniel Goleman's book *"Emotional Intelligence"*).

It's when we are instantly transported to a state of terror and can no longer think clearly. It might be called panic or an anxiety attack. But learning how to do a new behavior, make a change or think differently does not often (these days) expose us to potential death!

So although AMMY is trying to protect us, it often blocks our progress. Anytime we are presented with something like a new job, AMMY can send such bolts of terror through us that we can no longer learn or be effective, and we do stupid things - or worse, we give up!

The Inner Genius

In Seth Godin's book *"Linchpin"*, he talks about the lizard brain being *"hungry, scared, angry, and horny!"*

He mentions The TED clip of Elizabeth Gilbert the author of "Eat. Love. Pray", in which she talks about the "daemon" or inner genius that we all have. He says that the daemon has no control over the

AMMY as it tries to get you to *"shut up, sit down and do your day job"*, and not be noticed.

AMMY is extraordinarily clever at creating all sorts of distractions, rationalizations, procrastinations, fears, illnesses, worries and anything else that will stop your genius being released. Releasing your creative genius is stepping into the unknown and the unknown is a panic button for AMMY!

I remember as a little girl I was terrified of the dark - and yet as soon as the light went on, the fear disappeared. *Light does that to fear*! It helps to understand what is going on *physiologically* when we approach anything new. And by understanding our fears - we shine a light on them and see that really we are safe – and the fear is *usually* unfounded.

When they are unfounded, we need to retrain AMMY. Each time we wake up to an unnecessary fear that is driving our behavior, then say "thank you AMMY, but not now!" Repeatedly! With better understanding of what happens, we can learn to calm our AMMY down, *retrain* it and allow our genius to emerge and guide us!

HOW TO CHANGE – THE EASY AND FUN WAY!

Another habit we will be developing through out the book is to "FARC"! Neuroscientists have come up with a formula for change that seems successful and I have made a funny version of it!

To re-hardwire our brains we need to FARC! Which stands for:

F	Focus
A	Attention and awareness
R	Repetition
C	Celebration

Knowing what we know about the process of "FARC-ing", we have designed this book to make it as safe for your AMMY as possible, and to help you work through each stage.

As a young physiotherapist, I had a patient who had suffered a stroke. One day after weeks of working to help him move his foot on the paralyzed side, I saw his big toe move! So did he! We were jubilant!

I can't tell you how hard it was for him to create a new pathway in his brain to do this - such a small thing - but I remember saying to him: *"The first time you do this movement it's like a tiny hairline scratch is put onto your brain. Each time you do that particular movement, the scratch grows deeper and deeper until you have repeated it so many times, the scratch becomes a groove and the movement is now automatic!"* Which is a simple explanation of FARC- ing!

But a gazillion years ago when this happened, no one had ever heard of neuroscience! I *knew* that we had to find ways for him to repeat the movements in an isolated way – I believe it was inspiration! I knew that no matter what had happened to him, we could teach him new pathways to learn how to do the movements again.

We focused on a simple, relaxed exercise program isolating that one movement - which sounds easy but was enormously difficult for him. He was a courageous man who persevered in the face of tremendous frustration. We kept paying attention to the single movement, and also gave him awareness that it was possible because he had done it once. But it would take a *lot* of repetition and many attempts of what others would call "failing" and I would call efforts!

And we celebrated like crazy each time he did it! Well, he smiled a lot and I danced around the room shouting with joy and pride for him! *The celebration part is really important for the brain to cement the new learning's and rewiring.* Now, neuroscientists are helping people who have had strokes or other neurological damage years before regain movement and function - it's so exciting! Read *The Brain That Changes Itself* by Norman Doidge to be amazed at what is possible today! And all we have to do is keep FARCing!

KEEPING A JOURNAL

Keeping a journal is a great idea during your journey to joy - which is what I call reading the book!

You will be amazed at your heart insights! Make notes on what you (and your tribe) have learned, and how it affected you at the end of the week or each day.

And just as importantly, note how your behavior or changed thinking affected others around you.

You may choose to create a Tribe Journal!

Everyone contributes to it - fill it with photos and cards or anything you have done or learned that will contribute to all of you in some way.

If your tribe is your family – if you are using this book as the vehicle for teaching your children how to find and keep their inner joy - imagine the fun you will have doing this – and looking at it for years to come.

When you have finished playing your way through this book - what you have written will create your own book *"My* journey to joy!"

SCHOOL JOY

For the teachers who read this – you can use all the principles and ideas and joy-ercises in your classrooms!

Not only will it help you model joy for your students, but you can actually teach them how to rediscover their own joy! You can reveal the secrets of joy to them!

Sadly, not many parents will not be doing this – so there is a chance to change a child or teens life by including the lessons you learn from reading this book.

Create a school joy program based on what you are learning as you play your way through the book!

Joy Secret #1

Gratitude

"What you want is so near, so near!
It requires only the little shift,
The simple turn, from self to higher,
The letting go of time, worries, doubts.
Let the spirit of gratitude carry you." [1]
Claire Blatchford

Gratitude is the foundation for joy. That's the secret! Until you find and live with gratitude and appreciation, you will never find joy. *Living a life* of gratitude is our goal but…being joyful for a week is a great place to start!

It is difficult in our fast-paced society to focus for one day on gratitude, let alone a couple of weeks. For some, this will represent a new way of being in the world and can be transformational—it's amazing what sincere gratitude can do.

YOUR SEVEN MINUTES

Take your seven minutes now to reflect on how gratitude plays a part in your life.

- What does gratitude mean to you?
- Do you feel grateful a lot of the time?
- Are you grateful for many things?
- To whom and for what are you grateful?
- What types of things make you grateful?
- Did your parents behavior model gratitude?
- Did your siblings model gratitude or another adult in your life?

- How does it make you feel when you actively look for something to be grateful about in a difficult situation?
- What are you really thankful for in your life to date?

It may be difficult to answer these truthfully, but take time and really feel (consciously, with your heart) into the things in your life for which you have a sense of gratitude.

If you don't think about gratitude much at all, it's okay! The world we live in does not leave much time or space to enter into gratitude. Now is the time to create an opening in your life to *feel* gratitude and appreciation and allow it to flow freely.

Truly *feeling* gratitude or a sense of appreciation will have an amazing effect on your heart health, and how you view, and exist in, the world. It will also help others become aware of gratitude just by seeing your transformation.

This is a *very* important secret to unlock for all of us.

AMANDA'S TAKE ON GRATITUDE:

> *"To speak gratitude is courteous and pleasant, to enact gratitude is generous and noble, but to live gratitude is to touch Heaven."* [2]
>
> J. A. Gaertner

A GRATITUDE JOURNAL

My most poignant story of gratitude is about my mother. She was living in Australia when I moved to the United States. She was lonely, unhappy, unwell and in pain, and I felt so bad about not being there to help and support her.

She never complained about her problems or about missing me, but I know it was a huge struggle for her. It still causes me pain to think of how I wasn't there for her in person.

One day, when she was particularly down and in pain, I said, "*Mama, why don't you make a list of things for which you are grateful for everyday? Spend ten minutes reflecting on that list every night before you sleep, and do it during the day if you feel lousy*".

We spoke of this idea for a few nights and then I forgot about it. It did seem to help her though, as she was happier for a while after that.

She Created One!

I was going through her belongings after she died and found a little spiral-bound notebook that she had used as her gratitude book. I have not been able to read it all. And still can't and it's been 7 years!

Just thinking about it brings me to tears because she tried so hard! The effort it took her to write is obvious; her handwriting looked as it was difficult to write and the words are hard to read. She really did keep up her notebook for a long time. She never made a big deal of it, she just did it – that was her way. She would try everything in an effort to grow, to be free of pain, and to be joyful and more active – even at 80! She is a great role model for us all! So - if she can write a gratitude journal with all the problems she had, so can we!

What You Learned From Your Parents

For me, gratitude is something with which my mother blessed me. I have always been grateful for anything anyone does for me, or for benefits that come along – maybe because I don't expect such things, and so they are always a gift.

When I was a little girl, we didn't have much money. I knew we were in difficult circumstances. My parents were divorced when it was not a common practice and my father was an alcoholic, but I always seemed to have what I wanted or needed.

My mother would wake up every morning at 4 a.m. to go to work so she could then come home, take us to school, and be at home when we came home. She made great sacrifices for us and I have always been grateful for what she did. Knowing how hard she worked to give her children great schooling and everything they needed, has made me appreciate everything that comes to me – from anyone.

Some people have never experienced gratitude or had it modeled for them by their parents, or other adults when they were growing up. Those people may find this work on discovering, developing and embracing gratitude challenging, but it's worth the effort. By doing this, a whole new wonderful dimension is added to life.

Consciously Teach Your Children

Gratitude is not something we focus on teaching children – other than insisting they say "thank you"! Yet, it would be one of the greatest gifts we can give them. Teach a child gratitude and you teach them how to feel great about themselves and joyful all their lives.

If we think only of ourselves and expect the world or others to provide what we need, if we fail to see the world through others eyes as well as our own, life becomes a battleground over what we want and what they have.

Gratitude gently leads us to an awareness of others and their needs, helps our hearts and souls expand, and ultimately fulfills us more than we could have imagined.

It's not "things" that feed our deepest needs – it's love and gratitude.

Gratitude is The Opposite of Selfishness.

It is a view away from the self. It is seeing and appreciating anything that is given to you, especially what others have given you, done for you or sacrificed for you.

If nothing else, knowing that we are blessed with God's grace every moment, even though we may not deserve it, is enough to keep me eternally grateful. But I do have to remind myself consciously at times!

COUNT YOUR BLESSINGS

Blessings come as a *result* of using the spiritual gifts we have been given to overcome challenges, hardships or "burdens." *Receiving spiritual gifts*, and then doing something with those gifts, allows us to deal with difficulties.

Bad things happen, but with consciousness, surrender and receptivity, the spiritual realms can take anything and make it work out for the good. If we ask for, listen to, and receive inspiration, we are blessed in many different ways so we can then go and bless others with our gifts. Focus only on seeing your blessings!

Even when I struggle to find something for which to be grateful - I do it. When something bad happens or I encounter a challenge or difficulty in life, I try to conclude my thinking with, *"Well, I am grateful for..."*. Ok, so sometimes I need reminding and refer back to this book!

All the research on happiness is showing us that writing down or just focusing on the blessings at the end of every day brings about a profound change in our joy levels! It's a proven antidepressant.

Be Mindful

For example, I have had many days of feeling "down" for no apparent reason. I have everything I need and know I am blessed in so many ways. Yet I can't shake this feeling of misery. (No it's not hormones. Well, maybe!)

My only path out is to force myself *to focus on a feeling of appreciation for my blessings.* I actively look around me, become mindful, and *find gratitude* for my surroundings and the good things in my life: My health; the ability to walk and see beautiful scenery; my family; my friends; the satisfaction from my work – once I start, there is an endless list! *But I have to work to begin and stay with that thinking!*

Our challenge is to find the gratitude for *everything* in our lives – *even the hardships*! They are there for a reason. You just don't know it yet!

I felt thankful because I learn a lot through my "down" experiences. I learn patience, perseverance, tolerance, and the capacity to separate myself from the difficulty I am facing. It's not easy but the alternative is much less appealing!

It's All About You!

In difficult conversations, I learned to realize that what I was thinking and how I was behaving were increasing my frustration more than anything. Not the other person!

In any painful situation, we are given wonderful opportunities to learn more about ourselves, and practice being kind and tolerant, if not loving. This is particularly relevant in our personal relationships!

Of course, each time I have been through one of these challenging or frustrating experiences, I ultimately understand that it's all about me and how I respond to the experience - in other words, how I manage myself, and the choices I make!

This isn't such an easy lesson, but whenever we point a finger at another, there are three fingers pointing back at us. And a thumb pointing towards the skies where the wisdom of seeing the whole picture - not just our own little judgmental view - exists! No matter how much I wanted to, I could not blame anyone else for my reaction. And it was my choice to be a "victim" – or not!

It's tough at times to take responsibility for ourselves, and the lives we have created! It's much easier to be a victim and blame others!

At Least You Are Breathing!

Sometimes we feel there is nothing for which to be thankful, but it's not really true. If you can walk, talk, see or breathe that's a good place to start!

Work your way up from there. It's better for your nervous system, for those around you, for relationships, and generally for life! *Being grateful is a direct path to joy.*

Things we see as negative almost always lead to some type of blessing. Before you judge something that happens to you as horrendous - even if it is - try to imagine how this might be an *opportunity* in which you may be blessed. We never really know, after all.

For example, I have a friend named "Lady Dianne," about whom you will read more later. She was scheduled to have surgery to remove a tumor, but the night before the proposed surgery, the endocrinologist said she could not proceed since she might have Cushing's disease, a condition where the adrenal glands stop working.

Had the surgery proceeded as scheduled, her body may have failed to recover, even if the surgery was successful.

Despite the pretty nasty symptoms she was living with daily, Dianne's surgery was put off for two weeks. But how did the amazing Dianne look at this? As a blessing!

She said she was thrilled, as it gave her two more weeks to strengthen her adrenals before the surgery and to allow alternative strategies to work. She even laughed as she now had "an official reason to rest."

But wait, there's more!

Dianne was in the hospital already in anticipation of the surgery, but the neurosurgeon told her to go home. Since it was already 8 pm, this was unusual, as normally they would suggest she stay overnight and go home the next day.

Instead, she went home and slept beside her 6-year-old daughter, with whom she is very close. During the night, her daughter had an attack of croup that was so bad she went into respiratory distress. The child could have died had Dianne not been there.

What may have looked like an almighty problem - Cushing's disease - instead held within its hands the gift of Dianne's daughter's life. My personal experience (and Dianne's) is that faith in universal wisdom, the field, God, your higher self makes everything work out for the good - especially for those who believe in, expect or assume a good outcome.

If your heart is aligned with with that faith, as Dianne's was and is, you will be guided wisely.

LOOK FOR THE GIFT!

"Only an open heart understands
that everyone who enters our life is a guest bearing a gift.
Sometimes we must seek out the gift." [3]
Susan L. Taylor

A book that changed my life is *Illusions* by Richard Bach. There is a line in the book that says something like, *"Every problem bears a gift in its hand for you - look for that gift."* And, ever since then, I have!

Our past or current life partners, siblings, parents, experiences and friends – have been "prearranged" to deliver precious gifts - including the gift of spiritual growth. These gifts come whether we consciously want them or not! It's easier to be consciously looking for them and open to them.

Bless each of your relationships and feel appreciation and gratitude to the people as they teach us character building life lessons that no one else is willing to! And, remember, it may not always be the most pleasant experience for them, either!

We Bring Gifts As Well!

We, in turn, also give them valuable gifts with the learning opportunities we offer them. When we are with people with whom we interact easily and it's always fun, we may not be offered as many opportunities for growth. Do people who always agree with us challenge us to develop?

Maybe, but I suspect our greatest growth comes from the periods of trials and difficulties - where we have to stretch ourselves and be uncomfortable for a time in order to recognize and change our patterns and habits. Remember the magnificent butterfly emerges from the "dark night of the chrysalis".

In every difficult relationship or experience you have, look for the gift. *Find something in what is happening for which to be thankful*; that you can appreciate - even if it is only that you are still breathing!

The Blessings From Life Challenges

When I was 45, I "lost" all the money I had worked very hard to earn through a bad business venture. (I never found it again – ha ha!) Although that whole ordeal took five years; involved long, nasty court cases; was extremely stressful, and caused me to move to another country and be away from my family, I was blessed by it.

At this time this was not crystal clear to me! LOL. But with hindsight.....I would never have had the opportunity to work in the United States if it had not happened. Nor would I have wonderful Godchildren and people I now consider family over there. The journey in the U.S.A. was one of great growth for me.

True, some of that growth has been very hard, but all of it is useful and has led to experiences I would never have had if I had not "lost" all the money. Which, by the way, challenged my fear around security.

My pattern and habit from childhood was that money represented security, as my Mum was always worried about money. This experience of losing the money was a VERY powerful way to understand my security comes from within – not from money. And I am grateful for it!

You Have The Capacity to Change Things

If you feel everything about your life is miserable, be grateful you have *the capacity to change things, even if it is only your thinking that you change. In fact, that is the first place to start! How you choose to perceive things and the expectations you hold* will determine what you see and how you feel.

You can think (or tell yourself) your life is miserable, or you can realize you have free will, and then you can choose to make whatever changes you want. Be grateful *you have the gift of free will, but remember,* it comes with responsibility.

If your life is other than you would like, and all the people around you are "horrible", remember that you played a role in creating this situation, *(yes you did!)*, and you have an opportunity to make changes that will improve it, remove it, or transform it.

You have the power to connect to the higher wisdom through your heart, to change your thoughts and thinking process, and, often with the help of others, to change your circumstances, if you so choose.

You will create what you focus on.

Consciously Choose

We need to consciously make the choice to seek a life change, not knowing what will emerge or unfold, but asking for inspiration about what to do and opportunities to do it . Then we need to follow that inspiration.

Listen carefully for that intuition - "the inner-tuition" - and trusting that we will receive an answer from your heart. Our pure hearts inspire us with the right things to do - it's up to us to use our free will and do them, or not. For example, no one wants to die telling others, *"Don't do what I did"!*

When you look in the mirror at the end of your life, you want to see a life, and a heart, full of love. You want to know you loved as often and as well as you could - not fearing hurt, rejection, uncertainly or failure. *Living a life ruled by fear limits us in so many ways, and robs us of our joy.*

We are all born with the abilities and gifts to fulfill our life purpose, as well as with the capacity for free will - which is where our most important choices are made. *Changing your heart changes your thinking.* Which changes how *you feel* about yourself. Which changes your life! And others lives.

No one needs to know you are changing your thoughts about your life, yet it is an extremely powerful thing to do, particularly if you are in circumstances that stop you from making actual physical changes.

There is Always Something You Can Do

There are places and people to go to and ask for help; mental strategies you can create; exercises you can do; health practitioners to see if you have imbalances. *Just do something to change your circumstances.*

Ask for inspiration. Ask others you respect, those who genuinely love you, for guidance and help. In the meantime, change what you are *saying to yourself* about the situation you are in - and that can change everything else.

Reflect on what is currently happening to you, and look for the lessons, be thankful for them, and learn them! *Choose to believe* that in time, you will receive blessings from what you are going through.

(It's the emerging from the chrysalis phase!)

You may have to learn courage or the capacity to stand up for yourself; or to learn that you actually can change what you focus on, and your thinking and it *does* change your life.

Or perhaps you are meant to be learning patience, acceptance, kindness, compassion, or that you are not responsible for other adults actions, or one of the many other concepts discussed in the book. *Only you will know what gifts you unwrapped - packaged in seemingly tough lessons!*

LOSING SOMEONE YOU LOVE

If something really tough happens - like someone you love dies - grieve and mourn, but as quickly as you can, focus on how grateful you are to them, feel appreciation for what they gave you, and send them love.

After Mama died, I found that when I grieved, it was really for me and I wasn't able to feel her close to me. But when I *focused on sending her love and gratitude*, I could feel her presence and had a sense of peace.

I am sure she did not want to see me suffering, missing her, and feeling pain. I am sure your loved ones don't want to see you in pain either. They are probably going through a challenging enough time working out where they are, and what they need to be doing without having to worry about us grieving over them!

Of course I still mourn and grieve, especially when I give in to fear, but I only let those feelings flow for a short time. I consciously focus (there is that FARC again!) on sending Mama my love and gratitude, and soon I am feeling better and I can feel her again. I hope it helps her as well.

Through the pain of your loss, be grateful that you had time with your loved one in their earthly form. And they may not have left you anyway! My belief is that our loved one's spirit may no longer be encased in a human body, but his or her spirit is still with us in a different state.

Be grateful for their life and the extraordinary gifts you received from them. *Focus on what you did have rather than what you have lost or the regrets you have.* Then send them love and appreciation for everything they did for you.

Honor the ones who have passed with love, gratitude and joy. If you are still having trouble finding something for which to be grateful, we explore forgiveness later!

I, like many others, had one fabulous parent and one absent, rather difficult one. Both of them taught me invaluable lessons - it just took longer to understand the ones from my father. For me, the primary lesson from him was true forgiveness; it took me a long time to learn it, but when I did, it had a huge impact. And I still need to keep revisiting it!

BE A GOOD FINDER

"If you concentrate on finding whatever is good in every situation, you will discover that your life will suddenly be filled with gratitude, a feeling that nurtures the soul." [4]
Rabbi Harold Kushner

The pastor at our church in Dallas, Mark Craig, is an amazing storyteller. He once told of a research project where the scientists hoped to find the secret of success by studying a thousand "successful" people.

The scientists were stunned by their conclusion: The common denominator with all these people was not education, or socioeconomic status or parental wealth, but that they were all "good finders."

The researchers invented this term to describe how these very successful people looked at the world. In every person and every situation, these successful people found the good and actively looked for the good. Interestingly, as I was writing this, I made a typo and said they looked for God. *I don't think that was a mistake! LOL*

Be A Good Finder And A God Finder!

Maybe the secret is to be a good finder *and* a God finder. When we are constantly looking for the bigger picture and what is good, it's easy to be grateful.

Everything is a blessing when we see the world through gratitude. What is your "nature?" Are you "naturally" optimistic - do you have a "happy" gene? (Science is showing us that up to 50% of our happiness levels may be genetically determined!) but epigenetics teaches us we can overcome our genetic makeup in many cases!

Do do you think of yourself as skeptical? Pessimistic? Do you let things weigh you down? Do you always see the bad potential consequences of everything? Are you fearful most of the time? Do you recognize the fear?

Many people who have had difficult challenges in life have learned to be pessimistic (which is based on fear.) But babies are not born pessimistic! Babies don't pop out and say, *"Life is horrible!"* Just as we can learn pessimism, we can create *new habits of optimism!*

We Can All Be Joyful!

We are all born with the *capacity for joy*... our job, as adults, is to find that kernel of joy already present and nurture it. Try to find and nurture your joy day by day! Remember, JOY is an inside job – the spark is already there inside you!

Once you start, it can become a lot easier. If it's a struggle to find your joy, focus on gratitude, seek inspiration and ask to see the bigger picture and for guidance.

None of us has to listen to pessimistic people! Who wants to hear that the glass is half empty when it *really is half full!* You can change how you view things, *if you really want to.*

Here is your challenge: With every single thing that happens today, find something - no matter how small - that is good about it. *Find something good about every single person you meet.*

We *Can* Learn Optimism.

This book will teach you how, and there is also a wonderful book by author Martin Seligman called *"Learned Optimism: How to Change Your Mind and Your Life,"*

The best way to tackle finding something good about people and situations is to first catch yourself when you are being negative. Become aware of how easily and how much you fall into that habit or pattern, and start working on recognizing those negative thoughts before they are finished.

Replace them with good finder thoughts. Find as many good things as you can about your life. Find something good about your home, your car or your financial position.

Find something good about every single person in your immediate family and every colleague at work.

Think of the possibilities if you were to focus on only the good for this whole week. (Actually, if you did it for a month or a year, it would be even better!)

Another task for today is to put a note on your computer that says, *"I AM A GOOD FINDER"* - the brain loves a constant reminder!

REFRAME

This technique can change your life in a heartbeat! It can instantly change your perspective and the meaning of what is happening. Our perceptions and interpretations give meaning to events and interactions.

Have you ever taken a picture to the framing store to select a mount and frame? I am always amazed at how a different frame and surround can transform a painting making it vibrant and alive, or sucking the life out of it!

We can do the same thing for ourselves with words. Our words form the frame or mount! We can "frame" an experience as an opportunity, or a crisis, with the words we use to describe it.

If we hear someone say something negative, we can immediately reframe what that person said in our own thoughts, which changes the impact their words have.

It may help to think of what that person was intending to say - the real message behind the words. For example, what if someone says, *"We'll never have this done in time."* Instead of taking their fear or anxiety on board and feeling your stress and pressure mount, say, *"This is a great chance to see how much we can achieve under pressure. What an opportunity!"*

If people sneer at you – say it just to yourself!

You Choose – It Gives You A Sense Of Control.

If you utter or think the words, *"We'll never have this done in time,"* your body-mind immediately goes into stress mode. Stress chemicals pour out and pump through you, making you less efficient, shrinking your focus, and affecting your thinking and capacity to be clear and creative.

On the other hand, if you choose to reframe the situation through your words, you have a completely different mind set and "body set" - you have different chemicals racing around your body - ones that will help you focus and do the job.

Staying conscious of the big picture, and choosing words and labels that create a positive state generates creativity and enthusiasm.

It's simple and effective!

Consider this: A friend of mine had to go to the dentist for a crown. She could not have anesthetic because she is allergic to it. Unthinkingly, I said, *"Oh, that must have been terrible!"*

She replied, *"It's not nearly as bad as the effect of the anesthetic !"*

There are many ways we can reframe the words we use to make them beneficial for us and to help us feel gratitude. Catch your own, and

others phrases that pull you down, and replace them with a reframed version.

Lady Dianne

As I mentioned earlier, my great friend, Dianne (or as she laughingly says "Lady Dianne"), was diagnosed with a pituitary tumor. (That's a pretty serious brain tumor.)

She initially lost some sight in her left eye, and had terrible headaches and diminished sensation on the left side of her body. Instead of succumbing to terror and fear as most people would, she felt those emotions, but also used her will to laugh her way through her challenges.

Laughing, she reframed and said that now, she had an "official reason" to take a rest. As a mother of two small children, and as someone who is running one business and developing another with her husband, and who is *also* studying for her masters, she has a bazillion reasons to rest!

In my opinion, shared by many others, she is an angel and a queen of reframing. She has *found good in a terrible situation* and focused on that with laughter. Her chance of recovery was much greater than someone who succumbs to fear and pain. I am pleased to report she is doing well and no longer needs "an official reason to rest"!

Take whatever happens to you and go through the negative to the gift within it - that's what reframing is all about.

If we choose to, we can always find a gift in the negative things that happen to us...*or we can change our thoughts and learn to go with the flow and not even notice the negative!* TA DA!

GRATITUDE GLASSES – THE EYES OF YOUR HEART

It is impossible to have a heart full of misery and a heart full of gratitude at the same time. Do you recall the old saying about people who see through rose-colored glasses, meaning everything they see looks rosy, pink, happy and good?

Well, I believe there are people who walk around wearing black glasses! It doesn't matter what is really there - they see black in everything because of how they choose to look at it.

I would like to introduce the concept of "gratitude glasses." Put them on every morning and do not take them off until you go to sleep that night! *Make a circle between your thumb and index fingers. Put them over your eyes!* There.

You now have your own gratitude glasses you can take anywhere and use anytime! *Teach your children to do this! It's a great lifelong gift.*

What Color Are Your Glasses?

What color are your current glasses: Black? Rose? Bored? Angry? Frustrated? Lonely? Miserable? Disappointed? Resentful? Poor me? Cynical? Resigned? Compassionate? Excited? Optimistic? Or grateful?

I am so glad I have chosen to see the world and people through mostly rosy gratitude glasses - although it is something I work on daily. *Good finders wear gratitude glasses all the time!* If you don't want to use your thumb and forefinger - go out today and buy yourself a pair of fun, giant, plastic sunglasses - preferably heart shaped!

Okay, if you are not brave enough to *actually* wear them, buy them and put them on your desk. Have a second set for the car and a third for home and maybe a fourth beside the bed! These can be your gratitude glasses! If you can't find any, we have them at www.thejoyproject.com. I use them to see through the "eyes of my heart."

If you are feeling miserable, lonely, sad or depressed, consciously shift your attention to finding things for which to be grateful or appreciative. *Put on* your gratitude glasses! They re-frame everything! You will be amazed at how quickly you feel better. If nothing else, people will smile at you and if you explain why you are wearing the glasses, they will probably ask for a pair!

This is Another Powerful Tip!

If you can't sleep, or have trouble sleeping do the following activity just before you go to bed. Instead of watching some soul-disturbing television program, lie quietly in bed and reflect on your day.

Find three things for which you are grateful and focus on them until you fall asleep. It's even better if you write them down! Put your gratitude glasses on if necessary - or maybe you need to put them on your partner! Or you can both put them on!

Research has shown that writing things for which you are grateful in a gratitude journal, as a nightly ritual, has an anti depressant effect. That's what my Mama did. *When you wake up,* immediately find something *for which to be grateful.* It will transform the rest of your day.

Gratitude Glasses (GG) Make You a Good Finder!

Gratitude Glasses (GG) help you see traffic delays as happening for a good reason and possibly keeping you safe.

- GG wearers make the house they live in a home no matter how "bad" it is.
- GG wearers are grateful they have a family - even a dysfunctional one!
- GG folks see themselves as rich no matter how much money they have.
- GG alter the way you view what happened to you as a child. Filter what your parents did to you and for you through GG - you may be stronger, more resilient, more compassionate, and more loving as a result of your experiences.

Seeing our food through GG reminds us to bless every meal and to be thankful for it and those who prepared it for us.

GG wearers are always reviewing their blessings, feeling genuine appreciation and giving thanks for them.

THE ULTIMATE HEALING TOOL

*"God gave you a gift of 86,400 seconds today.
Have you used one of them to say, Thank you?"*
William A. Ward

The ultimate healing tool, along with forgiveness, is gratitude to God. If you don't believe in a religious or spiritual God, then be grateful to the spiritual realms, the Field, the Divine, the Universe, Source, Buddha, Allah or the wisdom that surrounds us. *Please see past any judgments you may have!*

If you can find it in your heart to be grateful for all you are and are not, all you have or have not, and all that happens to you, you will know joy.

There is a reason for everything. We may never know why something happened, but we know that situations can always be turned around - with work, faith and love.

How Do You respond?

"Stuff" happens and it can be a trigger for us to learn, grow, be and do more. How we respond to situations is the most important element. If you don't agree with this, think of two people in similar circumstances, or who are afflicted with the same disease. Why does one survive and one not?

Why did Dr. Viktor Frankel, author of *"Man's Search for Meaning"*, live through his incarceration in a Nazi concentration camp while others did not? Why do some people suffer abuse in childhood and move on to lead fulfilling and successful lives with good relationships, while others live the rest of their lives bitter and angry?

It's Always A Choice

I am not judging any of this - just pointing out that we always have free will and the ability to choose how we react, feel, think and live. There is always a choice.

It may be very painful; it may take great personal courage, resilience, counseling, persistence and love, but no matter how we perceive it, we always have a choice - even if it's only a choice what we focus on, how we think, feel and behave. That choice will grow into reality.

It may help you to read stories or view DVDs from people who have lived through horrendous or difficult circumstances to learn from how they were able to deal with their past. And how they learned to acknowledge and cope with their feelings to either emerge whole and healed, or to move on and enjoy their lives without complete resolution.

To paraphrase the bumper sticker on a friend's car: "Life is the teacher; gratitude, forgiveness and love are the lessons".

Make it a ritual to come up with at least five things for which to be grateful each day, and hopefully many, many more. Remember, you are a good finder, and a God finder if you wish! That makes it easy to find things for which to be grateful.

JOY-ERCISES

Joy-ercises are the exercises we give you as *tools to unlock the secrets and develop your new joy habits!*

Practice a variety of them for sixty six days so you can establish a new series of joy habits! They are not just exercises! They are JOY-ercises! They lead you to feeling great about yourself.

Although we are given a *lot* of grace for many things, *we usually have to do some work* to make the necessary changes. So do your JOY-ercises cheerfully and enthusiastically – they can transform your world!

GRATITUDE JOY-ERCISE 1: PRACTICE GRATITUDE TO THE DIVINE

> *"I thank God for my handicaps for, through them,*
> *I have found myself, my work, and my God."* [5]
> *Helen Keller*

Isn't it amazing how a power outage in winter can make us so grateful for the power that surges through our houses every day? That invisible power gives us food, warmth, light and a comfortable life. And yet, we are often completely unaware of this power that enables us to do so much.

Hmmm…what else is like that I wonder?

Of course it's God! God, Divine wisdom, the field, Spirit, the spiritual realms, Source, whichever works for you, whatever you call it, it surges invisibly through us and around us all the time, healing us; "powering" us up; blessing us; pouring grace into us; filling us with light; warming us; holding us; inspiring us; supporting us; guiding us; nourishing us, and loving us.

It might use Guardian Angels or other people as angels to do some of it's nurturing work. Situations can be turned into something good for us, help or teachers or whatever is needed for us at that time can "magically" appear.

Today, *find reasons to be grateful to your angels and guides, and for the wisdom of the spiritual realms* – guiding you through every minute – *if you ask them to* and *listen*! This should be an easy task!

Angels

Think how joyful it would be if you identified all the "angels" in your life who are helping you right now. Look for them. Acknowledge your Guardian Angels and other spiritual and human beings who are working for you, or with you, helping you. Feel appreciation for them.

And it's really great fun if you *tell* people you see them as an angel in your life! And thank them of course! Feel gratitude in your heart for them.

When in trouble, we spend a lot of time in prayer *asking* God and our angels for help - for them to fix things and take this or that away or *do* something for us. What if we spent some time today and every day just listening, and asking what we can do for them?

Perhaps we can be of service to them in some way by being kind to another person, or healing a broken relationship or forgiving someone - who knows what it could be.

I bet it would be interesting if you just sat and quietly listened tuning into God's "inspiration channel" - for seven minutes. Or longer!

And for those of you who don't believe in prayer, what is the first thing most of us do if there is a life-threatening crisis? If we are suddenly diagnosed with a disease or worse, our child is? We pray! It's amazing how prayer comes into a person's life in those crisis situations. And helps. Why wait for a disaster - begin now!

When you pray, feel how you would feel if your prayer was already answered. Really feel it. Have faith it is done. Make sure what you ask for is in the highest good for all! It's more powerful than we realize.

Without this connection to our divine source, there is no joy.

I remember my husband had an extraordinary experience that he didn't realize until later was God in action! He woke up one morning with a dream/ imagination/ sense that God had "spoken" to him. It was a deeply personal and relevant message for him - given in a very loving way.

He went for a walk (this is all while I was

sleeping soundly!) and was in awe of how bright and alive everything looked as he walked. The colors of everything were more vibrant. The squirrels more playful. The birds louder. And he felt joy. He felt the joy of everything around him. It changed him totally!

God - Or Good - In Action

You may not have such a profound experience – but when you are joyful are the colors brighter? The world lighter? Animals or people more playful? Your heart lighter or more peaceful? This is God in action!

That's the awareness you want to cultivate and share in your journal - joy is in the small things - the moments of *awareness, consciousness and connection*. This is not the big bang theory of joy! It's the little bang theory of joy!

Give yourself the time you need to fully explore gratitude to the Divine. When we feel truly grateful and connected to everything, when we realise we are really all one, we feel joy; life is great; things flow; everything happens with grace and ease.

Remember, babies are born with a capacity for joy, but some *action* must happen for the joy to emerge. As soon as babies can actually "do" things, they become joyful. When we allow babies and toddlers the freedom to explore and accomplish new movements or tasks, we can see the joy in their faces!

As we age and learn what our spiritual gifts are and how to use them, joy flows into us and shows in our faces as well! Rejoice with others who are in a state of joy - it can be contagious.

GRATITUDE JOY-ERCISE 2: PRACTICE WORKPLACE GRATITUDE

> *"We often take for granted the very things that most deserve our gratitude."*
> *Cynthia Ozick*

If you work, you may spend more hours at work than anywhere else so you might as well make it a place of gratitude and appreciation!

Go to work today with the specific intention of finding all the things you could be thankful for - and then be thankful for them!

Your boss, your friends, your colleagues, the intellectual stimulation, the chance to learn, grow and develop, the relationships, the people you meet, the challenge of your work - there are many, many things for which you may choose to be thankful.

You may have a leader who helps you believe in yourself! Belief in your own ability is a better predictor of success than actual skill levels - so examine your own beliefs about yourself today.

Does your boss build your skills and confidence? Do your colleagues see your strengths? If you don't like your work or the people with whom you work - be grateful anyway. It gives you a chance to practice being a good finder!

Actively look for things for which to be grateful - even if it is simply, "I am grateful that I am not out in the cold or hot or rainy weather. I am grateful I have a roof over my head. I am grateful I am paid for this." Remember that a lot of people out there would take your job and think they were the luckiest people in the world!

Remember, You Are A Good Finder!

If you clash with one or more "difficult" people, make the effort today to find one thing you think is good about them - one thing - and be grateful for that. A very wise friend of mine (Gayle) told me a wonderful story.

She was speaking with a young man who was dealing with a "difficult" lady at work - someone that no one liked or liked working with. My friend told him to see if he could think of one thing good about this lady. He thought for some time and finally said, *"She looks good in blue."*

She suggested to the young man that he return to work and constantly focus on that good thought; and if he was able, to tell the person what he liked about her. Several months later, Gayle caught up with the young man and asked him how things were going.

With great surprise in his voice he said, *"It's amazing. Everything at work has changed. I connect with her much better and she is contributing to the team a lot more and everyone is happier!"* Just one tiny little change like that can transform everything! You can do it! It's your choice.

You will be stunned at how your work life changes when you focus on gratitude and actively look for things for which to be thankful and feel sincere appreciation for all of them.

Others will notice the change and, wonder of wonders, you may even find yourself en-joying moments of work! (Do you know en-joy means in joy? You may find yourself being in joy.) Gratitude is very powerful!

GRATITUDE JOY-ERCISE 3: PRACTICE HOME GRATITUDE

"What a miserable thing life is: you're living in clover,
only the clover isn't good enough" [6]
Bertolt Brecht

Today is home gratitude day. Find as many things as you can that you are thankful for in your home: your family, your pets, your garden, plants, neighbors or community, your teenager's room (there's a challenge!) or that your home is a haven.

Be creative! Roam around your home and find as many things as you can. *Make it a family game.* Who can come up with the most things for which to be grateful? Make it a regular dinner table conversation - ask everyone *"tell us the three main things that happened today for which you are grateful!"*

If you hear yourself saying, "I wish I had a new sofa and the plumbing was fixed," catch yourself. Instead, say *"I am so thankful we have a sofa and I am saving to have my perfect sofa one day!"* Or *"at least we have water."* Or *"this roof does not leak and we are warm in cold weather."*

If your roof *does* leak - then be thankful there are *parts* that do not leak! Remember, you are finding things for which to be thankful, not to complain about. And *a complaint is a great opportunity to practice reframing!*

There is a wonderful Australian movie called *The Castle*, in which a family who lives at the end of the runway of one of Australia's biggest airports, fights to stop their house from being condemned. It's an ugly house on a lead-filled block but to this family, it's a home.

Daryl, the father, makes a very poignant speech about how their house is not a house - it is a home in which love, harmony and joy abound. It really doesn't matter what your *house* is like - what's important is how much of a *home* you have created.

A home full of love, joy and gratitude is a happy home - even if it needs work or renovation.

GRATITUDE JOY-ERCISE 4:
PRACTICE GRATITUDE FOR THE PAST

"Be thankful that you don't already have everything you desire.
If you did, what would there be to look forward to?"
Anonymous

Your activity today is to create a picture of "The Past" gratitude for yourself. There are many ways to do this. The main aim is to pull your memories from your body where they may be hidden and into your conscious awareness.

It's through this awareness that you can *actively* reframe and start to install a new script for your body and *create new habits and patterns.* (Remember FARC-ing? The A stands for awareness!)

Here is your big chance: Today your mission - should you choose to accept it - is to work through all the big events in your life that have been negative and reframe them, so *they are stored in either a neutral way or with gratitude* and appreciation for the lessons.

Review past relationships, past difficult life circumstances, your parents, siblings, teachers, school, college experiences, friends, anything negative that has happened to you in the past. Now find the gift each of those brought you. Drop to your heart and answer these questions:

- How did you grow as a result of each experience?
- How did your life change as a result of these people or situations?
- What would you have been like if it had not happened?
- What opportunities opened up because of them?
- What did you learn?
- Do you now have the ability to let go and move on, or to keep going in the face of difficulties?
- Did those relationships and situations help you know yourself or to grow spiritually?
- Did they help you decide never be addicted to anything?
- Did they give you strength of character, the ability to know right from wrong, or to not take yourself, or life, so seriously?

Without those experiences and *the choices* you made with them, you would not be who you are today. You would not have your unique strengths and areas of potential growth!

Bless those people because they are some of your greatest teachers. Be thankful for the situations because they have helped you grow - the toughest lessons are often the most powerful. If you can't find gratitude then at least see the bigger picture and be neutral.

Your heart will *really* thank you - anger and hostility are the most dangerous conditions for your heart.

Let Go!

A wonderful book called *Molecules of Emotion* by Candace Pert, the scientist who discovered endorphins, shows us that people who hang onto stuff that has happened to them in life are creating a basis for disease. Some researchers believe forgiveness is a major factor for healing in many cases of back pain.

If you choose not to forgive and let go, or not to find some gratitude in your heart, those things that you cling to from the past can make you bitter, twisted, fearful, angry or disappointed for the rest of your life.

They can sit and fester inside you and create the seeds of later disease. Let them go!! They only harm you not anyone else. It is past - there is no need to destroy the present for something that happened 25 years ago - or last week!

The past is just that - the past. *Focus on the present. That's where the gift is!* So let go, clear your heart and find gratitude today!

GRATITUDE JOY-ERCISE 5: PRACTICE BODY GRATITUDE

> *"Grace isn't a little prayer you recite before receiving a meal. It's a way to live".*
> *Jackie Windspear*

Your mission today is to spend the entire day expressing gratitude to your body! You are to say *nothing* negative, no matter what your stomach, thighs or face look like!

Treat your body with respect, give it grace, love it, and tell it how thankful you are to it. Be grateful your stomach is digesting your food and bless it today. Be in awe of how well your body works, despite the processed foods, junk foods and sugary drinks you might pour into it!

Be grateful you have hair and if you don't, be grateful you have a head! It's so sad that people only really learn to be grateful for what their bodies are, or do, when they become unwell or disabled in some way.

How often are we grateful for our ability to walk? Not until we can't any more. When do we value our ability to exercise, move and stretch and how important that is for our body and wellness? Only when we are confined to bed or for some reason cannot move as well as we once did. We treasure how great it is to not have pain once we have lived with it for a while.

Appreciate the enormous amount of intricate work your body does for you every single moment you are alive. Your faithful body is pumping blood, working hard, fighting disease, and bringing you nutrition. *Thank it by treating it well from this moment on.*

When you have flu or a cold or fever, be grateful your immune system is fighting off those germs. Our immune system is working for us every second of every day but how often do you thank it? As a gesture of gratitude to your immune system, tell your body that, *"Today I am going to help you by washing my hands carefully and frequently."* Then make sure you do it!

What about your blood and lymph systems? And your nervous system? How do you treat them? Do you know how much your nervous system is battered day to day with stress and yet keeps serving you as best it can?

Stress

Stress is a big factor in almost everyone's life - we *must* do activities on a *regular* basis to bust our stress.

Book a massage; go for a walk; have a bath and de-tox your body; exercise; rest; turn off all phones and any other communication device for 30 minutes every day; sit in the sun for 20 minutes; meditate; laugh; deep breathe; book a Qi Gong, Yoga, Power plate or Pilates class. *Ask your body what it needs, or ask your heart what your body needs - it will know!*

Rhythms, Routines And Balance

Problems can occur when we don't have *routines, rhythm and balance* in our lives and we push our body beyond its limits. It tries really, really hard to keep going, but there comes a point when it no longer can.

And then we find ourselves with a very serious condition from which we may never recover. For instance, most of us walk around dehydrated these days. We drink too much coffee, soda and sugary drinks and not enough pure, structured water. (See www. miracleproducts.com.au to learn about this critical resource. I use their devices.)

By the time we are thirsty, dehydration has already had an effect. This was shown to me dramatically one day in Dallas when I had a dark field microscopy session. It's an amazing process where we can see our blood's living activity through one drop of blood.

A couple of weeks earlier I had been thrilled that my red blood cells looked so round and healthy. Then on the day of this check up, it was very hot and I had not been drinking much water; when we looked at my blood - gasp - the red blood cells were all shriveled up and sad looking!

And I hadn't even felt thirsty. I learned drinking a little bit of *good* water often was important. Twenty minutes after we drank some structured water, our red cells looked fabulous again!

Be kind. *Be very kind to your body today.* It probably works harder for you than anyone or anything else in your life. Bless it, nourish it, say grace over everything you put into it and feel real gratitude and sincere appreciation for what it does for you.

And on top of all that - your body houses your soul. That by itself is worthy of true reverence. (More on that later!)

GRATITUDE JOY-ERCISE 6:
PRACTICE NATURE GRATITUDE

*"To educate yourself for the feeling of gratitude
means to take nothing for granted"*
Albert Schweitzer

How many times have you found yourself refreshed, restored and rejuvenated by a walk in the forest, by a stream or beside the ocean? Nature is full of invisible forces working for you all the time to create natural rhythms and currents that affect your entire being and soothe your soul.

Consider sunshine for a minute. Do we stop and thank the sun? Or the many forces that make life on earth possible? Sunshine is the most vital source of Vitamin D, which is essential for good health. What about clean air? It's only when allergy season comes that we realize what a blessing clean air is!

How often do we respect or revere the purity of rain, rivers, snow and other sources of water? Remember, without those, we would all die.

There is already a significant shortage of pure drinkable water in the world - *appreciate what you have now!* Make an effort to drink the best, structured water you can find. The quality of the water you put in your body can literally transform your health and vitality. *Treasure pure water.*

Think of the beauty that surrounds us - the trees, flowers, rainbows, sunsets, sunrises - all of which soothe our souls and feed our bodies essential nutrients. How often do you stop, look around in awe and wonder, and thank everything you see for bringing such beauty and

healing to you? We take it all pretty much for granted, don't we?

Be grateful for the winds that clean out the pollution we create! Be grateful for animals that bring us joy, comfort, and fascination: The trees which give us shelter: Bees that pollinate the foods we eat: Flowers, plants and herbs that bring us gorgeous scents, color, tastes and amazing healing: The changing seasons and the spectacular colors of fall, and the endless beauty that surrounds us and fills our hearts.

Without nature, your senses would be very bored! Even in the concrete jungles we have built, nature has a way of bringing her wisdom to us. Look for the little plants growing out of tiny crevices! Put a plant on your desk at work, or have one inside your home and revere it as your symbol for all nature does for you.

Thank the plants, and nature, every day for the oxygen they create and the life forces they bring you. Go for a walk and *feel one* with the natural world around you.

GRATITUDE JOY-ERCISE 7: PRACTICE HEART GRATITUDE

> *"It isn't what you have in your pocket that makes you thankful, but what you have in your heart"*
> Anonymous

Do we really have any idea of the truly immense nature of our hearts? People think the brain is the most important organ in the body but it's not! The heart rules the rest of the body and the Institute of Heart Math has plenty of scientific evidence to prove it.

Visit www.heartmath.org. It is a wonderful organization, teaching people how to appreciate their hearts and how to change their lives by paying attention to the heart and it's feelings. The heart is *not* just a pump that circulates your blood.

Your heart is your world! It's the way you deeply connect to yourself and everything else. *Your heart is what connects you to others. It,* not your brain, *is the seat of your innate intelligence. It's your source of intuition, inspiration, love and life. It's an alchemical vessel.*

Today is your day to spend time with your heart. It breaks; it hurts; it feels; it thinks; it constantly sends messages to the rest of your body orchestrating everything. *Your heart is the conductor of a magnificent symphony - you.*

Yet in our busy, rushed lives, we rarely stop and take time to tune into our hearts - to give them a chance to whisper to us. *Bless your heart today, thank it, listen to it, and through it.*

It is very wise, but it often speaks very softly - you have to listen carefully. If we regularly take time to listen to our hearts, we can be aware of a feeling or sense of *truly knowing* whether something is right or not. *Not an emotion, but a deep sense of knowing.*

I experienced this on the day of my first marriage. I remember walking down that aisle knowing I was doing the wrong thing. I should have listened! Some of you may relate to that! Although it did not last, I am grateful for the lessons that marriage taught me.

It has taken me many years to learn to listen to, and through, my heart and I still have a long way to go! Studying courses called *"Sacred Service"* and *"Spirit Healing"* (www.spiritualschool.org) has helped me a great deal. Both courses are well worth looking into for those of you interested in truly finding your heart, joy, peace and being of service to the world. Robert and Cheryl Sardello are amazing teachers.

Find the voice of your heart today. Listen to it. Listen *through* it. Bless it. Appreciate it. Thank it. *Keep talking to your heart and listening for its guidance in everything.* Today could be the day that changes your life!

Joy Secret #2

Compassion and Grace

"Each of us in our own way can try to spread compassion into people's hearts. Western civilizations these days place great importance on filling the human "brain" with knowledge, but no one seems to care about filling the human "heart" with compassion." [1]

The Dalai Lama

YOUR SEVEN MINUTES

- How would you define "compassion"? What does it mean to you?
- Who are people in your life you would consider compassionate?
- Think of a time when someone was compassionate with you.
- How did it feel? What did they do or say?
- How do you feel when you are compassionate with another?
- Where do you feel compassion in your body?
- Are you compassionate with others?
- Are you compassionate with yourself?
- Could you be more compassionate?
- Would others describe you as compassionate?
- Would you like to be more of a compassionate person?

Spend a few moments thinking about times in your life when you knew you were being selfish. What do you think selfishness does to compassion? Reflect on Buddha, Mother Teresa, Christ or any other being that has lived whom you feel embodies compassion.

AMANDA'S TAKE: WHAT IS COMPASSION?

"The whole idea of compassion is based on a keen awareness of the interdependence of all these living beings which are all part of one another and all involved in one another." [2]
Thomas Merton

My husband Ken and I were talking about compassion and he came up with a definition that resonated with me: *Compassion is being compelled, with passion, to take action.* That action may be to sit with someone, send them love or hold them in your heart and pray - as long as it involves doing something for another person.

I wondered if there was a difference between empathy and compassion. After much deliberation, I decided that empathy allows us to feel what others are feeling - we can sympathize, commiserate or have some sense of understanding - *but compassion actually causes us to take action and involves no judgment.*

Writing this made me recognize another gift my Mum gave me, a rare opportunity to experience true empathy and compassion when two of my friends informed me that their mothers were dying.

I had already realized that no matter how much we think we understand what another person is experiencing when they talk about losing someone they love, we don't really   understand until we have lived through, or felt, something similar.

Perhaps it's only then that we can be one with the other person's heart because of our own experience. This is real empathy - *where we can truly step into someone's shoes, and experience the feeling we are literally all one.*

My Mum's death totally transformed how I related to my friends and taught me more about compassion. I felt my soul was now able to be with another person's soul during their grief. As though my heart was their heart. I could just be there with them, not doing anything outwardly but doing something inwardly - holding them and their feelings in my heart. I wanted to do something, even if it was inner activity.

Compassion, to me, is that state where we can in some way see the other person for who they really are and what is going on for them, and we are moved to take action to support them.

We really sense what it must be like for the other person to be going through whatever it is they are experiencing, without taking on their feelings, and we want to do something to help them. Although sometimes we have no idea of the other person's life or why we feel this way, we still feel compassion and are moved to do something for them, even if it's just to be kind.

This is a heart-to-heart and spirit-to-spirit connection that is much more powerful than a brain-to-brain one. *Compassion is an ongoing activity - a way of living.* Compassion transcends time and space!

My Liver Goes Out to You!

The phrase, "my heart goes out to you" is common in our culture and it initially led me to think that the seat of compassion was the heart. Apparently, the ancient Egyptians thought the seat of compassion was the liver! They had a hieroglyphic that said *"my liver goes out to you."*

On reflection, perhaps they're right!

The liver deals with all toxicity in our bodies, and many believe negative emotions are stored there. If the liver is blocked with lots of toxic waste, it would keep us from being able to reach out to others. We would be too absorbed with negative emotions and ourselves.

Our hearts (and livers apparently!) actively go out to people through compassion, even if we don't understand why. Our heart gently surrounds those with whom we interact - they feel safe and loved, and if nothing else, they know we are there for them.

We don't really have to do anything other than hold them in our hearts because that is doing something. We may need to do more, but this is a start.

With compassion we can often see the larger picture - and we want to help in appropriate ways that still allow the person to experience what they need to, *even if it's suffering,* in order to make it through *their* life, *learning their lessons.* Compassion is healing.

Do you recall the poem about a man who dreams he is walking along a beach with God? As he looks back, he sees that at all the rough times in his life, there is only one set of footprints on the sand. He asks God, *"Why were you not with me at those times?"* God answers with love and says, *"Those were the times I was carrying you."*

I believe compassion is accepting, loving and supporting *yourself and others,* (especially your loved ones), *when they need it most* - in whatever way you can.

BEING PRESENT

Compassion is a quality that allows our gifts to be exercised.
When someone has a desire in their heart to do the right thing
but lacks the skills, knowledge or capacity to do it, and we can
help, we need to do what we can. Our responsibility is to help
others fulfill their responsibilities on earth - it's a flow from our
responsibilities to theirs and back.

If we remember that:

- we are all connected through our hearts,
- we are all part of the whole,
- we are part of every other living human and they us,
- we need to listen to their heart, with our heart, and
- we need to silence our judgments and listen through our heart to
  what we are being inspired to do, then we can "do unto others as we
  would have them do unto us."

As author Stephen Covey says in Seven Habits of Highly Effective
People, *"Listen with your eyes for feelings."* I want to paraphrase that
– *"listen with your heart for feelings".* To really listen to another's heart
language, we have to be *absolutely present and mindful.*

Are You Permanently Present Or Absolutely Absent?

Many people have very short attention spans and develop the habit
of being absolutely absent! Have you ever been talking to someone on
the phone and you sense they are distracted? When you hear the keys
clicking on their computer keyboard, you know they are not really
listening to you.

How does that make you feel? Have you done this to others?

Do you remember all the content of a conversation when you are only
paying attention to it half heartedly? The *biological center* for hearing is
in our heads, but we hear *the truth with our hearts.*

If you are listening with your whole being, you would be mindful,
more respectful and not focus on something else while another person
was communicating with you. Children pick this up very easily. Have
you ever had a child say to you, "You're not listening to me!" They're
experts at knowing when you are there with your whole heart. Or not!

Be open, be present, listen carefully and "hear" the other person's
heart (with your heart's "ears"). Remember the hologram: you two

are really a part of each other and a part of everything. *Offer absolute presence, love, support, grace, tenderness and more love.* That is part of compassion.

And it's not always so easy. I wish I did it a lot better. But I am doing the best I can - at this time, which is what we are all doing.

Helping Others To Fulfill Their Divine Mission

My friend Mary is one of the most compassionate people I know. I am convinced my Mum brought Mary into my life to heal me of Lyme disease and to become a soul sister. She is an amazing single mother of three children, one of whom is autistic. Her life is committed to those children, and through very difficult circumstances, she has remained one of the kindest, most loving people I have ever come to know. Her heart includes everyone - no matter who they are or what they do.

She seems to find a way to connect with every heart and spirit she encounters.

Mary truly perceives every person as a reflection of God on earth and works at *helping them do what God sent them to do.* She always tries to empower people and has a great capacity for discernment.

Through inspiration, Mary, a very spiritual person, a master herbalist and dowser, seems to know in her heart the truth about others - who they really are, *and the perfect thing to do to help them or be of service.*

Even if others are not behaving in the best way, Mary finds compassion for them, although she doesn't make excuses for or allow unacceptable behavior. She is very wise, soft and kind, yet incredibly strong, with integrity, all at once.

When I listen to the tone of her voice, I can really feel her caring and compassion coming through. Mary even taught me how to pray. The first time I heard her say a prayer, I thought, *"Now I know how to pray."*

I had not really thought about *how* I talked to God, but the way Mary did it was so beautiful, so full of love and compassion for others that I knew what I had been doing was not really praying; it was just asking for stuff and occasionally thanking God. I was not present and did not truly *believe* that what I asked for would appear at the perfect time.

I feel blessed to have met Mary - she has saved my life in many ways. Thanks to her, I connect before I pray, am much more "present" and I now believe that once I have prayed, *"it is done"*. And I can let go.

HEART CONNECTION

So what are the little steps that might lead each of us closer to living a life of compassion?

The more I research and write, the more I realize *the essence of compassion is connection* - connecting our head with our heart; connecting our heart to the heavens; connecting our hearts with other people's hearts; and all being connected with a "giant world heart."

 Compassion shines from the heart, along with love, kindness, acceptance, tenderness, caring, forgiveness and grace - many of the qualities we associate with God. I am convinced that the heart is the organ through which the Divine connects to us, connects to others through us, and therefore, connects us to them.

The heart connection is alchemical. It can transform everything. Connect now – head to heart, heart to heart and heart to the heavens!

SELF-CENTEREDNESS IS SEPARATION!

"The purpose of life is not to be happy. It is to be useful, to be honorable, to be compassionate, to have it make some difference that you have lived and lived well."
Ralph Waldo Emerson

After much deliberating, I have concluded that compassion is the antithesis of selfishness or self-centeredness. We can't be compassionate and thinking only of ourselves at the same time.

In my research, a frequent theme for compassion was recognizing that we are all part of the whole and *not* separate. *Like drops of water – we are part of the whole yet still individual.*

When we are self- centered, we are the center of our own little universe, and it's all we see. We lose the greater awareness of our connection, and responsibility to the rest of humanity, the world and the cosmos.

Sometimes we are self-centered in some areas of our lives and not others, or with some people and not others. *Selfishness is essentially a state of unconscious separation.* It is unusual to be in a state of compassion and selfishness at the same time!

Compassion requires us *to focus outwards towards others and simultaneously have a consciousness of the whole.* When we are self-absorbed, our focus is on ourselves and we are totally asleep to spiritual currents swirling around us, and the millions of other feeling souls.

We Are All One

Many people wonder about their purpose in life, saying *"There must be more to life than this."* Modern lifestyles seem to discourage heart connection, although we are more electronically connected than ever. *That heart connection is what really matters in life!*

Hearing and following Divine inspiration, serving others and acting with compassion gives us our sense of purpose. Realizing that there is no separation between any of us is the antidote to self-centeredness. We are all one. We are never really isolated or completely separate from others or God.

We are all affected by the same influences - the moon, sun and sea and the rhythms of the earth and cosmos. *We all make a difference - all the time.* Will the difference you make be positive or negative?

Once we realize we are all connected and that what we do will affect everyone, and everything else, how can we demand conditions that are for our sole benefit - ignoring, or not caring about, the effect on others?

It's Not All About You!

By separating ourselves from our higher selves and others, and wanting *only* what we desire to satisfy our own emotions, wants or needs, we create misery for ourselves and others.

In selfish mode, we cannot be in our hearts and connected. We are caught in negative emotions triggered by thoughts of *"What about me? What about my feelings? How dare they do that to me?"* As if "they" were terrible beings outside of us, and not a part of us!.

Whenever you find yourself blaming others - look in a mirror! *You will see a co creator of the problem!* It's confronting, but often there is truth in this statement!

These *self*-orientated thoughts create negative emotions of anger, jealousy, resentment, bitterness and disappointment that keep us separated from our own hearts, let alone anyone else's.

The Dalai Lama, one of the masters of compassion, says, *"If you want others to be happy, practice compassion. If you want to be happy, practice compassion."*

Developing the habit of compassion is a direct pathway to lifelong happiness! If you are not feeling joyful, have a long look at yourself and *wake up to your habits* - are you often in selfish mode? If so, immediately focus outwards, *seek to serve, do something self-less,* and be *full of compassion* for someone else!

GRACE

Compassion is also about grace - God's grace and allowing that grace to flow through us TO others. Grace is continuously poured over us. We are forgiven, blessed and loved continuously. We are given endless, unlimited grace yet we usually remain totally oblivious to it!

I am not sure we can give anything like God's grace but we can let what we are given flow through us to others. For those who find grace a difficult concept - it's about being unconditionally loved and *unconditionally loving others,* not condemning, giving up on them or judging them.

Our work is to become conscious of grace and pass it on - even if others don't appear to deserve it! We can share grace by being gracious, as well as being forgiving and loving.

We can also give someone the benefit of the doubt; assume the best about them; be compassionate instead of "right"; say nothing when we could criticize; speak only positively; think only good thoughts about another; put them in our heart; help them if they need it; and choose not to take offence.

Give grace to others. It's a choice! Make it a conscious one.
It takes a lot to continually forgive, bless and love, but it would be a great habit to develop, wouldn't it? Even if it took a lifetime!

It could be something we decide to do each day - to consciously give grace. Make it a morning mantra: *"Today I will be gracious, forgive, bless and love everyone."* Perhaps you are thinking, *"Be realistic!"* - or *"yeah right!"*

Well, how about, *"Today I will forgive, bless and love as many people as I can"?* Or be specific each day, and rotate through my husband/ wife/ children/ parents/ friends/ siblings.

Or start with baby steps - *"Today, I will give my partner the benefit of the doubt all day and I will choose to be kind rather than right."* Ok, that's not such a baby step! But you can do it – *if you choose.*

UNCONDITIONAL LOVE AND TENDERNESS

> *"Be kinder than necessary.*
> *Everyone you meet is fighting a hard battle".*
> *Philo of Alexandria*

Real unconditional love and tenderness are components of compassion. I speak more on unconditional love in Secret #10 – it's a big topic!

Tenderness

When I think about tenderness, I imagine the way a loving parent looks at their child; lovers looking at each other; or the way we hold a precious, fragile, delicate item. Our physical movements, eyes and voice tones convey tenderness.

In a gesture of tenderness, love pours forth from the heart, and is expressed to others in many ways. Are you so stressed and rushed in life that you grasp life, people and things with a tension-filled, vice-like grip? Do you unknowingly squeeze hard and harm or crush what is in your hands?

Or do you hold your life and loved ones as if they were precious - and treasure them by being tender, loving and gentle?

Someone who had seen me speak years ago sent a wonderful email - he was talking of the value of "dropping to his heart" before he connects with someone he cares about: *"When I am sharing with someone I care for and the question arises, "how do I drop down to my heart?" I simply share that it all starts with the tone... I feel what is in my heart and I express it ever so gently... my voice actually lowers and softens... all unconsciously by the way... and I know I am in my heart!"*

It's so easy to develop habits of being thoughtless, too direct, harsh, heartless, judgmental or making assumptions. That's what happens when we *react* rather than *respond.*

Respond From Your Heart

If we can just take a second, drop to our hearts and respond from our hearts, we become more conscious and tender, and make better choices. True strength comes from the gentle wisdom of the heart.

Listen to your *voice tones*-they are the key indicator of how much tenderness is present. Be aware of how your eyes feel; we can "feel" tenderness in our eyes.

And last but not least, notice your hand gestures. I have watched parents who touch their babies in such a tender way that tears come to my eyes; and lovers who touch the cheek of their partner in a way that conveys more love than any words could. A tender gesture is very powerful.

These four components – being present, self-less-ness, grace, unconditional love and tenderness - seem to work together in my heart to bring me closer to living life with compassion for myself and others.

Compassion has to be a conscious choice – until it becomes a habit. Make a decision to be more compassionate and more conscious of compassionate behavior, and then keep practicing!

COMPASSION JOY-ERCISE 1 AND 2 – PRACTICE SELF-LESS-NESS!

> *"In separateness lies the world's great misery; in compassion lies the world's great strength."*
> *Buddha*

This is a two-day practice. For today and tomorrow, *focus only on others and how you might help, support and bless them;* and allow grace to flow *through you to them.*

These two days are not about you at all. Not even a teeny bit! They are all about you doing something for others - being in the activity of compassion and *serving others* with love, kindness and tenderness.

Do something for a family member that you know will delight them. Do a chore that is not yours just to save the other person from having to do it. Do volunteer work. Help your neighbor or community.

Pay the toll for the person behind you. Find an old person living alone and do some manual labor for them, or better - do it, and then spend some time visiting with them. There are a million things you can do to focus on and help others!

The purpose of these activities is for you to not think of yourself and your wants or needs for two whole days. The more difficult you find it, the more interesting you might find the results.

Remember to do all of this with a heart full of compassion and caring for others, which means your intentions are sincere and pure and your true heart is in it. If you do it just to have others say what a saint you are, then it won't work!

Perhaps a mantra these two days could be, *"Can I do something to help you?"* If they say "no," send them love or hold them in your heart because that is doing *a lot*!

You may be surprised to see how different the world appears during and after these two days, how many people are affected and how your interactions with them seem to change.

COMPASSION JOY-ERCISE 3
– PRACTICE COMPASSION AT WORK

You can transform every aspect of your work (and life) with compassion. Imagine what life would be like if we actually encountered customer - service people who had compassion for our suffering!

I know my best experiences have been when I have felt someone genuinely does care that I am frustrated, upset or disappointed, rather than simply saying *"I'm sorry you're having these problems"* as they read from a script! *Heartfelt compassion transforms customer service.*

We Never Really Know What Is Going On For Other People

Imagine too what life would be like if you had compassion for your colleagues - even if prior to now, you have judged them idiots. Give them some grace!

People may be confused, stressed, overloaded, have a difficult situation at home, not be trained well or have a hundred other reasons for not performing the way you think they *should*. *The habit of compassion can transform your relationships with colleagues.*

How You Feel About Yourself

The best bosses I have ever had are those who really showed me compassion. They knew I had plenty of areas where I needed growth, but *they still believed in me*.

They treated me with understanding and kindness when I made mistakes, and they worked with me to help me learn and supported me. I felt good about myself around them and the most important thing in life is how you feel about yourself! It transforms everything!

If you are a boss - do you think the people that you lead feel the way I did? Helping people feel good about themselves is the secret for sensational relationships! *Compassion transforms leadership.*

The Power Of A Compassionate Heart

Maybe your life would change if you viewed everyone at work through, and treated them with, a compassionate heart. They might "miraculously" turn into great colleagues and bosses and they would wonder what kind of personality transplant you had undergone!

Your mission this day is to be compassionate with everyone at work. Develop these habits:

Be *selfless* - focus outward and not towards yourself, sincerely offer to help people and be understanding. If you see someone stressed and rushed, *find* a way to support them.

*   Be *gracious* - pass the grace that is given to you onto as many people as you can. Be patient, respectful and tolerant; forgive them; give them the benefit of the doubt and just be kind!
*   Be *present* and connect heart to heart.
*   Try your best to *unconditionally love* (or accept) them as they are.
*   Be *tender* with them. See them through tender heart eyes. Everyone is fragile and vulnerable at times. Be kind again! And again! And *always* be gentle and compassionate with them - and yourself.

COMPASSION JOY-ERCISE 4 and 5
– PRACTICE COMPASSION AT HOME

> *"The purpose of human life is to serve,*
> *to show compassion and have the will to help others."*
> *Albert Schweitzer*

Okay, these are the easier days! But this activity is *so* important, and there are *so* many people involved that you have two days to practice! It's easy to have compassion for our children. We give them endless space to be who they are, faults and all!

Compassion For Your Partner

But do we do that with our partners? Siblings? Relatives? We are more likely to give compassion to our friends than to any of our relatives, or our partners!

And yet, it is our partners who are our greatest teachers in life. They volunteered - though maybe not consciously - to *help us grow and develop emotionally and spiritually*. Find it in your heart to have compassion for them – as I said before, you may not be an easy task!

When we practice the negative habit of being self-orientated, *we see our partner as the problem*. We don't even know we are *projecting* onto them all of our "stuff" and not really seeing their heart. We see the image that we have created based on *our past* and *fears* - not the truth of who they really are.

What's Your Story?

Life is all about the stories – the *fairy* stories - we make up and tell ourselves about others and situations - not reality! What story are you telling yourself about everyone and everything in your life?

When we are compassionate, we know we are all one, we see a bigger picture and understand our partners have taken on a big task, and that without them, we might be stagnating. That's the *story we choose to tell ourselves*, which makes it easy to find gratitude for them and their gift.

We understand the challenges they face with us, and have a sense of the difficulties they experience as they help us grow.

Teenagers Are Special!

Teenagers deserve compassion, as they may be the greatest teachers of all! Try to remember what it was like when you had hormones coursing through your body and you loved and hated your parents at the same time.

It's amazing how we are seen as brilliant by our toddlers who want to be around us all the time, yet those same toddlers grow into teenagers who avoid us like the plague and think we are embarrassing, controlling and total morons!

Our work is to love them, discipline them and teach them with compassion, despite what they think of us! *It's not easy, but someone has to do it and that someone would be you!*

Remember that compassion is a blend of forgiveness, self-less-ness, presence, unconditional love, grace and tenderness. And at times, it requires us to be firm and set boundaries.

Teenagers, too, need to have compassion for you and the huge job you have taken on with them - but we are more grown-up than them, so it's more our responsibility.

Forgiving And Focusing

These two days are all about *constantly forgiving* (yourself and others), focusing on others needs, *giving* everyone at home as much grace as you can - *especially when they don't deserve it,* loving and accepting everyone *just as they are* (a big one for most of us), and being as tender as you can with them.

Look for the habitual patterns of behavior you have adopted in your family and *re-pattern them to include compassion.* Think of these patterns as simply cast in sand - awaiting new impressions to be pressed onto them. A good or blessed pattern will change everything.

Make it a family practice or game to develop compassion and gratitude as the default habits! Who can be most compassionate? Who can be most grateful – for the most things! If you can't manage any of the above, then work on having a tender voice - show your love and compassion through your voice all day!

COMPASSION JOY-ERCISE 6
– PRACTICE COMPASSION FOR YOUR ENEMIES!

> *"Compassion compels us to reach out to all living beings, including our so-called enemies, those people who upset or hurt us. Irrespective of what they do to you, if you remember that all beings like you are only trying to be happy, you will find it much easier to develop compassion towards them. The true aim of cultivation of compassion is to develop the courage to think of others and to do something for them."* [3]
> *The Dalai Lama*

The above quote from the Dalai Lama pretty much says it all. Can you find the courage in your heart to think of others and do something today to help your "enemy"? The concept of enemy is pretty foreign to me because unless we are at war, our day-to-day life is not usually full of "enemies".

However, we often have people who have hurt us, who annoy us, humiliate us, frighten us, shout at us, belittle us, are unkind to us, offend us, or cause us difficulty, frustration, disappointment and pain, or are simply "mean" to us.

The*se are the "enemies" that we need to have the courage to forgive* and see if we can *help* in some way. If we can't love them, then at least we can hold them in our hearts for some time, *so our hearts can work miracles,* and try to think kindly of them.

This takes courage and "will forces" - a *conscious* act of will to do something that does not feel "natural." If you practice, it will soon feel natural - and great!

If the concept of actually helping these so-called enemies is too much of a first step for you, then maybe you can think of this person or people in a way that is *neutral* rather than negative! From neutral, you can move to thinking something kind or good about them. Then you can try understanding how unhappy they may be to behave the way they do, or how difficult life must be for them.

Move to feeling for them in your heart, and from there you will be closer to compassion. This may take a little longer than one day - but start today! *You'll be surprised at who benefits the most.*

COMPASSION JOY-ERCISE 7
– PRACTICE COMPASSION FOR YOURSELF

"If you have no compassion for yourself,
then you are not capable of developing compassion for others."
The Dalai Lama

Reflect all day today on "How compassionate am I with
myself?" Many people habitually judge themselves harshly. Do you
allow God's grace to flow *through and to* you for the mistakes *you* make?
Or do you beat yourself up as a failure or loser?

Mistakes bring learning. If you've never made a mistake, you've missed a
lot of learning opportunities. Some of our biggest and most beneficial
lessons (which do not seem so beneficial at the time) come from our
biggest mistakes.

Imagine what a toddler learning to walk would do if every time he
or she fell down, we shouted at them, told them what silly idiots they
were and used the kind of phrases we use on ourselves all the time.
Pretty soon, they would cry and not attempt to walk anymore.

We limit ourselves in the same way when we give ourselves no grace,
mercy or compassion. Are you hard on yourself? Do you drive
yourself mercilessly?

Do you judge yourself harshly, or talk to yourself in a disrespectful
way? Do you deny any feelings you have and just swallow what
happens to you and never allow yourself to feel pain? Do you keep
inventing terrible stories about yourself and your past?

Do you load yourself with guilt, or accept others dumping all the
blame on you and not accepting any themselves? If yes to any of the
above, stop doing this today!

We Are All Doing The Best We Can

We are all human, doing the best we can, and we need to give
ourselves a lot of grace and compassion. Today, your task is to be
endlessly tender and loving with yourself. Be gracious to yourself for
things you have done in the past *and move on, let them go.*

Allow yourself to feel some of the pain that may have been suppressed
for a long time. It really is okay to feel the pain - as long as it comes
out and you deal with yourself compassionately. (Best you do this with
someone you trust and when you have time to cry.)

Give yourself permission to feel whatever your heart needs to. Recognize and release stuff that is held inside and blocking your progress – perpetuating old habits and patterns.

Set this intention before you climb out of bed every day: Today I will be compassionate (loving, tender and grace-giving) with myself. I will pay attention to my true self, the one that lives in my heart, and not the selfish, spoiled personality - which is the "front" I put on for the world to *supposedly* keep me safe.

Allow your heart to guide whatever you say to yourself and how you treat yourself today. That judgmental, nasty, critical, nagging voice will be silent - all day and hopefully for a lot longer!

You have been doing the best you can with what you've had, so pat yourself on the back and give yourself a ta-da!

You'll be gentle and kind to yourself as you "learn how to walk" again - this time on the path of compassion.

Joy Secret #3
Hope

If you lose wealth, you lose nothing.
If you lose health, you lose something.
If you lose hope, you lose everything.
Mr. Gojani, a refugee from Kosovo

YOUR SEVEN MINUTES

I met Mr Gojani at a conference in the USA shortly after his family had fled their country and his quote was inspiring for me. The challenge for today is to give yourself at least 7 minutes to focus internally and review the concept of hope.

Here are a series of questions that might help you work out your thoughts and feelings about hope.

- What does hope really mean to you?
- Think of hope as a noun and hope as a verb - what's the difference?
- How is hope different from wishing?
- Can you think of situations in life where you were full of hope? What difference did it make to your life at that time?
- How did you feel and act?
- How did you treat others?
- At other times, when you felt hopeless or uncertain, how did you behave and feel?
- What things or situations tend to make you feel hopeless?
- Recall times where you were driven by fear instead of hope.
- What outcome did you experience when fear was in control?
- What is the difference in how you felt/acted and treated others when hope was your guide?

- Recall what you said to yourself when hope was your companion and compare that with a time when fear ruled your thoughts?
- Which made you feel stressed and heavy?
- Which made you feel more relaxed and light?
- What happens in your life when you operate from fear?
- What happens in your life when you have hopeful expectations?

AMANDA'S TAKE:

"But we also exult in our tribulations,
knowing that tribulation brings about perseverance;
and perseverance, proven character; and proven character, hope
and hope does not disappoint."
Romans 5: 3-5

RESILIENCE

Having been a mostly resilient, optimistic person the majority of my life, I am blessed with taking the hope road most of the time. I truly believe that there is hope in all situations, and that all things happen for a reason.

I challenge myself with finding a way *through* the circumstances, rather than giving up and feeling hopeless.

My belief is that there is always - *always* - something we can do to change a situation - even if it is something internal like changing our thinking. Which of course changes everything!

I was blessed with a couple of great friends who held my hand when I "lost" all my money at the age of 45. I am so grateful to them for their love and support - and the hope and courage they gave me. With that support, I could recover and continue when everything looked bleak.

Sometimes we need help to bounce back and be resilient. If you are going through a difficult experience, seek out people who are optimistic and hopeful; avoid those who are full of doom and gloom - negative people can destroy your spirit and your ability to be resilient and persevere.

At times though, negative people can make us stronger! They force us to develop our strength of character and be all we can be, as long as we don't succumb to their negativity or hopelessness!

Many really positive, resilient people came from backgrounds where their families or circumstances seemed hopeless, yet they made a decision early on that they would never be like that! See – there *is* a reason for everything!

WHO IS REALLY THE NEGATIVE PERSON?

If the world seems full of negative people to you - it's time to review *how you actually perceive the world*. Are *you* actually the negative one?

When I was in my twenties, I was overwhelmed with how many problems people I met were experiencing - or that's the way it seemed. I never met people who were happy - until I had a blinding flash of the obvious! I suddenly recognized that I was basically asking people with my attitude and non-verbals, *"What is wrong with your life?"*

I would pay attention to what was going wrong rather than what was right and wonderful *in my own life*. And then I asked them to validate my misery! Once I had that "ah-ha!" moment - my life changed and so did everybody else's! Suddenly there were all these happy people around me. It was an unforgettable lesson and gift! LOL.

I also realized that I was not vibrating at a very high level and needed to look at how negative *I* was being! But if the people around you *really* are negative, then change the way you view the world *and* find new friends or move on!

THE SEED OF RESILIENCE LIES IN HOPE

An Eastern proverb tells us to *"fall down seven times, get up eight!"* That's *resilience*.

It's a useful habit for every aspect of our lives. We can't learn, be great salespeople or in relationships without resilience. It makes us better leaders, parents, employees, friends or spouses/partners! *With resilience, we can make mistakes and learn,* rather than see ourselves as failures.

Smart resilience is when we learn from each fall, and rise wiser and able to deal with the next challenge (which may be a life-changing wake up call) in a different way. It's difficult to have resilience without hope or the courage hope gives us.

A woman I spoke to recently described her very difficult situation. Her father had died two months previously; her mother was not doing well as a result; her job was in jeopardy; one daughter had post-partum depression; another daughter with a mental illness announced she was pregnant, and her third child was diagnosed with a brain tumor.

Needless to say, she was exhausted and very stressed. Although she was feeling overwhelmed and it seemed that not much else could go wrong, *she held onto hope and faith,* which gave her the resilience to keep going and support everyone.

She did more than have faith that God would give her the strength she needed; *she consciously used her will to hold* that faith no matter what happened. She had faith in herself that she could continue to not just cope, but also to handle the situations with equanimity.

The most powerful, joyful way to solve issues is to hold a vision of what is possible, ask for and follow inspiration, do your work and then surrender attachment to the outcome. She believed - and often reminded herself - that good would somehow emerge from these seemingly endless crises and she *chose* to remain hopeful.

How resilient are you? If you don't seem to have much "bounce-back ability," you might need to focus on developing hope and faith by hanging around people who have a lot of it. These people can help as they light *your* candles of hope and faith!

Choose to monitor and change your language, and what you are putting your attention on and thinking. Catch yourself repeating negative and hopeless phrases in your head. Read inspirational stories of hope and faith and how others have found hope and courage.

These are just some of the many practices - *notice they are practices, since they require some action on your part* - that can build your hope, faith and resilience. To rediscover our joy, we usually have to do some sort of work!

HOPE VS FEAR

> " *We can easily forgive a child who is afraid of the dark; the real tragedy of life is when men (and women) are afraid of the light.*"
> Plato

Remember, *we are living lives of habits and patterns ruled unconsciously by fear!* Fear for me is the opposite polarity of hope.

We can travel between the two poles, but if we don't make a *conscious* effort to spend most of the time at the hope end, we will unconsciously live in fear that blocks life forces and joy.

Hopelessness is often triggered by a fear of something - perhaps a fear of failure; of not being good enough or lovable; of losing something, someone or some battle; of humiliation (FOWOT – fear of what others think!), poverty or separation. Or the fear that whatever we are facing is so large we cannot conquer it.

So many people compare what they have with what THEY THINK *others have*, and fear they are missing out – yet it's a *fairy story* they tell themselves. Concocting fairy stories about others lives does nothing to add joy to yours. How can you ever really know how others live or what they have?

There are many fears ready to grip us at any time. We have to be vigilant!

The Difference Between Joy And Happiness

My favorite way of describing the difference between happiness and joy is this: most of us are running wildly through an endless pitch black corridor desperately searching for a light switch.

The dark consists of all our fears. Suddenly we find a light switch and rush to turn it on. Light! Relief! Our fears are gone. We are happy.

Whew!

But then the ight bulb dies; or the power fails or worse – someone turns the light switch off – and oh no – we are plunged into the unhappiness of fear again. If this happens a lot – hopelessness follows!

When we stand in that darkness and breathe, when we resist the panic of fear, we see a light shining from somewhere. We look around and *realize that light is shining out of us!*

And the longer we look at it, the brighter it becomes. *That's our joy! You carry that joy with you 24/7,* it's yours! You will never be in the dark again – *it's the ultimate fear eradicator!*

As a little girl, for some reason I don't understand, I was afraid of the dark. I was particularly afraid of the scary monsters that lived under my bed!

I let my fear become so overpowering that I gave into hopelessness and stayed in bed, too scared to move. It was always amazing to me that as soon as the light was turned on, the room was "safe" again.

Most of our fears are like that - they dissolve when light is shone onto, or into, them. *JOY is the constant light within us, the constant light within us that guides us from fear to hope.* When all appears dark, we aren't aware that *we have closed our eyes! We are not seeing the light shining from within us!*

Hope opens our eyes; it gives us courage; it acts like a candle in a dark room; it lights up our surroundings and shines into the future, showing us the way and dispelling the fears that create obstacles on our paths.

HEART THINKING

In Proverbs 23:7, we are told, *"As a man thinketh in his heart, so is he."*

Fear disappears when we have clear thinking in our hearts. By clear thinking, I mean that we have tuned into our inspiration and know exactly what we are sensing and supposed to be doing.

Imagine there is an ongoing battle between light and dark in the heart. Being connected to our higher selves and the spiritual realms gives us the light; our own negative thoughts are the dark!

If we clearly *choose to focus on the light,* the fear or darkness disappears as the light rays shine through us and we shine the light on our darkness.

If we can *consciously* operate from the light in our hearts, then fear will never grip us again - or not for long anyway! When we use our heart's "knowing" to guide us, we are filled with hopeful expectations.

Wake up to the unconscious fears ruling you, think with your clear heart, seek inspiration about what you are to do, connect to the spiritual realms, do the work, and press on.

PATIENCE

Patience goes hand in hand with hope! Many times *we need to wait for the right timing* - although we want what we want NOW, or for things to be fixed or relationships healed *immediately.*

Often, that's not what is best for everyone involved! We need to *wait patiently, with a heart full of hope,* for

Divine wisdom to operate and guide us. And sometimes, we have to surrender all control (not that we really have it anyway) and get out of the way!

It takes effort, consciousness, persistence *and work (willpower)* to do this. But it's worthwhile work!

HOW DO WE CONNECT WITH GOD'S LIGHT – OUR JOY.

First, look around you! Everywhere we look, there are miracles that unfold each day - whether it's the sun rising, the flowers blooming, babies being born, the seasons moving, or our bodies working every minute in amazing ways.

Second, look back on your life and remember what seemed the worst event in your life at the time, and how it miraculously turned out months or years later to be the best thing that could have happened to you (hint: think past relationships!).

Third, listen to your heart. Recall all those times in life when you felt some kind of guidance. People hear inspiration differently, so you may "hear" God as a booming voice, or a feeling of heat or fire, a burning in your heart.

You may hear a clear, distinct "voice from your heart" giving you wisdom, or a whisper that tells you something you *know* is the right thing to do. It may even be a clear thought without words! Or you may just feel wonderful peace and rest. Or be given a vision.

Remember a time when you were in crisis, you prayed, and things worked out from there. *This is one way you tap into your heart's "knowing" - by asking and listening.*

Fourth, ask for a sign. Ask for spiritual guidance to be so clear in your life that you know it is there and real; so clear that there is no way you can doubt its' presence or influence or inspiration. Florence Shinn has a great affirmation *"Infinite Spirit, give me a sign; don't let me miss a trick."*

Fifth, pray! Pray for your heart to guide and show you the truth. Pray for the divine design of your life to unfold with grace and ease. Pray about everything you do – preferably before you do it – believing that once you have asked, it is done! Follow the guidance you are given. Be thankful for all that happens.

With inspiration, the right action and faith, things will always work out for the good – *in Divine timing and often unexpected ways!*

HOPE AND HEALTH

> *"There are no hopeless situations,*
> *only people who are hopeless about them."*
> *- Anonymous*

Many studies have shown that optimism and hope play a vital part in the healing process. How people view a diagnosis or their situation can determine whether they live or die. *"Stinking thinking"* (hopeless, pessimistic thinking) can often contribute to or cause illness.

Lance Armstrong's classic comment – *"cancer picked the wrong person this time!"* has inspired thousands. With a spirit like this, his immune system is much more robust than those with hopeless thinking.

People who are full of faith and hope are often those who have inexplicable "miraculous" cures. Being full of hope makes us seem, and feel, vibrant, colorful and alive.

It means we are more likely to take the actions we need to take to find second opinions, new practitioners, treatments, strategies and information. *Hope gives us a courageous spirit.*

Hope increases our life forces – it's like "spiritual breathing". It strengthens every cell in our body and heals us. Have you ever noticed that when we are fearful or stressed, our breathing stops?

In moments of fear or stress - we gasp, freeze, take shallow breaths and lose the capacity to move, listen or hear. Why do we say, *"We were paralyzed by fear?"* It's because fear instantly stops our life force.

What a doctor or any health or complimentary practitioner says when we are ill needs to be very carefully considered. They must allow some place for hope in the patient's hearts.

A heart filled with hope can transmute everything. If we suffer from a serious illness, who knows if a new cure will be found next week? Who really knows if a miracle will occur? Who really knows what prayer will do? Who really knows if there is someone healing this condition in another country?

All things are possible! And your job is to have faith that if you are meant to find this cure, you will - so go look!

And if you feel a particular healthcare practitioner has little hope for you, it is critical you find one who shares your hopeful heart. No person can give you a sentence! They can tell you what they found, and what they have learned to date, but that's all they really know at that time.

Who knows what experiences other people have had that would transform your spirit to one of confidence and hope? *Never give up.*

You never know, *hope and faith may be the only things needed to keep you alive and make you well,* or to allow you to follow whatever your path is, whether it involves healing or not, with peace and equanimity.

LEARNED HOPE – IT'S A CHOICE

What's the difference between people who give up on a situation because it's "hopeless" and those who try and try again? The difference is persistence, resilience, hope, *and what they say to themselves , what story they tell themselves.*

Some of us don't realize we have old patterns and habits of negativity, which leave us depressed, fearful, un-motivated, helpless *and* hopeless.

When we fall into the trap of being victims, we give up all responsibility for ourselves and can't see or appreciate how we have contributed to our circumstances.

Many times we blame others or find excuses, such as *"I couldn't help it;" "It's not my fault;" "There was nothing I could do."* There is often no truth in these kinds of statements.

We always have a choice. We are blessed with free will - which means *we make choices* in how we behave, respond to, or deal with something.

Sometimes it's hard for us to hear this, and we resist, because it means *we have to take responsibility* for what happens and how we respond. *It means we have to stop blaming.*

We are never alone; there is a spiritual world full of angels who are always sitting beside us, waiting to help, *but we need to ask!*

Things are never hopeless while the angels are there, *and they are always there* in some form - even after fear blocks our breathing.

What Do You Say To Yourself?

Stop saying negative things to yourself about any situation. If it works for you - tell yourself, *" I can do all things in Him who strengthens me."* When you feel negative or hopeless, take some time and focus your attention on your heart area and if possible, connect with your spiritual "helpers". You may notice your body relaxes and you feel peace and hope.

Often the phrase used to describe hopelessness, or the state where one loses the will to keep going, is "dis-hearted". In this state, *we have disconnected from our hearts,* and Divine wisdom. If we make the effort to reconnect with, and operate from the clarity in our hearts, we are choosing hope.

Listening to our hearts knowing expands us; it connects us with the spiritual realms; it gives us courage; it works together with faith; it heals, and it builds. Our hearts are clear when we are truly connected to our higher selves.

Ask The Questions

Fear stops life forces flowing, separates us from our spiritual nature, paralyses us and is the basis of almost all negative emotions like anger, jealousy, disappointment, lack of self esteem, defensiveness, thoughts of inadequacy, cowardice, and frustration.

Anytime you have a negative emotion, stop and ask yourself, *"What am I frightened of here? What fear is behind this behavior/thinking/response?"*

These are extremely powerful questions and can transform a situation by shining a light on the fears that lurk in the dark, unconsciously controlling our moods and behaviors. Keep asking the questions until you have shone the light of hope into every little nook and cranny of your being.

Eliminate fearful self-talk and replace it with hopeful inspiration!

WHERE DO YOU FEEL HOPE?

We know hope *grows* in the heart, but it takes work to be able to identify where hope is felt in the body.

When you relive a situation in which you were really hopeful, or

at least had some hope for a positive
outcome, can you remember any
physical sensations? How did you
breathe? Did you feel really alive?
Remember - hope is linked to life force
and our spiritual and physical breath.

What did your voice sound like? How
much energy did you have? Maybe you
felt light? Did your world actually look
brighter? Or was there a sense of peace? Maybe you felt calmer?

Make sure that the next time you feel full of hope, you pay special
attention to finding the place where you feel it in your body.

Do you have actual physical reactions to fear? Most people do,
although we are often unaware of it. Does fear "grip" you or do you
have a "sinking" feeling in the pit of your stomach or feel heaviness
somewhere? Do you clench your jaws, grind your teeth, not sleep, have
diarrhea, neck pain or back pain, lose your ability to focus, or become
confused, angry and aggressive? Or do you become hyper-alert? The
list could be endless.

*If you can identify the bodily sensation of fear, then you can recognize it, shine
light on it, and by identifying it for what it really is, make it evaporate!*

Well, maybe it doesn't exactly evaporate, but you at least will be
conscious of the *real* issue. And it might just be eradicated!

FOCUS

Focus on the difference between where you feel fear and where you
feel hope.

The more you can differentiate, the more awareness you have, the more
consciously you can choose how you wish to think and feel. (And it's
part of FARC-ing! Remember - Focus, Attention and Awareness,
Repetition and Celebration!)

It always *seems* easier to let fear rule the day and some recent research
indicates we have "fear loops" operating in our brains automatically.
These then drive our patterns and habits. *To change them we have to wake
up, become conscious of and actively stop them!*

We can avoid facing them; hide; succumb; be the victim; be hopeless,
or take no action. It may seem easier at the time and you might even

feel better because your brain initially rewards the old behaviors, but it's not the way to be truly alive and joyful.

We need to wake up, know we are spiritually supported, guided and loved and have the faith, strength and courage to stand up and *face our fears*. Move away from what is causing those fears, or challenge them and fill ourselves with hope instead.

I find that if I am in a fearful situation, I surrender it to Spiritual wisdom - and it's amazing how it works! I ask for guidance help and for this situation to be handled for me - and voila!

But to do to that, we need patience, the ability to let go and to be conscious of when we are being driven by fear!

A clear heart will always show us the path of hope. Our fears mostly focus on memories of the past, uncertainty about the future, potential hazards, problems and danger.

A balance between the two stops us from doing dangerous or silly things, but allowing fear to unconsciously *dominate* our thinking stops us from feeling alive.

Hope is always available to us. So are our spiritual helpers! If we choose to ask for help, look for and focus on hope, fear begins to dissipate.

Just believing hope exists can increase it! Hope gives us courage, persistence, willpower, resilience, strength and joy. Hopelessness takes them away. *How you choose to think makes ALL the difference!*

WHY BREATHING MATTERS!

People respond differently to similar situations because of:

* their unconscious fears,
* the choices they make,
* the way they look at things,
* how they pre-program themselves,
* old patterns and habits, and,
* how much life force they have.

Focusing on our breathing - especially our "spiritual" breath (imagine you are breathing in light and love with each breath - in and out of your heart) - can help reprogram our old patterns and increase our life forces.

It's Always Sunny Above The Clouds

There is always hope. Always. No matter how bad things seem, if you seek God's direction and wait, the sun returns. *It's always sunny above the clouds!*

Things pass. Time heals the heart. Joy comes back, even after tragedies of monumental proportions.

HOPE JOY-ERCISE 1: PRACTICE HOPE AND FAITH

> *"Hoping does not mean doing nothing.*
> *It means going about our assigned tasks,*
> *confident that God will provide the meaning and the conclusion.*
> *It means a confident, alert expectation that God will do what He said He would do.*
> *It is imagination put in the harness of faith.*
> *It is a willingness to let God do it in His way and in His time.*
> *It is the opposite of making plans that we demand God put into effect,*
> *telling Him both how and when to do it."* [1]
> *Eugene H. Peterson*

Today is your day for putting your faith in something bigger than you! It doesn't matter whether you call that entity God, Love, Buddha, Allah, Universe, Spirit, the Divine or Spiritual Wisdom, as long as it has meaning for you!

As you go through all your tasks today, recognize there is a much larger world than you can see with your eyes. Try to sense the spiritual nature of the world. See and feel how full of hope and life things really are. *There is vast spiritual wisdom in action.*

About six years ago, my husband had what we call a "God experience" . He woke up one morning unsure if he had been dreaming or not, but he knew it was real. God had "spoken" to him. Not in big booming words; but in gentle, persistent tones.

He was told that he was an excellent man repeatedly – despite him saying *"But God, what about that….; and what about this…."*, to which God would answer *"you are an excellent man, and I love you"*.

This happened while I was sleeping next to him and when I woke up he was gone! He had gone for a walk and his life had changed. Honestly – he was a different man!

He said that as he walked everything looked and felt different. Animals and plants seemed more alive; the colors were brighter; the sky bluer and he felt optimistic and full of joy!

I believe that day he was able to see the spiritual realms around him; he tapped into that eternal hope and faith; he became aware of the whole. We can all do it – we just need to connect to our higher selves - and we can do that in many ways.

Are You Doing Your Work?

Check to see you are doing your part in your life responsibly. Look for the hope and light inside what appears dark, and if you can't find the light, hold onto faith or pray to find it. Allow the future to unfold without pushing or needing or wanting what *you want* to happen *now*!

Put your faith in the fact that someday, you might understand the "grand plan" of your life. If you could see the big picture, *you would see that many outcomes, which you may have thought were the worst in the world, were in fact the best.*

Perhaps a relationship breaks down and you separate. At the time, you are crushed. You feel no hope. You can't go on. Of course you can and you do! And with hindsight, you look back and thank God for the blessings.

For example, if you had not ended your previous relationship, you would never have met the real man or woman of your dreams! Or you may not have made the trip of a lifetime. Or you might eventually realize that the person you so adored had a lot more baggage than you realized, and it was in fact a lucky escape!

Remember The Gifts!

Who knows what the "disabled, troubled or difficult" child brings as their gifts. Our friend Mary's son was diagnosed with severe autism. She was told there was nothing to be done, and that there was no hope.

That wasn't the right thing to say to Mary! As a result of the gift of her son Michael, Mary has discovered her incredible capacity to heal, and many treatments that have helped hundreds of people that were never used before for autism, or other health issues.

Mary's life has not been easy and still isn't. But she does her work cheerfully and diligently. She continues to make the effort to help Michael and others heal. She believes and has absolute faith and a knowing, that he will be healed.

She has fought and continues to fight with amazing courage to make things better for him. She makes things happen when she is told it is impossible. *Nothing takes away her joy, faith and hope.*

This is the same story shared by many courageous parents who maintain hope in the face of seemingly insurmountable problems. And every parent who has fought this battle will tell you that the gifts and joy their child has brought them are immeasurable.

We don't know what the future holds and I don't think we are meant to, because that takes away the element of mystery, and the opportunity to learn the lessons and the discipline of faith and hope.

Our lessons may not be learned if we don't experience some suffering, pain, loss, sorrow or uncertainty. If we are never uncertain, fearful or confused, faith and hope are not practiced. They can't become the new habits.

We need to practice new habits—they are like muscles. Use them or lose them! Having faith in something bigger than you is also a practice! It's seeing things through the filter that there is a spiritual wisdom operating in your life! *Everything happens for a reason – you just may not understand it yet.*

HOPE JOY-ERCISE 2: PRACTICE FINDING WHERE HOPE LIVES IN YOUR BODY

> *"If you lose hope, somehow you lose the vitality that keeps life moving, you lose that courage to be, that quality that helps you go on in spite of it all."*
> Martin Luther King, Jr.

Today is the day for you to clearly identify where hope lives in your body!

Find a place where you can sit uninterrupted for a while. Take a few deep breaths and then as vividly as you can, recall and then "relive" a situation where things did not look good and you were driven by fear. Pick a moderate fear scenario, not a terrifying one!

What did you feel and where did you feel it? Now think of another challenging situation where you were hope-filled. What were the sensations in your body? Write down the differences between the two memories as clearly, and as descriptively, as you can.

Describe the physical sensations; what your feelings were; where you felt them; what they were like; how you behaved; and how others responded to you. How connected did you feel to God or the spiritual realms in both conditions?

Write down anything that you can think of that was different between the two situations. Once you are conscious of the differences, you can be more aware of the polarity - hope or fear - from which you are operating at any time.

And if you find yourself at the fear and darkness end, move towards hope and light- like the brightness or contrast bar in a computer. As we move the cursor towards one end of the bar, the screen image and all we see lightens *or darkens*.

As we slide up and down the hope/fear continuum, our whole world lightens as we move to hope, and darkens the closer we travel to fear. Write notes at home and at work that say *"Hope!",* and post them in very prominent places to remind you to *choose* hope and faith, and not fear or hopelessness. Put one on your desk or in your drawer as a reminder. Perhaps a little one on your mobile phone! Or put one on the wall of your bedroom so it's the first thing you see in the mornings.

These notes may sound silly but they work as symbols to remind us that we can choose hope any time we have the courage and will to do it. It also helps you to FARC – the "A" part – *attention and awareness; and the others - Focus, Repetition and Celebration!*

Go to bed recreating that feeling of hope inside you.

HOPE JOY-ERCISE 3:
PRACTICE TELLING YOURSELF A GREAT
FAIRY STORY

"Consult not your fears but your hopes and your dreams.
Think not about your frustrations, but about your unfulfilled potential.
Concern yourself not with what you tried and failed in,
but with what it is still possible for you to do."
Pope John XXIII

We all make mistakes. Well, maybe not you! But the rest of us do! *We are all constantly learning how to do things better, and doing the best we can with what we have.*

These are not new ideas, of course, but we would think they were if we watched how most people treat themselves. I bet you would never say to your best friend (or even your enemies!) the sorts of things you say to yourself.

There are times in life when you may be in a very difficult situation that you cannot escape from or change immediately. You can still have courage, awareness or *consciousness*, a plan, a dream and hope to change or remove yourself.

If you choose to operate with hope, everything changes. It's magical, but then *anytime you consciously bring God or light into your life, it's magical.* But you already know that now! You have experienced it if you have been able to throw yourself into the joy habit practices so far! Look at yourself with hope-full eyes. For example: You maybe feeling unhealthy and overweight, but know you *will* lose weight; you *do* have the strength to do this (whatever "this" is!) Things *will* improve. Things may not change in the time frame in which you want them to, because the Divine design for you may be another, much better plan.

If you FARC, you can change! (Focus, Awareness, Repetition, Celebration).

So be patient. *And wait with a heart full of hope.* Think of all the aspects of your life and/or body with which you are unhappy or disappointed, such as your weight, appearance, smoking, addictions, finances, relationships.

Examine how you view those aspects and what you say to yourself about them. *Are you using fear-based judgments or hope-full thinking?*

We all live our lives based on the "stories" we tell ourselves. Our stories are based on our perceptions - which are just that - perceptions and not true reality. These *FAIRY stories* become our beliefs. *And they rule our lives.* What story are you telling yourself about yourself? About your situation? About your options and choices? About others?

These stories are unconsciously programming everything you do or feel. *It's critical you become conscious of the story you tell yourself.* Remember, it is JUST a FAIRY story - it's *imagined* - you can change a story anytime you like and give it a happy ending!

A hope-filled heart will give you strength and courage to continue the journey - and change your story. If your concern is an abusive relationship, be honest about the reality of things changing, and seek help wherever you can.

Perhaps if you are at the "hope end" of the pole, you won't be driven to eat so much? Perhaps, just perhaps, fear was driving you to eat?

Or if you have hope, you won't fight as much, or feel so maligned, in relationships and life. Or with hope, you will have the courage and strength to give up smoking/ drinking/ addiction.

Who knows what miracles will happen when you operate from hope! Wait patiently, with positive expectations; take the right action with a heart of hope; feel gratitude, remembering and knowing that there is always hope for you - it's called Divine Grace.

HOPE JOY-ERCISE 4:
PRACTICE FINDING THE FEARS – AND MOVING TO HOPE

"When it gets darkest, the stars come out."
Anonymous

In *Freeing the Soul from Fear*, my wonderful mentor and teacher Robert Sardello suggests fear is always present in our world. Yet most of us are unconscious of how much fear rules our lives. *Learning to live and work with hope in our hearts can help balance that fear, and create a hopeful heart.*

Today is the day to find places in your

life where fear makes you behave in ways you don't like, respect or admire. Or where your AMMY takes over and you have no clue of what is happening! Being unconscious of fear allows it to grow, fester and prove itself right! Your AMMY says, "See - I told you to be frightened. See what happened because you didn't follow my advice?"

Not all fear is bad, of course. Fear or feeling the need for caution, can be a warning sign of truly dangerous situations and can help you make safe decisions. I don't step out in front of moving cars or walk down dark streets in dangerous areas, or do things that I have a strong feeling/knowing not to do!

But many of our fears are imagined - beliefs that have sprung wrongly from our imaginations and stories. Remember my fear of the dark and bogeymen as a little girl?

Today, review your fears and decide whether each fear is warning you of something real, or if it's imagined and falsely ruling your life. Where you recognize fear is driving your behavior, stop and see if it is the best motivator for you. Are you really in danger? And if not, *reframe* the situation from a hope-filled perspective.

Speak From Your heart - With Hope

Occasionally, I am frightened to say something to my husband, colleagues or friends - afraid they may react with anger or defensiveness or be upset. But in reality, nothing bad will happen if I say what I need to *say, kindly, honestly, and from my heart.*

They may react angrily, but is that really a reason for the paralyzing fear in me? In fact, it may lead us to a resolution. If I don't address what is bothering me, *that fear creates a barrier between us,* a silent ongoing tension that is very real, and I behave in a fearful, resentful or angry manner.

The results of that are usually far worse than if I chose to operate with hope, tried to speak from my heart, and addressed what was bothering me. Resentment can build up and up, and it influences how we interact with those around us negatively in every way.

We might think our resentment goes away, but it doesn't! *We need to ask for what we want or need instead of just resenting the other person not reading our mind and knowing what we need!*

Hope Gives You Courage

Hope gives me the courage to say what I need to say. For example, if I read an email and am concerned that there was an undercurrent of irritation in it, I can sit and fret and worry about it until it is a real issue for me. My AMMY takes over and makes me fearful that I have unknowingly done something wrong.

Instead of this, I could call the person and from my heart, say, *"I read your email and I was wondering if I have done anything to upset you?"* Said in a soft, concerned voice from my heart, this usually has a positive response, and brings about resolution - *if there was anything to resolve! The critical part is to be honest with yourself and speak from your heart.*

Pick one situation you are dealing with at the moment, and see if you can detect any fear surrounding it. If you do, find or breathe in hope, and see what inspiration comes with hope in your heart.

How many times have you been afraid to say something or do something until finally, when you blurted it out with a spirit of fear or anger, you found yourself in all sorts of strife! When you finally find the courage to face the same sort of situation with hope in your heart, dealing with it is easier!

Most of our challenges and difficulties are in our *imaginations* - in the stories we tell ourselves about what will happen. They are rarely real.

Turn the light on (by that, I mean put hope into your heart), recognize the story for what it is – a fairy story - and see how the "bogeymen" all go away!

A heart that is thinking correctly fears nothing.

HOPE JOY-ERCISE 5: PRACTICE HOPEFUL EXPECTATIONS

> *"There is no medicine like hope, no incentive so great, and no tonic so powerful as expectation of something better tomorrow."*
> *Orison Marden*

Today is the day of hopeful expectations. In other words, *you are to go through this day expecting good things to happen*, and for situations to work out perfectly, as spiritually planned, no matter what *you think* they should look like!

Before you start driving or traveling to work, *expect* the traffic to be

smooth, flowing easily, or for you to find a seat in public transport. If that isn't the case, be hope-full that there is a good reason for any difficulties and that it will become obvious to you at some stage.

If you are full of anxiety about a meeting that you have been dreading, stop! Say *"Thank you AMMY but not now!"*

And immediately become hope-full about it by surrendering the situation to Divine wisdom, or "pre-living" it in the way in which you *would like to see it happen.*

Imagine yourself *living through the experience* with all those hope/body sensations that you became aware of in earlier habit practices.

See, hear and feel the meeting having a *positive outcome* with you *feeling* and operating in a hope-full and therefore, courage-full way throughout. *Then*, walk into the meeting with *your new courage, true heart and hopeful spirit.*

If someone who scares you is approaching and you stop breathing, seize up, clench your fists or sweat - know that fear has "gripped" you. Stop. Take a breath. Say *"Thank you AMMY but not now!"*

Replace those fear sensations and language with hope-filled courage, and from that new position, interact with this person with cheerful enthusiasm! You might be stunned at the difference!

On your way home, be hopeful about how the evening will work out. See, hear and feel things going well; your relationship being smooth and easy; imagine your teenager succeeding in life despite the fact they appear to be totally uninterested in anything except aggravating you right now!

Feel what it is like to go through a day with hope, and hopeful expectations, instead of dread, worry, resignation and expecting the worst.

Take notes and decide which feels better. Then make your choice of how to operate - from your heart's wisdom or your imagination, fabrication or old fairy story! This will determine your expectations for the day.

Finally, make a list of all the things about which you would like to be hopeful. *Really feel the hope in your heart as you write* - it's not enough to *just* write it down.

You have to *consciously work* to eradicate the fears, *feel* the hope and really *believe* in the possibilities in each situation. Breathe those possibilities into your heart. You already know what it's like to wait full of dread and anxiety - waiting for the worst to happen.

So today and from now on, even if things don't work out the way you wanted them to, be full of positive, hopeful expectations, which will keep you in a good frame of mind while you are waiting. Maybe that will prepare you to be in a better state to take what does happen and make something great out of it!

How you feel is up to you. Actively hold onto hope!

HOPE JOY-ERCISE 6: PRACTICE TACKLING SOMETHING DIFFICULT WITH HOPE

> *"Most of the important things in the world have been accomplished by people who have kept on trying when there seemed to be no hope at all."*
> Dale Carnegie

Gratitude Glasses Or AMMY Glasses?

Think of a difficult situation in your life right now. Are you looking at it through "glasses" made of fear or of hope? Are you letting AMMY take over? Do you have your gratitude glasses on or your AMMY glasses?

Do you have a sense all is, or will be, as it should be? Do you believe that, even if something unpleasant has happened as a result of someone else's free will run amok (i.e. someone doing something that upset you or harmed you), good can come of it? *What fairy story are you choosing today?*

Sometimes people who say, *"Everything happens for a reason,"* passively wait for the world to come to them. *Believing things happen for a reason does not mean we can sit back and do nothing.* We must work to be conscious of what is going on, fulfill our responsibilities, and play our part.

If you don't know what to do, then say to yourself, *"I don't know what the best thing is to do, but I will have faith, do the right thing, be grateful, feel appreciation, be loving, kind, compassionate, hopeful and see what unfolds".*

Your Story

Pick one of the most difficult life challenges you have right now. Check the story you tell yourself about it. Reinvent your story so it serves you better!

No matter how hopeless it seems, work with your will, and use faith and hope in yourself, others or the scenario, to instill yourself with the courage you need to do something. It may be to work on forgiveness or make plans to talk to others, or find a way to love them fully or accept yourself and them.

If there really is nothing you think you can do, Think again! You can always accept the situation and look at it with hope-filled eyes and heart, knowing that spiritual wisdom is at work and can change anything - *in an instant*. Pray.

You may do nothing different except change your thoughts, stories or feelings, *and everything might change!*

Hold Onto Hope – It Takes Effort

Hold onto hope that you will be guided with inspiration to know what to do, even if you don't know *now*. Hope-fully expect that insight and clarity will come to you, or the right people will appear, or the right situation will emerge.

Your job is to be watchful and listen carefully for that inspiration and trust in the wisdom given to you.

Be conscious of which thoughts control you. They may be AMMY running amok! Remember, AMMY is interested in your *survival - not your success!* If you are uncertain about what will happen - find hope - and *expect* that good will come of it.

When it does, it may not look like "good" to you, but with the benefit of hindsight, you might see it turned out much better than you imagined!

"Hope springs eternal," as Alexander Pope wrote in 1733. It can keep us going, motivated and persisting when others give up.

The Heart And Hope

The heart is an alchemical vessel in which hope is used to transmute everything difficult into something beneficial.

Put all your problems in the heart, fill it with the philosopher's stone of hope, and see what emerges. (The philosopher's stone was the secret, magical ingredient used by alchemists to transmute base metals into gold.)

I never give up. Never. It drives my husband crazy! Hope gives me the energy to have persistence, creativity, resilience and optimism. And sometimes that persistence takes the form of patience - but not very often! I have to work on that one!

I do try, however, to make sure that what I am striving for is also what I believe to be in the highest good of all, and not just me forging on until have my own way. If I can't actually do anything, then I check my story and wait for inspiration to come for the next step.

I know there is always a next step! I just wait in hope, not in despair. Well, sometimes I feel despair, but not for long – because I check my stories and search for hope!

We will never have accurate knowledge of the future – it's the *future!* We can't know today what tomorrow will be like – *but we can sure imagine it with positive feelings, hope and no fear.* No human really *knows* what will happen – but *choosing hope opens the way for the realm of alchemy and miracles!*

HOPE JOY-ERCISE 7: PRACTICE HOPE-FULL NOT HOPE-ING!

"The very least you can do in your life is to figure out what you hope for. And the most you can do is live inside that hope. Not admire it from a distance but live right in it, under its roof."
Barbara Kingsolver

There is a difference between wishing and hoping. Hope without faith is empty - it's simply wishing. Hope filled with faith is active. It spurs us on to do something.

We can wish all we like that things will change or be different, but *wishing places all the power externally.* We wish someone would come along and fix things so everything would be fine, but we do nothing to contribute! We don't take an active role. We don't do our "work".

I think many people say, *"I'm hoping this situation is going to improve"* *without actually engaging in the whole process!* It's just a word they use to describe the feeling of, *"I have given up and am resigned to what will happen."* (This is often accompanied by a sigh!)

These people may still be living in and ruled by fear, but just saying they are hopeful! They are really wishing things were different without willingness to be involved *actively or consciously.*

Take Action

Our work is *to hold hope and faith especially when things look bad.* We need to *take action* - to *choose* hope, *step into* hope, and put hope into our hearts to trigger the alchemical process.

We must hold onto faith, move, *do something* to see the world differently or *change* the way we react. We must *become conscious* of what sort of expectation we have - one of hope or one of dread?

When we really are full of hope, we are filled with light and actually feel lighter. We vibrate at a different rate and are actually different beings. Our hearts are different; we are conscious of the decision to operate from hope; we have done something to make that possible.

My husband, Ken, had an interesting experience with hope and our friend Mary, a health practitioner. She assessed him and told me the things she had found, which I was to share with him. They were not necessarily easy things to hear, and I was being led by fear when I worried about his reaction.

But when I did tell him, using hope and courage as my companions, coming from my heart and with compassion, he said he was filled with hope and light deep inside. When Ken heard what Mary had found, he felt, at last, that someone had really identified what had been core issues for him.

I believe Mary is inspired in her work, and Ken sensed her spiritual connection to us, and he felt that what she spoke was truth for him. That gave him hope. He was able to hear it in the right way and not react or be angry. Hope spreads!

Ken has since been able to find that same sensation and fill himself with it, rather than disappointment or another fear-based emotion. And he can *choose* a very different way of approaching the world now, especially when he catches himself having negative thoughts.

Find The Fear And Breathe!

Both of us still fall back into our old fear-based habits at times - but *now we can recognize them, breathe, and choose to become hopeful and expect good things to come.*

See if you can feel the difference between actively making your heart full of hope and just passively *wishing* for things to be transformed.

As Norman Vincent Peale said *"As hopefulness becomes a habit, you can achieve a permanently happy spirit."*

Hope comes with knowing, and *choosing to remember,* that the spiritual worlds will help when you need it and *ask* for it. Go on - you *can* do it!

Joy Secret #4

Reverence

YOUR SEVEN MINUTES

> *"Always and in everything, let there be reverence."*
> *Confucius*

What does reverence mean to you? The following questions help you understand how reverence is a life changing habit to develop.

Unfortunately, it's not a common conscious practice – and we don't teach it to our children. *Reverence in its pure state is the ability to see The Divine in everything and everyone, and be in awe of that spiritual magnificence. Everyone you meet is a spiritual being.* They *deserve* reverence.

Do you remember reading of a reverential "fear" of God? From what I understand, this "fear" of God is not really fear – it's actually a state of reverential awe - having true respect for the power, love and presence of the Spiritual realms.

- What does reverence mean to you?
- Think about the things - or people - you handle or treat with reverence.
- What or whom do you revere, honor or respect?
- Do "things" keep coming up for you more than people or the spiritual worlds? Money? Possessions? Having more than others?
- Hopefully, you think people are awesome for their qualities, and not their money or fame!
- Does being in nature make you feel reverence?
- Where do you feel reverence in your body?
- How do you show reverence?
- How do others show you reverence?

- What are your behaviors, how do you use your body and what is your voice tone like when you feel reverent?
- If others treat you with reverence, how do you feel?

AMANDA'S TAKE:

> *"The moment I have realized God sitting in the temple of every human body,*
> *the moment I stand in reverence before every human being and see God in him*
> *- that moment I am free from bondage,*
> *everything that binds vanishes, and I am free."*
> *Swami Vivekananda*

NAMASTE AND TRUE RESPECT

Have you ever seen the way the Nepalese, or some Indians and Buddhists, greet each other?

They put their hands together as if in prayer, and bow their heads and say *"Namaste,"* which has a variety of meanings around a similar theme:

"The spirit in me salutes the spirit in you";
"I greet that place where you and I are one";
"The light within me sees and honors the light within you"
or simply - *"I see the God in you."* This is true respect.

Would that not be a great way for us all to greet people? To be constantly reminded that in front of us stands an incredible, awesome being of light, worthy of awe and wonder?

SPIRIT IGNITERS OR FOOFERS?

Every one of us has a pilot light that lives inside our hearts, and *everyday*, with *every* interaction, we can *choose* to *ignite* that flame in others - or blow it out – to "foof" it like a candle flame. We can be spirit "foofers" (those who blow the pilot light out) or "igniters"!

Reverence ignites the pilot light of our spirit - and of others.

Reverence, like forgiveness, needs to be a way of living, and the greeting of Namaste can be the trigger to remind us (many times daily) to treat everyone and everything with reverence - to be a spirit igniter! That's your mission, should you choose to accept it!

You might feel silly walking up and saying Namaste to people in our culture, so when you meet someone, try to meet their spirit with your reverent smile or handshake - and just silently say Namaste to them! Try to be present and make any greeting more meaningful than just, *"Hi, how are you!"*

Are Things More Valuable Than People?

At a class I attended years ago, someone brought out an ancient treasure: a 3,000-year-old rose quartz Buddha. You should have seen how people handled that Buddha and rightly so! It was worth millions of dollars, but priceless in terms of what it represented. It was "irreplaceable".

But... *it was just an object*. I didn't see anyone else there handling another human in the same way! How easily we can do that - have reverence for, and handle with awe and wonder, an external object whose value we measure by huge amounts of money or its uniqueness or irreplaceable nature.

Yet we don't realize that in front of us every day stand one-of-a-kind beings of unimaginable beauty, spirit, value and worth. How do we treat them?

Disasters like the Christchurch earthquake or the Japanese tsunami really put things in perspective - all the possessions, the things, washed away or destroyed. What really mattered? *The people.*

When did you last view a human with awe, wonder and reverence? We do it all the time with film stars and famous people - our culture has made them objects of awe and wonder, or horror in some cases!

But when did you last view someone with whom you live or work with true respect, *humility*, awe and wonder? We seem to have forgotten about reverence in our culture, and it's time to bring it back to consciousness - along with humility.

If we were all treated with, and treated others with, humility, respect, awe, wonder and reverence, the world would be a very different place!

I love this spectacular poem by Hafiz, one of the best-known Sufi poets from Persia, translated so beautifully by Daniel Ladinsky, in *"I Heard God Laughing, Poems of Hope and Joy"*.

My Brilliant Image

One day the sun admitted,
I am just a shadow.

I wish I could show you,
The Infinite Incandescence,
That has cast my brilliant image.

I wish I could show you,
When you are lonely or in darkness,
The Astonishing Light
Of your own Being. 1

Imagine what the world would be like if we respectfully and humbly greeted each other daily with "*Namaste*", and could truly feel and see the astonishing light of each being or at least imagine that it was there and greet it!

Picture how different our world would be if our politicians, corporations, corporate leaders and community leaders all remembered and operated with true reverence.

ARROGANCE AND CRUELTY - ENEMIES OF REVERENCE

> *"Whoever undertakes to set himself up as a judge of truth and knowledge*
> *is shipwrecked by the laughter of the gods."*
> *Albert Einstein*

One of the definitions of cruelty is heart-less-ness. If we are in our *hearts*, we behave with gentleness, kindness, respect and reverence. If we operate from our *fears or insecurities*, we can be competitive, manipulative, controlling, political or just plain old mean!

It feels to me that the opposite of reverence is a blend of arrogance, pride, and cruelty - a disregard for the life in others and therefore of life itself - *all arising from unconsciousness and detachment.* When we don't have true respect and humility *within us, and for ourselves*, it's hard to show to others. We are too busy *proving* we are great!

We don't even have to be arrogant to be cruel! We can be cruel unconsciously, or more sadly, on purpose.

Our tongues can be very cruel. Be careful and mindful of what you say to others and about others. Are you considering them with reverence? Or is your program *"it's all about me"* and proving how good you are? Words can ignite someone's spirit, or crush it, in a heartbeat. Make sure your words are spoken in a tone of reverence.

Our actions can be cruel, disrespectful or humiliating. Even our non-actions! Such as not communicating with people - although sometimes there is a real reason for not communicating, and if you are in a position where you cannot communicate, pray for those people from a distance.

We may give someone the "cold shoulder," or have little "clubs" at work where we exclude people, or we may exclude people from our family circles. There is no reverence in these behaviors.

How do you treat others - *always with kindness, humility and true respect* or differently from that?

How much respect did Mother Theresa command throughout the world? And how did she treat everyone? With absolute reverence and love.

HUMILITY

Humility goes hand in hand with reverence. *Humility and reverence both acknowledge the source of our light.*

We are born with these capacities, they are part of being human but *we forget;* we lose consciousness. Our egos, with all their fears, take over and we *practice* the habits of insecurity, unkindness, arrogance and pride – instead of making reverence, humility and respect our default habits.

We need to reawaken our awareness of humility and reverence - and weave them through every aspect of our lives.

Once we comprehend the spiritual significance of, and spiritual influence on, *everything* in our world, and that *we are all connected; we are the whole and* part of the whole, then we automatically operate with reverence and humility – we can no longer be cruel or arrogant.

We will be so aware of the awesome, true nature of everyone we meet that we can go past their "personality", and ours – because we will see our own true nature! Instead, awe, wonder, humility and reverence will reign!

Michael Grinder, one of my mentors, (www.michaelgrinder.com) runs great courses. He says of non verbal communication, *"We are in love with the influence of power, when we should be in love with the power of influence."*

It's true too of the influence the spiritual worlds can have on us - if we ask, and allow them to help and guide us. Develop a habit of reverential awe for that power – it is there to support us.

The more we connect to our source, and see others connected to the same source, the easier it becomes to see the astonishing light in everyone which includes YOU! Pure Joy!

REVERENCE FOR THE WORLD AND NATURE

> *"To believe that every tree, plant and insect can talk takes an open mind.*
> *Go by yourself into nature and sit quietly.*
> *Then pick up a rock and listen to your thoughts.*
> *After a while, put that rock down and pick up another rock.*
> *Your thoughts will change.*
> *These are the voices and the wisdom of the stone people.*
> *Many of the stone people are very old and very wise."* [2]
> Don Coyhis

You cannot NOT make a difference! It's either positive or negative. Your choice! Whatever you do affects what happens to others - AND the world.

It affects all the humans around you (and maybe further away), nature, and other living creatures. It ultimately affects what happens on Earth. Every time we pass something into our air or water system, we are affecting all the life, animals and humans that rely on that system, and they feed into many other systems.

It's a connected world. Are you someone who consciously cares for the Earth? Do you treat *every* aspect of our precious planet with reverence? Do you discard trash into the ocean or out your car window as you drive along, completely unaware and uncaring of the consequence?

Do you *recycle* if you have the chance? This is a way of showing reverence for the earth - instead of polluting her with all our landfill and toxins. Do you think carefully about *cleaning products* that you use? Support companies that are passionately committed to enhancing our lives and the environment.

Do you keep your *car* in good shape so you are not constantly spewing out products that harm us, and the Earth? Do you take the *shopping cart* out into the parking lot and leave it where it can roll and hit another car? Or do you abandon it where someone else will have to collect it? Are you *considerate* when you drive? Do you think the road is yours and everyone else is an idiot?

These are all small daily things that you can do if you choose to live and behave with reverence, with true respect and humility. You can make a big, positive difference to everything.

If you choose to act unconsciously, disregarding the outcome, you will have a destructive influence. It's your choice, again! *WAKE UP! What you do really matters!*

I wish all companies would treat the earth and people with reverence – creating a truly respectful and awe filled culture, instead of revering only the dollar, bottom line and profits.

Joy Is The Precursor To Success

We know that joy is the precursor to success; it's the new competitive advantage. There would be a lot less corruption, improved profitability and productivity and many more fulfilled employees, if companies focused on true serving and reverence as a mission statement, and were not consumed by goals based on power and greed.

For instance, why would anyone treat a service-oriented person with less respect than they would a corporate executive? Without those service-oriented people doing their jobs, there might not be a corporate executive!

These people who are the first point of contact with customers, are often the most important people in the company - *they are in charge of how others feel about your company and products;* they *create* the relationships that determine a sale, loyalty or great word of mouth advertising. They truly deserve great respect.

Large companies who care little for their employees or customers, and which consequently offer appalling service, have lost touch with what is really important for their businesses i.e: *how people feel.*

The fast track to corporate success happens when there is a focus on building relationships through serving, reverence, helping, supporting, taking care of employees as well as the customers, paying attention to how people feel, and creating an environment in which people can be the best they can be – with all the secrets and habits of joy embedded in the culture.

Great Leaders

I believe one of the reasons my husband is such a great leader is that he is naturally humble, and has a real reverence for the people who work with him. He sees their potential and possibilities (their astonishing light – even before they see it!); he believes in them and *he helps them see their own light.*

His book, *The People Pill,* is in some ways a study of reverence in the corporate world. The companies he led had soaring profits under his leadership, and I am not just his biased wife! The actual figures are astounding - and he did it by growing people, and treating them all with respect and reverence - and fostering a culture where others did the same.

Through Simon Sinek, I heard of a company called Barry Wehmiller. This phenomenally successful global, multi billion dollar company has a guiding philosophy. Their guiding philosophy - a credo - that people literally filter all decisions through is: *"we are developing great people to do extraordinary things."* Now that is what I call the reverent corporate philosophy of a JOY focused company! Reverence needs to be a part of everything we do. It's a wonderful daily habit.

HANDLING OBJECTS WITH REVERENCE

How do you put objects on a table? Do you "chuck" them down or throw them from a distance? It doesn't really matter what the item is, if you throw it down without any thought, you are creating a spiritual gesture of disrespect.

Think about it - when you see someone take your business card the way the Japanese do - with two hands and with great reverence - how does it make you feel?

It makes me feel honored and respected. If you take someone's business card but just shove it in your pocket - what have you just told that person non-verbally?

It's the same with anything another person gives you - a document, parcel, gift or food. *Be present; be conscious and grateful; take it from them respectfully, treat it with care, and place it gently down.*

Try doing this for just one day - handle everything as if it was something very precious that had been given to you to keep safe. You will be amazed at how different you feel!

If you do this consciously and repeatedly until it becomes a new habit or pattern, you will find that you enter into *a state of reverence* - your cells will start to vibrate in harmony, in resonance, with reverence, and it will have a dramatic impact on everything that you do - while you remain in that state!

Throwing anything that isn't meant to be thrown, carries that spiritual gesture of violence. If it's a football or a basketball, it's okay to throw it! But even then, how it is thrown is important. If the ball is thrown with the *intent* to hurt someone, it is neither respectful, nor reverent, to the person - or even the principles of the game.

As The Mother (Sri Aurobindo) said in one of her books – *"everything always depends on the way in which things are done; not only what one does but the spirit in which one does it."*

REVERENCE FOR FOOD AND OUR BODIES

Do you treat food with reverence? Do you see it for what it truly is - *your life renewal force*? Do you say Grace and not only thank God (or Spirit, Angels whatever you believe in), the cook, the farmers and the food for the work they did in growing, but also nature for providing you with this nourishment?

Many of us don't even *stop* to eat. It's very difficult for our bodies to *receive* the nutrition from the food if we are doing two other things as well as eating. We drive, work on the computer, do tasks, shop and catch up on our to-do list while we eat. Is that treating the food or our bodies with reverence?

On my Qigong retreat, we were silent for 2 weeks. We had to *do nothing but eat when we ate*. It was incredible! I chewed much more, tasted much more and really appreciated the food. That's the value of being present – it allows you to feel reverence.

I would recommend everyone tries eating in silence or at least paying sole attention to eating (in silence) for 10 minutes every meal. I love the way the French, as a culture, *appreciate, savor and honor their food* and the *process* of eating. It's a great habit to develop.

How we prepare food is very significant! Do you eat out all the time like so many people do these days? *Pick your restaurants carefully* so there is some awareness and love in the preparation of this nourishment you are providing for your body.

Most of us see eating as some process that has to happen to stave off hunger, rather than a *vital source of nourishment and life forces.* If we habitually prepare food with love, care and reverence, those qualities go into it and feed us spiritually as well! If we just "throw" something together and shove it into our mouths - the gesture of reverence is absent - and much of the physical and spiritual nutritional value!

When you put the food on the table, do you slam it down or place it with care and love as if it was a gift? If waiters did this and approached their jobs *and guests* with reverence, I bet they would earn a lot more in tips!

REVERENCE FOR YOURSELF AND YOUR SOUL

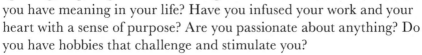

How do you treat your mind? Do you fill it with images of negative, cruel and harmful sights? Do you watch violent movies or programs? Do you compare yourself with others constantly?

Or do you educate yourself and learn new and interesting things? Do you actively seek uplifting, inspiring activities or images? Do you have meaning in your life? Have you infused your work and your heart with a sense of purpose? Are you passionate about anything? Do you have hobbies that challenge and stimulate you?

What are you doing for your spirit? Do you take time to just sit quietly in natural surroundings and allow the peace of nature to restore you? Do you have faith in a higher power and take time to attune to it?

Do you attend classes or do anything to learn or grow spiritually? Do you read uplifting books? Do you have friends who are joyful and encouraging? Do you see your life as a service to others?

Do you beat yourself up with your negative internal dialogue? You can change that dialogue by *waking up to the source of them – the fears that drive your old patterns, behaviors and habits.*

Create a list of things that make you feel positive and light. Read it every day. Say them out loud! Speak with reverence to *yourself,* not just to others. If you forget to see God in yourself or other people; if you struggle to treat yourself with reverence - at least treat *everyone else* with true respect.

And that means no screaming, shouting, aggression, hitting, cruelty, abuse or violence. It means having self control, compassion, caring and acting with kindness. Hopefully that will lead you to living in, and behaving with, reverence, one of the most critical habits and secrets for a joy filled life.

Pretend when you speak with someone that the person is God or some spiritual being. I know humans are not God, but they have a God - like spirit inside them - so do you!

God Lives Here

Would you dare to shout at or speak to a Divine Spiritual Being in a disparaging, belittling or nasty way? I doubt it. *Imagine that people walk around with a little sign on their forehead* that says, *"God lives here"!*

Treat them as if you had a Divine Being standing in front of you - they will wonder what has happened to you! And if they ask, you can answer - it's love and reverence.

The habit and gestures of reverence, both the physical and spiritual kind, is something we can weave into all our daily activities and it will lead us to humility and joy. More motivating for many, it will lead to true influence, as others will be affected profoundly, and positively by you.

Focusing on developing the habit of reverence may help you develop a sense of purpose or meaning in life; it will certainly be rewarding and fulfilling, and bring you satisfaction in more ways than you can imagine.

REVERENCE JOY–ERCISE 1:
PRACTICE REVERENCE FOR THE DIVINE

> *"Millions of spiritual creatures walk the earth unseen,*
> *both when we wake and when we sleep."*
> *John Milton*

No matter what your spiritual belief system, we need to treat God (or your equivalent of God) with awe, wonder and reverence. Remember as you read, if you don't believe in God, substitute with the words that have meaning for you.

Today is your time to find *awesome respect for the spiritual realms.* For angels, guides, the nature spirits and all living things. Too often we forget about all the angels that help us out - on earth and from "above."

I believe we have guardian angels and that there are many "angels" in human guise who help us through our lives! They come in all shapes and sizes and appear magically at times we need them. It is only afterwards that we do realize we were "touched by an angel." Isn't that awesome?

This is the realm of miracles and things way beyond our understanding, so j*ust be grateful that we are living in a world where miracles can and do happen all the time.* Be very reverent towards this whole amazing, awe-inspiring spiritual world of which we are members!

Look around you today and try to feel them in all you do, and be aware of all the beings that are with us as well - like loved ones who have passed, and angels who want to help us. *We just don't always know how to look, sense, feel, and listen for them.*

It's relatively easy to learn this new habit - be quiet, look with your heart and listen. Consciously ask and look for the help you are offered.

At the wake after Mum's funeral, I was standing on the balcony talking with one of her oldest and dearest friends, my surrogate Mum, Billee. A turquoise butterfly flew right by me - two stories up. I saw it and instantly *knew* it was Mum! It was the strangest thing. *I just knew it.*

Several days later when I was really missing her, I was with some friends on their farm. For three hours I was surrounded by all manner of turquoise bugs - butterflies, dragonflies and others I could not even recognize. *Turquoise was Mum's favorite color!*

Since then, she has sent me many butterflies - they appear outside my window, on billboards, in airports, magazines, t-shirts and cards. The inner knowing that it's her makes it true for me.

The Spiritual Realms

I have told this story many times now, and almost everyone has a similar one. Those who have crossed the threshold are always with us - *we just need to wake up and recognize their presence!* Have you had an experience in your life like mine?

How could you not be filled with wonder and reverence at the amazing ways they can connect with us?

Think of all those times you have needed a guiding hand - and although you didn't know it at the time - you were given help.

It's often only when you stop and reflect on those situations that you can see the guidance they gave you! Thank God and His "team" for all they have done for you; for all the help they have sent you; the blessings, gifts and grace He has bestowed on you; and for His ongoing forgiveness. We have a lot to revere!

Treat the spiritual realms with respect; do not ignore them; look for them and acknowledge their help; listen carefully for what they say to you; take time with them every day and sit in awe, wonder and gratitude for everything you have been given.

Align your will with the divine design of your life. It works out better in the end. Much better! I love what C.S. Lewis wrote: *"There are two kinds of people; those who say to God, 'Thy will be done'; and those to whom God says, 'All right, then, have it your way!'"*

The price is much greater if we do it our way!

REVERENCE JOY–ERCISE 2: PRACTICE REVERENCE FOR LIFE

> *"By having a reverence for life, we enter into a spiritual relation with the world. By practicing reverence for life, we become good, deep and alive."*
> *Albert Schweitzer*

A life-threatening illness or event usually transforms a person's perspective – of everything. Have you met anyone who has survived cancer; fought off another terrible illness, or had a near-death experience?

Almost everyone will tell you that they have a new reverence for life; and for everyone and everything in their world; they now enjoy every moment.

Why do most of us wait for a crisis to make us appreciate what we have? Because most of us are *asleep* to the true nature of the world and take our life forces for granted! We are unconscious of the beauty, joy and wonder of being alive. We are living life at half-mast.

Imagine you were told you had a month to live. That's all. One month. How would you live in that last month – *not what would you do, but how would you live?*

I had originally meant to type ""*How* would you live if you had a month to live?" Instead I unconsciously typed "*How* would you live if you had a month to *love*?" It's a sign of Mum helping me again! *This may be the most important question in this whole book.*

If you truly only had one month to live, living the way of love would be the best possible way to spend it!

It is at critical times like this that many people discover their true spiritual nature. Many people who have never prayed before, or believed in prayer or a God or anything spiritual, start to pray with fervor at times of crisis. They develop faith, which Gandhi says, *"is nothing but a living, wide-awake consciousness of God within."*

Everything In Your Life Is Truly A Gift

If you had only a month to live with love, you would suddenly start treating life, yourself and others with great reverence - and you would recognize how precious it is.

You would see everything in your life as a gift - your family, your friends, your colleagues, difficulties, challenges, even your enemies would look pretty good at that crisis time! You would feel gratitude and awe for *everything* that happens, and you would deeply feel the spiritual realms that lovingly surround you.

I imagine you would look appreciatively at natures magnificence and the tiniest things would bring joy, wonder and awe; and *you would suddenly see the bigger picture* and not be caught in petty squabbles.

You would not waste time watching mindless television, and instead communicate lovingly with your family and friends. I hope you would explore and share your feelings and be aware of others feelings. I hope you would be honest and truthful. Live life like this now - don't wait for a crisis!

Relish Every Moment

Art Buchwald, the famous American journalist, was told in 2006 that he was going to die. His kidneys had failed in June, and he was given three weeks to live and went into a hospice. He was cared for and nurtured, spent time with his family and friends, and relished every moment of life.

As he told the story later, he was full of joy and had a great time, and developed a deep sense of reverence for life. Five months later, he had to check out of the home because his kidneys were now functioning! Joy, reverence, gratitude and relishing every moment of his life, restored his life!

He died several years later, after he had written another book called, *"Too Soon to Say Goodbye!"* (published by Random House).

Today is the day to look at how you respect and revere every aspect of your life. Start being conscious of every wonderful moment you are given - whether it is disguised as a challenge, or is an obvious blessing.

Become full of reverence for it, and for *everything* that happens, and for all those who are in your life. Be glad, joyful, grateful, kind, and relish every little thing that happens - all the pain, challenge, difficulty *and* the fun.

Treat your life as the precious and wonderful gift it is.

REVERENCE JOY-ERCISE 3: PRACTICE REVERENCE FOR NATURE

> *"Gratitude bestows reverence, allowing us to encounter everyday epiphanies, those transcendent moments of awe that change forever how we experience life and the world."*
> *John Milton*

PROJECT 1:
FEEL AWE, WONDER AND REVERENCE
FOR NATURE

Go out today and find some aspect of nature to bring those feelings and consciousness to you - plan a weekend trip to immerse yourself in it. If that is impossible, find some spectacular photos and lose yourself in them.

Put those photos up on walls around you so you can be aware of, and feel, the majesty of nature with awe, wonder and reverence. Or watch some of David Attenborough's extraordinary DVDs on wildlife and nature. There are many incredible shows about nature that inspire us make us gasp in awe!

On a trip to Nashville's Opryland to speak, I was in one of many long corridors on the way to my room. For those of you unfamiliar with this famous, amazing hotel and conference center in Nashville, it's enormous!

It covers 5 acres and you have to walk miles (it seems) to reach the rooms and it is very easy to find yourself lost in all those corridors. I was irritated and lost when a family emerged from another corridor. They were obviously lost as well!

The father was angrily pushing a luggage cart that was very overloaded and the mother was frustrated, looking at a map trying to work out where they were. They had two small children aged about four and six who were having the best time, dancing and jumping with excitement even though they were in a windowless corridor!

The Wisdom Of Children

This, for me, was a blinding-flash-of-the-obvious moment! Suddenly I saw the children's awe and wonder contrasted directly against how we have come to live our lives as adults. The adults were frustrated, angry and upset. *The children were finding the joy in the situation* - they were full of awe, wonder and laughter, and made the experience fun by playing.

As adults, we are so engrossed with *"being on a mission"* (like finding the room), *doing* stuff, and *having* stuff that we forget to flow, look around and feel awe and wonder for where we are!

It's easy to be filled with awe when we look at a magnificent view, experiencing the amazing beauty of nature and the incredible silence. But in everyday life, we can lose that sense of awe unless we consciously *seek it* and *hold it*.

Consider the ocean and its unfathomable power, or look at the night sky and all its vastness. Think about the Grand Canyon, or being in ancient forests, rain forests, beside rivers and isolated streams. Each of these can fill us with awe, wonder, reverence and feed our souls. There is something in the silence, vastness and wisdom of nature that makes us become conscious of reverence.

Go out today and become conscious of the amazing power of the natural world surrounding you. Keep doing it until you have created a new habit - living with reverence.

PROJECT 2:
EVERYDAY REVERENCE

Find a way to look at everyday life situations with awe and wonder - like those children in the halls of Opryland did!

We all did that as children, so we all have the capacity to do it - just as *we have the innate capacity for joy*. We would be so excited over the smallest things! Go and watch children play on a beach for an hour and you will see pure, unbridled awe and joy in action!

Joy sits patiently inside you waiting for the day, like today, when you will awaken to it. No matter what happens today - find a reason to be in awe and wonder.

Look at your colleagues and family with a sense of awe for the incredible spiritual beings they are. They may be covered with a pretty ordinary personality, but they really are "astonishing beings of light!"

Be amazed at the technology of your car - it can take you places and you never need to think about it - unless it doesn't work! Find yourself in awe of how the universe or God or Source arranges everything so perfectly - no matter how messy it looks to us!

I am always amazed by people who can create machinery, make art or carve wood into glorious shapes. I'm also fascinated and awed by people who manage very difficult lives and still smile, or by people with severe handicaps who are so grateful for what they have. I stand in awe of doctors, carers and healers who can work magic.

I look at everyone with curiosity, fascination and wonder - how can they do what they do? *Everyone* - no matter who they are or what they do - has something amazing to give to life - and to us. We just need to be *curious* and look beyond ourselves to see it.

I see the world as an alive, swirling mass of awesome, amazing, wonderful, mysterious stuff just waiting for me to learn about it, and it's very exciting! Remember the children in that corridor? Your mission today is to experience everything with a sense of awe and wonder. You will be surprised at how much gratitude and joy you feel at the end of the day.

REVERENCE JOY–ERCISE 4: PRACTICE REVERENCE FOR OTHERS

> *"Everybody can be great because anybody can serve.*
> *You don't have to have a college degree to serve.*
> *You need only a heart full of grace."*
> Martin Luther King, Jr.

Namaste. That is your meditation and task for today. Silently greet every person you meet, and every animal and plant you encounter with this word.

In your imagination, feel yourself performing the gesture that goes with it, as you bow with reverence to the life force, to the "I AM" in front of you.

It's not weird to be greeting all life forms in this way. Plants are precious - they give us oxygen, herbs, food and a gazillion other things. They have their own life force - some see that life force as a spiritual being.

Are you not amazed at how a seed can fall on the ground and, despite all the obstacles it has to overcome, emerge as a gorgeous flower or some nutrition-filled substance for you or animals to eat? When you see a bunch of flowers or a single bloom - try to grasp the amazing powers that went into the bloom being there.

Animals are equally complex. Think of how they live, and

survive, despite what humankind is doing to them and their environment. When you see a squirrel or birds downtown, imagine what they have done to adapt to concrete jungles, not to mention how they can now eat junk food! They are not healthy, mind you, but they are eating it to survive for as long as they can.

Look For The Inside God

Remember, a Divine spark *is in every person you see. Including you!* The beggar on the street, the janitor, the cab driver, your colleagues, the person who collects your trash, the corporate executive, the gardener, cleaning person or council worker, bus drivers, sales people, cash register clerks - *everyone!*

And most importantly, that spiritual Divine spark is in your family members. *Today is a special day for your family!* You are going to treat them all as the precious spiritual teachers they are. They give us more opportunities to grow and develop than anyone else ever could. Remember, you may not be the easiest person on the planet to live with, in truth!

Be in awe and wonder that they chose you! Be filled with reverence for them and gratitude that they *are* with you, and willing to stick with you. If they chose not to stick with you, be full of reverence anyway, because their departure may turn out to be the best thing that ever happened to you - no matter how bleak it looked at the time.

Look for what is inside other people's hearts - this is their true nature and who they really are. Everyone is an astonishing being of light inside his or her heart. You are blessed to have these people as part of your life.

The blessing may not be obvious at this moment, but live in joyful, hopeful expectation that you will one day soon see that blessing. You will be filled with awe and wonder at the magic that happens when you develop the habit of reverence and you live with, and actively *feel and show,* reverence and respect for all.

REVERENCE JOY-ERCISE 5
PRACTICE REVERENCE FOR YOUR SOUL AND SPIRIT

> *"There is a beautiful creature living in a hole you have dug"* [3]
> *Hafiz*

This is your day! The day for you to discover for yourself what a spectacular and awesome being you are.

Try not to let judgments and critical thoughts come pouring in as you read that last line - they are the "hole" we have dug for ourselves. The more negative self-talk we have running in continuous loops in our minds, the deeper the hole and stronger the patterns we create. Look at yourself through your heart today - *feel who you really are.*

When we ask someone, *"Who are you?"* they mostly reply with what they do. *"My name is Amanda and I am a speaker"* or a banker, a manager, a nurse or mechanic, and so on.

That's not *who* we are! *We are souls and spirits constantly waking up, creating our lives, merging with, and connecting to Spirit and humans.* It's the layers of personality and ego that block our vision of who we really are.

People like the Dalai Lama and Mother Theresa can see through all that ego and personality stuff because they know who we are in our hearts, and they wear the glasses of compassion, which, like X-ray vision, cut through.

Pretend for today that you are the loving parent of you - the child! This is the day you are going to see your real self. When you see yourself as the Spiritual being you *really* are, you will *automatically* treat yourself with reverence.

There is something for your soul to do in this world - some special purpose that only you can do. Find that calling. You may be a little flawed – we all are - but that's because we're human. You are *not* a loser, victim, failure, hopeless, difficult, troubled or any other *label* you, or someone else, has attached to you.

We are all responsible, special spiritual beings: we need to acknowledge our limitless nature and capacity; and be actively doing what we were meant to be doing here on this journey – to joy.

Treat your purpose and spiritual work with reverential awe. *Your work* is to discover what that purpose and calling is, to learn about it, and do it the best you can.

So today begin to find out who you really are and what your spiritual purpose is and begin to fulfill it! Have a chat with your spiritual advisors and ask them who you are and what the Divine plan is for you.

Just for today, watch *only* uplifting DVDs; read spiritual books; listen

to or attend a spiritual class; spend time on your own; reflect on your limitless nature; and see yourself as important, special and valuable.

Surround yourself with beauty - flowers or photos or scenery; have wonderful aromatherapy oils burning so your sense of smell is pampered. *Pure* aromatherapy oils and their scents can lift our spirits tremendously. Hang out with people and friends you love and go away for relaxing weekends or days.

This may not sound like you are treating yourself with reverence, but you are each time you do activities that help you relax and reconnect with yourself, God, your family and friends. You are doing something spiritual *and* acknowledging your true nature, coming into harmony with it.

REVERENCE JOY–ERCISE 6
PRACTICE REVERENCE FOR YOUR BODY

> *"He who loses his reverence for any part of his life,*
> *will lose his reverence for all of his life."*
> Albert Schweitzer

This is a big day! Hopefully it is the start of a new way of treating *your body - the temple that houses your spirit.*

I don't want to hear any laughter about your body being a ruined or crumbling temple! If, however, it is not a temple in great shape, today is the day to begin to change that. *Without your body, you have no life on earth.*

It really is a temple and it does house your soul and spirit so it's pretty important in the big scheme of things. If it functions well and is healthy, then you have more energy to do your spiritual work.

There may seem to be a lot to do here - but just choose aspects that resonate with you and it won't seem so daunting!

First, acknowledge and thank your body for keeping you going as well as it has to date, and humbly apologize for the stresses to which you have exposed it. And then promise to take better care of it, starting today.

Rhythm And Routine

Our body needs to be in harmony with the world and nature's rhythms. We need about seven hours of sleep most nights; we need to balance sedentary activity with exercise, which is critical for a healthy body; we need rhythmic patterns of eating healthy foods and drinking plenty of *pure, structured* water; we need sunlight on our skin; and to balance stress and stimulation with relaxation, and much more.

How much rhythm and balance do you have in your life? Examine your life and *identify* your patterns today - and then pick one that is not so nourishing for your body and change it. The brain often has loops of these old "bad" habits running continuously. It even rewards you for not changing!

Change takes persistence, consciousness and of course FARC-ing! So keep FARC-ing as you work your way through this book (Focus, Attention and Awareness, Repetition and Celebration).

Perhaps you can set a sleep rhythm, where you go to sleep, or at least are in bed, by 10 p.m. and wake up at 6 a.m. This gives you a great length of time to sleep - and it may seem artificial, but try it before you scoff! Going to bed at the same time each night and waking up at the same time are valuable tools for good health.

Many people are sleep-deprived these days, yet good sleep is one of the most essential requirements for treating your body with reverence. Sleep revives, restores and renews every cell and life process.

Choose to regularly exercise. (After checking with a medical professional, of course.) At the very least, buy a pedometer and make sure you walk the ideal number of steps for you a day - it's not as bad as it sounds! (If you are exercising *too* much, do less!)

Hugs and massage are not just relaxing - they are critical. The skin is the largest organ in the body and it performs many important functions such as de-toxing and it needs a good scrubbing periodically!

All humans need touch - babies born prematurely who are massaged and touched frequently are out of their neonatal units faster than those who are not touched and they have fewer developmental problems. That's how life-giving touch is to humans. Book a massage for yourself today.

Do some research on magnesium sprays and use a good brand daily - most of us need more magnesium but do your research first to make sure you need it. I use Miracle Mist made in Australia.

Bust Stress

Find ways to bust stress. Illegal drugs, excess alcohol and smoking are not great choices! They don't really work.

Create an *"unwind" ritual* for your journey home each night. You can have a notebook in the glove box and before you start the car to go home, write down your to-do list for the next day, then replace the notebook, drive home and *be present* when you arrive instead of being worried about work.

Or hang your troubles on a "trouble tree" outside your front door so that you walk into your family free of those burdens. If necessary, you can collect them again the next morning when you leave home! They are rarely still there.

Meditate at the same time every day. Pick a time that works for you and then just do it. For 5 to 10 minutes, sit and focus on your breathing, a color, silence, or the sound "ohm". Do this several times a day for shorter periods if you are really under pressure. Do *something* that de-stresses you every day.

Doing these things will be treating your "temple" with reverence and the respect it deserves. Give your body a chance to help you like it wants to. Today, stop the things you are doing to harm it. If you reflect for a while – you will know what they are!

It's *your choice* whether to FARC or not – to change or not.

REVERENCE JOY–ERCISE 7: PRACTICE REVERENCE FOR YOUR FOOD

Grace is not just a prayer we mindlessly say over our meal! *It's a way of transmuting our food into physical and spiritual nourishment.*

Decide that from today on, you will only put the best quality fuel in to power your body. No more sodas, ever! No more diet drinks (studies show they contribute to obesity and are loaded with chemicals!). No trans fats either. Read all the labels on your food. Minimize the amount of processed and prepackaged foods you buy. Make more of your own meals and prepare them with love and gratitude. At least for today!

Buy as much *organic* food - or at least hormone free - and antibiotic - free food - as you can afford. Especially potatoes and other root vegetables, as ground vegetables absorb more pesticides and chemicals.

Eat chickens and eggs that are truly free-range - the rest can be loaded with hormones, and may affect our own hormones, body systems and the environment.

Buy the book *"Nourishing Traditions"* by Sally Fallon (or find it at your library) and decide to cook meals at home as much as possible from now on.

Stop eating out every night, or having take-out, or eating prepackaged foods. The nutritional value of most processed foods is minimal. *And they are not generally prepared and cooked with love and care!*

Have as much vegetable variety as you can and use what is in season. Try to eat local products as much as possible, as they are fresher and may still have some of their nutritional substances available to you! Make the effort to find food that has been allowed to mature on the vine, tree or plant.

If you can't buy food that is fresh from the vine, find manufacturers who pick organic food fresh and freeze it right in the field. Having chosen your food with great consciousness and prepared it with love, care and thought, say grace over every thing you eat or drink and be thankful for it.

Thank the plants and animals that contributed to this meal, the people who grew it and prepared it and ask for it to be blessed, nutritious and healthy for your body in all ways.

Then eat it slowly and thoughtfully, with appreciation and reverence. *And chew each mouthful 30 times! YES, you can do it!* Doing everything with reverence means you look for and see God in everything you do.

Making a habit of reverence is a real pathway to joy!

Joy Secret #5

Generosity Giving and Receiving

"We make a living by what we get,
but we make a life by what we give."
Winston Churchill

YOUR SEVEN MINUTES

Really take time to reflect on these questions. Dive in deeply as they can wake you up to what is really going on in your life! The answers can change everything when you have "AH HA" moments. Takes note on today's answers.

Within these questions are clues to your core fears – the most essential ones to eradicate. There are, in my opinion, three major fears that are the root cause of all our issues in life! The first - not being worthy of love or not being good enough; the second – fear of being unsafe in some way and the third – fear of death or separation.

- Are you a giving person?
- In what spirit do you give? Is there any resentment, resignation?
- Are you kind to everyone?
- What is your motivation when you give?
- Do you have a generous heart and spirit?
- Is it easy for you to give freely - not just things, but of yourself?

- Would you consider yourself a generous person?
- What would your friends say if you asked them if you were generous?
- Who is the most generous person you know - not just, or only, financially.
- How well can you receive and accept love or gifts or blessings? Is it easy for you?
- If someone compliments you, how do you respond?
- If someone is generous with you, how do you feel?
- Do you believe you deserve good things?
- *Do you believe you are lovable? That you are worthy of love? Worthy of others generosity?*

Some people do nothing but receive (or take!), and rarely give! These people can have an "entitlement" mentality - they believe that they deserve to be given everything.

- Do you know anyone like that? How happy are they?
- How happy are their families? What is the quality of their relationships?
- What do you think a generous spirit means? Does it include kindness? Caring? Thoughtfulness? Empathy? It's much bigger than just giving!

AMANDA'S TAKE:

> *"The wise man does not lay up his own treasures.*
> *The more he gives to others, the more he has for his own."*
> Lao Tzu

MAKE GENEROSITY A WAY OF LIVING

When people see or hear the word generosity, the first thing most think of is money! Money has its place, but more important is the deeper habit and spirit of generosity and making it a way of life, because generosity is an important component of unconditional love.

What are we willing to give? What is our motivation when we do give? In what spirit are we giving?

How many times have you agreed to do something as a compromise in some relationship; you didn't *really* want to do it but you "did it to keep the peace"? When you did whatever it was – was in a spirit of resentment, graciousness or kindness?

Most of us at some unconscious level want to make the person pay emotionally! We let them know we are not happy or only doing it to keep them happy. *If you agree to do something, be responsible for your decision and do it consciously, wholeheartedly, with a generous spirit!*

Someone with a generous spirit is continuously giving in many senses and ways; it's natural for them. They're consciously kind and thoughtful. They share their hearts, time, love, thoughts, lives, joy, gifts, possessions - and their money! Some of the most generous people I know have very little money - but they are very rich!

Imagine living with a spirit of generosity in all aspects of your life. What would you be doing differently from how you live now? Consider every aspect of your life. Make a list!

Be generous with your thinking; give people the benefit of the doubt and avoid judging, while being discerning. Give your time - it is the most precious gift for anyone. Share your knowledge and expertise and try to help everyone succeed. Be thoughtful and kind i.e. think with and give from your heart.

Are you the sort of person who sees that a couple needs some time alone, and offers to look after their children overnight? Or if you know someone needs help and cannot afford it, you gift it to them? My friend Mary does all this in the spirit of helping others – her spirit is truly generous in all ways – it's just natural for her.

Most of the rest of us need to practice to make generosity a habit! Then it will more naturally flow from us and for us!

IT'S ALL ABOUT THE FLOW OF LOVE

The Dead Sea is dead as a result of water entering, but leaving *only* through evaporation. There is no flow of water in and out. It leaves a highly concentrated, salty residue and neither plants nor animals can live in it. Flow is the critical factor here, as it is in many other areas like love.

We live in a world held together with love, flowing through everything we do - we just need to trust it is there, *receive* it and *share* it. That way we don't become like the Dead Sea, full of toxins like bitter feelings, negative thoughts or resentment and anger. We need to let love flow *into us then through* us to others! This is the foundation for creating a habit of generosity and a secret to joy.

Generosity and gratitude go hand in hand. When we are grateful for love, our lives and all that we receive, we understand how important it is to share the gifts in order to keep the flow of love going. That's what generosity is really about - the flow of love in our world.

Anything given with a loving spirit is a wonderful gift.

It doesn't matter what form the generosity flows in - it may be knowledge; time; money; kindness or thoughtfulness, or any number of "things."

What is important is that there is a *loving intention*, which keeps love flowing out of you. That unconditional love comes to us from the Spiritual Realms, not to hoard, or keep and use selfishly. It is there to help us, so we can prosper, grow and develop, but *also there to pass on and help others prosper and grow.*

When we are generous, it expands our spirits; brings us light and joy; lights up others lives, and always has a win-win outcome!

THE IMPORTANCE OF RECEIVING

Almost as important as giving is the ability to receive. Without the receiving, there can be no flow. What is given hits a brick wall, slides down, and sits like a blob on the ground!

We need to be able to receive Spiritual love and blessings - *and* love from others. (And to do that, *we need to believe we are worth loving – which of course we are!*) Often, we are given blessings and healings, which we don't accept or receive, and they "sit" in our auras, waiting for us! All we have to do is say *"thank you"* and allow them in.

Why not try it this minute? Stop reading and take a couple of breaths – connect through your heart to God, Spirit, Source, your angels or love and thank them for the healing and love they have waiting for

 you. Imagine that love and healing flowing into you as a bright, golden white light - filling every nook and cranny of your body. Receive with grace and appreciation!

Babies and toddlers are giant sponges of receiving! They love to be loved. And in turn, they give so much joy and love back. They know about flow!

Are You Really Loveable?

Modern lifestyles and cultures often leave children feeling unlovable, fearful, unworthy, and unhappy, despite the best intentions of their parents. They have great trouble as adults receiving love, acknowledgement or recognition, and allowing it to enter their hearts, because they were so hurt or wounded.

One of the most powerful practices you can do it to honestly examine your deepest feelings and *beliefs about how worthy you are to receive love.* If necessary, change the story you tell yourself. Create a new one based on truth, *not perceptions. We are ALL worthy of love and love-able!* No matter what we have, or have not, done, we are loved and always will be.

As an adult child of an alcoholic, I didn't realize until I was about 50 that this was an issue for me! I am mastering it now, but it unconsciously influenced every aspect of my life!

I share this with you just to show you that despite 20 years of self-development, reading and studying, it was only a few years ago that I read a book called *Adult Children of Alcoholics* and had several blinding flashes of the obvious!

Suddenly lots of things made sense. I had always believed that my father's alcoholism had no effect on my childhood or me, as my mother loved us so much, and we just didn't see him much after I was five. But I was wrong!

I didn't then become a victim to it, using it as an excuse, but it did shine a light on areas that were causing destructive, negative habits and patterns in my life. Once recognized, they can be healed!

If there are stories, habits or patterns of behavior that you need to change to feel better about yourself - make the commitment and an action plan.

Just taking time to reflect on whether we feel worthy to receive love, help or blessings is something the vast majority of people never do. So good for you for doing it!

Become conscious of anything holding you back from freely giving and receiving. I bet a lot of people really love you - even if they are not your parent! Ask someone you trust how lovable you are! I bet you will be thrilled with how much love they truly have for you!

Sometimes I think we love dogs or other animals so much because we can actually easily *receive* love from them – it's unconditional. We are wary with humans because their love is often not so unconditional! Remember, generosity is a core component of unconditional love. Have a generous spirit with yourself as well as others.

If you *open your eyes and open your heart at the same time,* and realize *the story* you have been telling yourself is not true - you may be surprised at just how lovable you really are!

Quirky maybe - but definitely lovable! And you will see how much others love you.

IT'S MY PIE AND I'LL KEEP IT IF I WANT TO!

Sharing makes the pie bigger! Always. Like the loaves and the fishes! Generosity has an expansive quality about it. When we are generous our spirit goes out to others, our love envelops others - we are described as "big hearted" or having a "big spirit."

The opposite is withdrawing our being and spirit from others and *from love.* We shrivel up and become isolated, wrinkled, mean old critters! Perhaps it establishes the mindsets for us to shrink away from our responsibilities, as well.

I wondered what the opposite of generosity was and concluded that it's a state of separation, shrinking away, selfishness, blame, stinginess, isolation, meanness and fear. Which made me think about selfishness and what it really means.

Wise Selfish Or Foolish Selfish?

We all are selfish in some way, in certain areas of our lives. We think about ourselves, and we need to be introspective for growth and development - this wise *selfishness* is necessary. It helps us set boundaries that can keep our stress levels down.

"Foolish" selfishness (as the Dalai Lama calls it), when we think only of ourselves and ignore the impact we inevitably have on others, can be harmful. We are all intricately connected. We cannot not make a difference! E*verything we do has an impact. Everything.* Make sure that your impact is positive!

If we think only of what we want, have and need, and ignore the fact that we are all connected, *part of the whole and have the whole within us -* we are forgetting that *we always affect others, and they us.*

We are all part of a giant community - our souls are connected at very deep levels. Cutting off that connection isolates us, makes us shrink away, and become "foolish selfish". It harms us, and others. *The opposite of generosity is separation - disconnection from the whole,* which leads to fear. Those fears probably led to the disconnection and make us forget that everything we do affects everyone else at some level.

Generous, giving people *can trust –* themselves, others, and often believe in a Divine plan. Think of the effect that has on life. They are not focused on hoarding and protecting what they have - or fearful of losing what they *think* they have. They have an *abundance mentality.* They recognize the oneness of everything and their role in the whole.

We Disconnect From Spiritual Love

Being unhappy, stingy, selfish and mean-spirited stunts us and disconnects us from Universal love and light. Mean-spirited people almost visibly shrink and darken - physically and spiritually! Their mouths are tight, their brows are furrowed, they hold tightly onto things, they are miserable, and they hunch over and grumble a lot - think of Dr. Seuss Grinch!

They are very fearful of losing *all* they have if they give *any* of it away. In your heart you know none of us "own" anything or "have" anything! Disconnected people are rarely grateful; they almost always feel they deserve more, that someone received more than they did.

They are into comparisons: *"I want what the Jones have"* or *"Why can't I have that?"* They want, and believe they deserve, all that you have, and feel no desire to return the generosity. Maybe it's because they can't receive love easily and they think love might come if they have more stuff!

FOMO!

Non generous people live with two giant fears – they are not good enough *and* F.O.M.O.! Fear of missing out! A lovely nurse told me about this fear after a recent conference. Do you know people who live a life ruled by this fear?

Disconnected, mean-spirited people unknowingly stop the flow of love.

They receive and keep out of fear, not trusting that giving is what keeps love flowing to them and to others! We are supposed to receive and share! Sometimes this type of behavior is called a poverty mentality - if you have some of the pie, there will be less for me!

That is so *not* the way the cosmos works! *We always make the pie bigger when we share with, give to, and help others.* It really is a matter of *trusting* the flow and being discerning rather than fearing.

If you help others at work by giving them your time, the benefit of your knowledge, and the wisdom of your experience, it will usually improve *your* position - not that you do it for that reason, or with the expectation of receiving anything in return.

This is especially effective if someone asks you for help first! Remember, it's sometimes good to wait till someone asks for help! LOL! This is the big lesson for me! Once asked, you can choose to give freely, no strings attached. Check every so often that what you are sharing is actually what they want, *and importantly, need!*

As a consequence, people will respect you and see you as an expert. Other people will also notice - perhaps your boss, and the next thing you know, you may be promoted! So instead of keeping all your wisdom to yourself, thinking, *"If I keep this to myself, I am in a better position," share, expand, grow, focus on giving to others,* and allow the love to flow back to you and watch your life become full of light.

The Right Motivation

Having a generous spirit also means you have the *right* motivation - *to give without any expectation of a return.* You give because you want to give, not because you expect a return or reciprocal arrangement! Do it especially if you *don't want* to help or give! And do it with a great spirit – it's a wonderful practice to build your new generosity and kindness habit.

Sometimes, if I am on a plane and a child is screaming and out of control, I will consciously send love to the child. I surround them with white light and love and it's awesome how often they settle down almost immediately!

Giving love is always appropriate, and often most effective *when we don't feel like doing it,* yet still make the choice to do it. *People don't even need to know you are giving. You can just send them loving thoughts!* It's enough that you know *you* are doing the right thing and sharing love.

BE GENEROUS WITH EVERYONE

> *"Thousands of candles can be lit from a single candle,*
> *and the life of the candle will not be shortened.*
> *Happiness never decreases by being shared."*
> *Buddha*

Some of us are generous with our own families and no one else, and some of us are generous with others and not our families. Review your life and see if you give your family enough of you - your feelings, thoughts, time, energy, love and care.

Feeding them and clothing them is good, but it is not generous. Being generous and *giving them you* is how to show you really love them, and how you model the flow of love. Mind you, we think we *know* how to give love to others in our families and others we love – but - we give love *the way we want to be loved! And it's not always the way others want to be loved!*

Here is a great question to ask anyone you love – and in fact anyone at work but you have to change the words! With family or friends ask *"what do I do that makes you feel I love you?"* At work, ask *"What do I do that makes you feel I appreciate and value your contribution?"*

You are to have only a loving, and receptive response to this question at home – no judging! And then t*he key is to do what they say makes them feel loved!*

There is no point in asking if you are not prepared to follow through on it, and *do* what makes *them* feel *loved.* It's not about you – it's about them and *what makes them feel loved.* You might think you know how to be loving, and make others feel loved - but you don't *really* know until you ask!

Are you bright, happy, kind, entertaining and witty in public or with strangers, and miserable and unkind at home? If so, perhaps you might want to consider your spirit of giving and think about where your generosity is hiding!

True generosity has a purity in it that comes from having no motivation other than to *give love* (the way others want to be loved), to *be love* and to *share* it with others. Bring light and joy to their lives – light their candles – and make sure the flow of love continues.

GENEROSITY JOY-ERCISE 1: PRACTICE BEING GENEROUS WITH YOUR SPIRIT

> *"Every man must decide whether he will walk in the light of creative altruism or in the darkness of destructive selfishness."*
> Martin Luther King, Jr.

Altruism is the quality of unselfish concern for the welfare of others. Today is your day to be creative and see how you can joyfully be generous, and allow your spirit to shine its incredible glow on others.

It would be wonderful if we could actually feel how bright our light is, and help others recognize their own astonishing light! We are all designed to be the candle that lights a thousand others. *It's our choice whether to do it or not.* Will you do that today? Your mission today is to go out and consciously "light as many candles" as you can.

Feel light and be light-filled, *feel* great and joyful, then spread that joy and light. Laugh, be happy, have fun, and create joyful moments for you *and for others. Be a walking joy spot!*

If you are not feeling joyful, remember Psalm 118:24 says, *"This is the day the Lord hath made and we will rejoice and be glad in it."* Notice it's a *conscious* decision - we *will* rejoice and be glad! Keep repeating this to yourself or something similar, until you feel it in your heart.

Create ways to feel good, be joyful and give joy. Skip, dance, play, laugh, sing, admire nature, admire others and tell them they are wonderful and that you love them. In France, it's called "joie de vivre" - the joy of living! *Use your joy today to bring joy and color to others.*

Or perhaps you will just sit quietly, hold someone's hand and be with them. Whatever they need, generously give it to them. Whatever it takes - commit yourself today to lighting up others and the world with your astonishing generous spirit. *Consciously seek joy in everyday life – it's already there – and in you!*

GENEROSITY JOY-ERCISE 2: PRACTICE BEING GENEROUS WITH YOUR TIME

> *"Give like the rose gives its perfume –*
> *effortlessly, unconditionally because it is its own nature."*
> Swami Vivekananda

Just because you *can't* do everything, you still need to *do everything you can*.

Time is one of the most precious commodities we have. Love is *the* most precious and we can *choose* to give love by giving our time. This is an investment with an abundant return. After we have passed, what you have given will live on in those we loved, and in those they love and so on.

Today is the day for reflection on the time you give to others, especially your children, partners, parents and friends. Is it really so important that you have a fancy expensive car and large television in every room, if it means you have to work so hard you rarely see your children while they're awake?

If you have a hobby or sport that takes you away from your family in the only spare time you have, you need to find a balance between giving to yourself, and giving to those who love you.

Parents who are elderly and living alone need special attention. We think they are just fine and we call infrequently - and yes, they have their own lives, but many are older and more fragile than we realize. Most of them need more loving care than we currently give them. They often find it hard to ask!

One of the hardest things I had to deal with after Mum died was the quality of the time I gave her when I was with her. I spoke to her every day; would visit her in Australia twice a year, and tried to do things she would like to do. *But* I would also fix up everything that *I thought needed* to be fixed up, bought and sorted out. I was very busy *doing* stuff for my Mum but I didn't spend nearly enough time just *being with her*.

It might have been just sitting and saying

nothing sometimes; or having a drink with her and chatting, or telling her about what I was thinking and feeling, and what was going on in my life. It might have been just listening to her talk about whatever she wanted to.

I know in my heart that my Mum wanted this more than anything, but I could not see it with my eyes, because I had all these things to do for her. *I didn't see with my heart – I let my head get in the way.* Learn from my lesson!

Let Them Love You Too!

Balance the "stuff" you have to do around your loved ones with just *being* with them and loving them - and *letting them love you.* Even if you can't be with your parents physically, call them at least once a week and do nothing else while you are on the phone other than be present and loving.

Hear them with your heart and they will feel loved. This may be your last conversation with them so always make it a good one! People debate the merits of quality versus quantity of time we spend with people, but I reckon we need both. *We need to give lots of good quality time – but ask them* what quality time means to them!

Try to spend more time with your parents if they are still alive - and even if they are not - their love is still there! Even if you only have five minutes, it's still a wonderful gift when you are there in body, heart, mind and spirit. We so often feel frustrated about the time we have to spend with people when we are rushed or busy, and *it usually shows when we're with them.*

If this is the way you find yourself, it's better you spend less time with them but have the right spirit. To be really present while we are with someone else means we have to give them our undivided attention and listen. Stop the judging and self-talk that says, *"I don't have time for this"* or *"Hurry up, will you?"* or even, *"Here we go again, the same old story."* Be kind if not loving!

Most of our parents made a lot of sacrifices for us. It's a small price to pay to return some of the love they gave us in the past. It's all about flow, remember? *Make time today to be fully present with the most important people in your life* - and then make some time for yourself.

Consciously make generosity a habit. See if you can establish a rhythm where you can continue to be there for them, and yourself, in some way. You will see great joy in the eyes of the people for whom you do this.

GENEROSITY JOY-ERCISE 3: PRACTICE KINDNESS - GIFTS FROM YOUR HEART

> *"Let no one ever come to you without leaving better and happier.*
> *Be the living expression of God's kindness:*
> *kindness in your face, kindness in your eyes, kindness in your smile."*
> Mother Theresa

Giving from your heart means that you are open and honest; you gently share how *you feel* (not just spew out your emotions!); you *give for the right reasons*, in the *right spirit*; you are *kind*; you have *compassion*; you *genuinely* care; and you do *everything* with love.

It's through our heart that we connect with our highest selves, so *to give* from your heart is to give to others as God gives to you - always with love, always freely, and always with grace, *even when we don't deserve it.*

Gifts that come from the heart are the gifts that money can't buy. These could be letters to your parents, partner or children that tell them what they mean to you; how special they are; what you love about them, and much more.

Mum used to write me these letters and of course, I would always cry when I read them! I had them all carefully stored when I moved to the U.S.A. One of my greatest regrets in life is that a storage shed I rented was flooded and the company didn't let me know. Without my knowledge, that company threw away many of my material possessions, including the most treasured ones, those letters from my Mum. I am still working on forgiveness! But at least I have the *memory* of those letters, if not the actual papers.

After she passed, I was cleaning Mama's apartment and I found the letters I had sent to her. She had kept them together in a special place in her apartment. You will never know how much a gift of the heart will mean to another person. If you haven't written a letter like that to someone you love, today is the day! You might feel like you want to write five of them. Wonderful!

A gift of the heart can be sending loving thoughts to a person or holding them in your heart, or something you have created lovingly that they might really treasure or enjoy. It might be as simple as giving your attention. Just noticing someone and saying *"Good morning"* may be transformational for that person. Try a kind word, a small compliment or even a big one!

Smile at someone with kind eyes; send a supportive glance to someone who is being yelled at; write a friend a letter; send an email to say *"I am thinking of you."* Send flowers for no reason. Jot down a note that says how much you value the effort someone put in for you, or write a note that tells your child how proud you are of them, and how much you love them.

There are a thousand ways you can be the "living expression of God's kindness." Chances exist every day for you to do that. As Wayne Dyer says, choose to *"be kind rather than right".* Today is the beginning of *a new life of giving from your heart - consciously and willingly!*

GENEROSITY JOY-ERCISE 4: PRACTICE GIVING TO YOURSELF AND RECEIVING IT!

Don't give up; just give! To yourself as well as others.

Many people are generous with others and really mean-spirited to themselves. They never give themselves any love, kindness, credit, care, grace, any thing, or any time for resting, recuperation, joy, spiritual renewal, learning, fun, balance, being alone, health or exercise.

If we live like this, we burn out and don't have the energy or spirit to be generous because it's all we can do to survive from day to day. And often we become martyrs - a state that definitely doesn't have a spirit of generosity! We can't continuously give to others without allowing something to flow back in. The most renewing source is Universal love! *Remember it's a flow.*

If you are not surrounded with humans who give unconditionally to you and balance the flow, you can always go directly to your spiritual source that, who is pouring grace and blessings out on you continuously. Ask for *and receive* those blessings. We are even told *"ask and ye shall receive"* - our job is to let that love into our hearts.

For the full flow, there has to be *generous giving and active receiving.* Are you giving yourself enough time and gifts to keep you in that flowing stream?

An example of a gift is *the gift of time to yourself.* Give yourself permission to do something you love to do; exercise; stop and have a quiet moment somewhere; go somewhere special to celebrate; play sport; hang out with friends you haven't seen for ages, or even to have a bath and read a book.

And doing things *for* yourself doesn't mean you have to do things by yourself! Find ways to make something you perceive as an onerous chore fun and rewarding! If you could teach your whole family that this activity is rewarding and fun, there might be several of you sharing the housework and then everyone wins.

Listen today for any words you say to yourself that are not full of grace and kindness. *Who are you to say you don't deserve grace when your Divine self has decided you do!* You may never be perfect - no one will.

All you can do is *be the best you can be that day. Forgive yourself and do your best again the next day.* These gifts of *self-love and unconditional self-acceptance* are a lifetime journey for most of us. (Self-loathing is easy!)

I remember walking beside the beach in Greece when I was 23. I was in a bikini, tanned, young, vibrant, healthy and happy. I bet I looked radiant. Three men walked past and one said, *"Nice face, short legs!"* Fortunately I thought it was funny, but do you know, 29 years later I still remember it!

And if I am really honest, I did sometimes wonder after that if my legs were too short. Now at 59, I really don't care and know my husband loves my legs! I love my legs! They work really well, are strong, a good shape, and are the perfect length for me!

Can you transform similar experiences in your life? Can you love and accept yourself, and acknowledge the fact that you are doing the best you can, given all your skills and knowledge right now?

It doesn't matter what you do to recharge your battery or how you are generous with yourself or how you reconnect with the flow - but *to reconnect is your mission for today.* Make the commitment to give yourself these "gifts." And then make sure *you receive the joy* – enjoy - every moment of it. You deserve it.

GENEROSITY JOY-ERCISE 5: PRACTICE GIVING YOUR BLESSINGS

> *"Be generous with kindly words, especially about those who are absent."*
> *Johann Wolfgang von Goethe*

Words are very powerful. So are the non – verbal messages you send. You can bless people or harm them with your spirit, words, looks and gestures.

Today is the day to look at *how you use your words and non-verbals:* Do you use them to bestow blessings and kindness or to criticize, belittle, drag down and destroy? Do you give people the benefit of the doubt or assume the worst?

Today say and think only positive or kind things about others -especially if they are not in the room. Say or do only things that lift others or situations up or fill them with light. Many problems, dramas and difficulties are set up in workplaces and families because people talk about others behind their backs. This is so destructive, and we do it all in the name of "being objective!" No, we are not! We are judging.

Most of us are doing it with *a mean spirit,* gossiping and being political to prove we are in the right and others are the wrong. A generous spirit will not complain, judge, gossip and discuss flaws while another person is not there - or when they are there, either!

If our God judged us as we judge others, and metered out blessings based on our behavior, I bet most of us would be given very few. Just because you smile as you say something nasty doesn't take away the sting. In fact, the nasty phrase you say lives forever – in the other person's memory. Be careful – *very* careful of what you say – especially in anger.

Check your workplace and home for gossip and back biting today. If you find it, walk away from it and choose not to be involved unless we have to do or say something to end a bad situation or protect others. If you are the instigator of gossip or back biting - stop! Never again are you going to gossip, "metaphorically backstab", or "discuss" anyone else.

Always be a blessing to others and if you can't, then say or think nothing other than something kind! Find a way to bless those around you, *even if you don't like them*. Ask yourself, *"How could I be a blessing to...?"* And then do it with the right heart and generous spirit. At some level, that person deserves it, even if *you* don't think they do.

Maybe the blessing would be that you ask them for a meeting so you can discuss "your differences" in a mature, adult way, so the whole workplace (not just you two) can have more peace and harmony.

One dictionary definition of blessings is "Something promoting or contributing to happiness, well-being, or prosperity." What can you do today that will promote or contribute to someone else's happiness, well being, prosperity, their success, joy or sense of worth – to ignite their spirit? How can you help someone feel loved and to love themselves better? Ask how you can bless others as you are blessed – stay in the flow.

GENEROSITY JOY-ERCISE 6: PRACTICE RECEIVING WITH GRACE

> *"Human life runs its course in the metamorphosis between receiving and giving."*
> *Johann Wolfgang von Goethe*

Worthy Of Grace?

There are a gazillion references to *receiving* in the Bible. I bet it's even a law of nature to receive, accept, and then bless others! If flowers could not receive the warmth from sunshine, they would not survive. If the flowers did not in turn bless the bees with pollen, the hives would not grow and so on. All cycles and rhythms would be stopped without both sides doing their part.

How are you at accepting blessings or gifts from others? Or from yourself? Or from the Spiritual realms? Receiving with grace means the ability to accept anything given with love, and to allow that love to flow into us - *even if we don't feel we deserve it.*

Grace is an unearned gift. It comes from a Greek word, "charis" which implies a kindness bestowed upon someone that he or she has *not earned. Choose to consciously live in such a way that you feel, deep down, you are loved and worthy of love.* We need to feel we deserve good things and blessings in our lives.

Do you, deep inside, feel that you don't deserve time, gifts, acknowledgments, blessings or anything else from anyone? That you are not worthy? Is that the belief you hold because of a past story? Be honest. Search deeply. These stories are very deeply embedded and hidden!

This is when working with grace and the concept of grace is critical for learning to accept. We receive grace *whether we deserve it or not.*

Takers And Boundaries

Do you feel as if you are a one-way stream of giving - that everybody wants, wants, wants from you? Frequently, people who are very generous run into people who are very good at taking! Do you feel surrounded by takers, people who don't give anything in return? If you are, *focus on the choices you have made* that have led you to this situation and review them!

Are you really being taken advantage of or have you forgotten that you offered to give initially – and perhaps didn't set boundaries? Or that it might be *your responsibility* to give as a parent, for example?

Are you accepting the gifts given in return? Often when we feel taken advantage of, people really are trying to give to us, but we don't see that or accept it. *Most people want to return generosity.*

Be discerning and honest. If we are habitually generous, there are some people out there who may knowingly or unknowingly take advantage of us. If you feel someone is taking advantage of you, you may feel resentment, and it's okay to have that feeling. It's the *story* that triggered the feeling and *how you respond to that feeling* that matters.

Often we feel resentment because we are not receiving what we want – but *we don't take responsibility and ask for what we want or at least discuss it!* We expect others to guess.

Instead of bitter feelings, be conscious of all the factors operating; be aware, discerning and discuss the situation with the person; or if possible, set yourself up so that they can't "take advantage" of you again. *Set some boundaries* that help them understand what is acceptable and what is not!

Bathed In Love

Do you ever feel love flowing into your heart, great peace or a sense of being "bathed" in love? This can be a Spiritual grace being poured out on you. I notice this the most after I have been giving love out to others, or serving them.

Once I had an image that I was a toddler sitting in God's enormous hand. I have never felt so safe, loved, relaxed and protected. That was the gift of grace for me.

Maybe you will receive intuition, inspiration or be uplifted by something that comes to your heart - these are gifts. Make time so you can receive these inspirations or intuition. Sometimes it comes in the shower - we don't even have to work at it! *We just have to ask for some help!*

Only you can decide what you need to do to be able to recognize and receive love, inspiration, intuition, or other forms of blessings. *Your task today is to quietly contemplate receiving and accepting love.* Do you gratefully receive by sitting with your higher self and allowing it to fill you with love? Or do you do it by being in nature and allowing her to soothe your soul? Or by spending time at the ocean, and feeling at one with everything?

Do you need to silence the "tormentor" in your thoughts who fills you with fear? If so, replace it with the voice of love and reason – and know that *you are a worthwhile, lovable person, despite what you may or may not have done.*

Blessings In Disguise

Remember, some of our blessings may come from other people (often angels disguised as people!) so be on the alert. You never know where or when a blessing will appear! *It is your job to receive that blessing with grace, allow it to truly enter your heart, and let it flow out to others.*

Of course, there are always those who bring a gift in the form of a criticism. How do you receive criticism? Does it crush you, or make you defensive or angry? Receiving negative comments in an adult and mature way means being able to hear them, look at them objectively, assess what truth there is in them, and then work with what you find.

Thank the person if they have opened up a valuable area of growth for you - even if it is painful. And if you find no truth in it, perhaps you can discuss it and learn to see it from their point of view. *There are blessings everywhere if you have a spirit of receiving and giving!*

GENEROSITY JOY-ERCISE 7: PRACTICE ASKING AND RECEIVING

"If ye abide in me, and my words abide in you,
ye shall ask what ye will, and it shall be done unto you."
John 15:7

Did you ever read a little book called the *"Prayer of Jabez"*? There was a story in there that really stuck with me. Someone had died and was being given a tour of heaven by St. Peter. They walked past a large building with no windows and the newcomer asked what it was. St. Peter replied, *"You don't want to know."*

The man was insistent though, and finally St. Peter agreed to show him inside. They walked into the building, which was lined with miles of shelves. On these shelves were millions of beautiful white boxes - each tied with a gorgeous red ribbon. The man asked, *"What are they?"* and St. Peter replied,

"They are all the blessings people never asked for while they were on earth!"

There is so much help and support available for us if only we would *stop, ask and listen.* Blessings come in every form you can imagine. Some of the ways they come "wrapped" include help, intuition, gut feelings, inspiration, friends, warnings, healers, surprises, money, answers to hardships, struggles, trials and great moments of joy.

Ask for all the blessings that are yours today! Ask, believe, and you shall receive! The critical point here is to *believe*. You may not receive the exact thing you think you *want*, but with faith, you will be given the *perfect* thing you *need at the right time*! And it will be *so* much better than what *you thought* you wanted!

So ask *(with the right spirit)* for what you want – *believe* you have been heard and that you will be provided with the *perfect thing for you at the perfect time*. *Keep believing* it until you see it. *Feel* it is already done. Then let it go.

The best thing for you, with the highest good of all, will happen – but maybe not in your desired timing or format – so be on the alert! Your part, your work - is to hold your faith – it's called believing even when you don't see anything as proof that what you want is on the way! You could ask for signs and then be amazed at what is sent! As Martin Luther King Jr. said *"Faith is taking the first step, even when you don't see the staircase."*

Forgiveness

YOUR SEVEN MINUTES

> *"Forgiveness, it has to be seen, is not a one-time, one-moment act,*
> *but is a spiritual path."* [1]
> *Robert Sardello*

Dwell for the next seven minutes on people whom you feel have hurt you or on people:

- with whom you are angry
- with whom you are disappointed
- with whom you are frustrated
- you feel hostile or resentful towards
- who annoy you and "make you crazy."
- whom you think have "done the wrong thing by you"
- who are past partners or parents who abandoned you
- or siblings who were never kind to you!

In fact…anyone who annoys you, "makes you crazy", or generally offends you!

Think of things you are hanging onto. Or stuff you have done for which you feel shame or disappointment.

At the end of this "dwelling," you might be a seething mass of anger, pain and other nasty emotions! But that can be a good thing, because it will give you some sense of *the work you need to do this week,* and show you where to focus your forgiveness activities!

This secret is the one where you are going to start freeing yourself of the burden of resentment, anger, hostility, offense and hurt. *And remember to forgive yourself as well – it's a big one and most of us need to do it!*

AMANDA'S TAKE: FORGIVENESS AS A WAY OF LIVING – WITH TRIFOCALS!

The Way Of Forgiveness

Joan Borysenko, a pioneer in the field of integrative medicine and the mind/body connection, once said, *"Forgiveness is not a set of behaviors, but an attitude."* I would like to paraphrase that and say, *"Forgiveness is not a set of behaviors or actions, but a way of living."*

If we keep in mind what my wonderful teacher Robert Sardello says about forgiveness being a spiritual path, choosing to live "the way of forgiveness" may transform everything in your life – and maybe the world! From now on, would you be willing to filter your life events through the lens of forgiveness?

Forgiveness Glasses

To keep with the theme of glasses - we need to wear "forgiveness glasses" *all* the time.

I believe we need trifocals! *Love* would form the outside frame and *gratitude, compassion* and *forgiveness* would be the three parts of the lens. They are a combination of almost all the secrets you have so far mastered! Hope and reverence could form different lenses you can use when you need them!

From the minute we wake up, we need to wear these glasses so we view our world through our joy and peace-enhancing habits. We would look at, and live in, the world with a new awareness of what is *really* going on.

Life is not all about us all the time! Our egos would like it to be, but it's not. I believe our life on earth is really about being loving, believing in the spiritual realms and doing what we are meant to be doing, which *is to bring the talents we have been given into being,* and make the world a better place.

We will always begiven the resources to do what we need to do if we *ask, believe* and *follow the inspirations.*

Using Our Spiritual Gifts And Talents To Co-create

As we do the things we are meant to be doing, listening for inspirations and following our calling, we learn, grow, move forwards and find joy.

If we just sit around and watch television, play violent video games, don't work or serve in some way, or do only what we want, our gifts and blessings will wither, because we are not using them and contributing something to the world. *We are put here to be co-creators with the Divine realms* - we are continually blessed for that to happen, but if we fail to understand this purpose we lose connection with our joy.

Remember that by keeping our (invisible) forgiveness glasses on, we are choosing to be more discerning, live consciously, aware of all the spiritual activities that are really going on around us, and *we understand our opportunities and responsibility to grow up, make a difference and become wiser.*

We become less self-centered, more accepting, less likely to take offense and stop seeing ourselves as helpless victims, reacting rather than responding to what *we perceive* is going on.

Look After Each Other

Once upon a time, cultures had ceremonies to help in identifying the truth and right action. Sadly, most communities no longer support the rituals, ceremonies and sacraments that at one time pulled people together in a sort of a group intervention to facilitate forgiveness.

These were rituals that would create a chance for the guilty to repent and make amends. People were enabled to move on with their lives in those societies, or at the worst, suffer banishment. Without these societal interventions, we now have to use "do-it-yourself forgiveness kits"!

In Luke 17:3, we are told, *"Be on your guard! If your brother sins, rebuke him; and if he repents, forgive him."* So if we see some injustice, our job is to do all we can to stop it - *safely*; you may have to silently forgive the transgression but try not to let it happen again - to you or others.

If someone treats you badly, it's *your* responsibility to tell that person they are hurting or offending you and request they stop treating you that way – *you set the boundaries* of what is acceptable to you or not. This gives them an opportunity to apologize (or repent!).

If they don't, you can choose to forgive them and avoid them in the future. There has to be a level of forgiveness so *we* can heal, but *we* need to take action as well. We are not forced to forgive, but *we have been given the capacity to forgive as a gift* - for us, and the world.

The greatest benefit from forgiveness is to *us*, not the "forgivee!" We are not just healing ourselves when we forgive; we are helping to heal others and the world.

Rather than condemning, judging or criticizing another, if we can say to ourselves, *"There but for the Grace of God go I"*, or better still - *"There go I"*, we acknowledge we are *all* part of the hologram, which means we are part of each other and everything!

By making the choice to forgive in whatever way we can, we are set free. Ask for help for the people you need to forgive, and also to help *you* see their true spiritual nature. We may not achieve it this lifetime, but at least we can try!

The "forgivee" may not even be aware of our gracious behavior! But neither are we conscious of the grace that is continually bestowing on us and yet, it is still given to everyone and doesn't require acknowledgment!

Living Forgiving

Forgiveness begins in our perceptions – which form the *story* we tell ourselves about what happened. The story determines if we feel offended and cements our belief of whether we need to forgive, or be forgiven. *It's impossible to forgive without our perceptions being changed.*

Perceptions are the way we view and interpret "reality", but without consciousness, it's never true reality – it's just the *fairy stories* we have created around our perceptions. We don't see reality – we perceive and judge. *Problems in life are largely about perceptions, not reality!*

Constantly wearing forgiveness glasses changes every aspect of our lives. If someone cuts us off as we are driving - we can curse, shout and raise our blood pressure or.... we can say, *"Great - an opportunity to practice forgiveness!"* and smile as we look at them kindly and say, *"I forgive you."* We never really know what is going on for other people – that person may have just come from the hospital or be heading to one! They may drive away thinking you are a jerk, never knowing they are forgiven or even that they needed to be!

If you chose not to take offense there is nothing to forgive! If you did react, your choice to forgive means you have normal blood pressure, can think clearly, and are less likely to go on and do something dangerous yourself!

What if someone at work does something that irritates you? Remember you are wearing forgiveness trifocals. As soon as possible, examine your perception of the situation and then ask yourself, *"Hmmm, is this REALLY the truth and am I choosing to take offense, be hurt, feel pain, resentment and anger because of my story?"* Even if people mean to offend you, it won't work unless you take offense!

If you don't take offense and remain in a calm, relaxed state and choose to think that they are just behaving badly because they are distressed in some way, there is no need to forgive! A wise person told me once *"I never take offense – so I never need to forgive!"*

If you can see others as they *truly* are – spiritual beings of astonishing light - give them grace, chose not to take offense and deal with *your own* perceptions and judgments, there is no need to forgive anyway!

Try to see every person as a loving God would see them - which would be with loving concern, grace, acceptance, understanding and compassion. Throw gratitude into this mix, as they are teaching you something and giving you a chance to practice forgiveness!

FORGIVENESS CHANGES YOUR LIFE

> *"If we practice an eye for an eye and a tooth for a tooth,*
> *soon the whole world will be blind and toothless."*
> Mahatma Gandhi

How great was this statement by Mahatma Gandhi and how clear was his thinking? He and the Dalai Lama are two incredibly influential people who would have more reason than most of us to be filled with revenge, anger and hostility. And what did they do?

They chose the path of peace, compassion, wisdom and understanding. They chose not to take offense because they lived the secrets of joy! They forgave when necessary.

Making the secrets of joy into habits sets you up for a life of worthwhile accomplishments, inspiring others and profound legacy.

Revenge and resentment are destructive, and an enormous waste of our time, life forces, and energy. We only have to look at wars to see what world damage they can do. Who wants a blind, toothless world! Stop it now!

When some people perceive they have been mistreated, they brood about it forever. It sits inside them festering and rotting away their insides - even after the "offending" person dies!

The brooding affects our hearts, health and everything we think and do at some level. It's a continual drain on *our* life forces, *not* the one who "transgressed." Remember – they transgressed *according to our perception*. Forgiveness, surrender and letting go are often the only things that will restore our health - both physical and spiritual.

It's okay, and obviously unavoidable at times, to feel pain, hurt and fear, which usually form the basis of anger anyway. The sooner we choose to work with forgiveness, to live in forgiveness, the sooner we start moving out of our pain and misery.

We must not feel revenge or hold grudges. They cannot coexist with joy. Identify these negative emotions, recognize how harmful they are and resolve to forgive, and move on. Do not infect your children with your revenge. Children have no knowledge of revenge – no concept of it – we teach it to them by modeling. Are you sure it's what you want to teach your children?

If we carry these negative feelings, they grow in us. *We* are the ones now injuring ourselves because *we* are not moving on - the negativity insidiously damages us and reinforces the "offense" every time we think of it. This state actually casts a shadow on other aspects of our lives. How sad.

We choose anger, brooding and stagnation over forgiveness, peace, joy and growth. Are you sensing a common theme here? *Forgiveness is all about setting you free.* The fact that it may help others, the spiritual world, and heal our physical world is a side benefit!

Fear is Usually At The Root Of Ongoing Un - forgiveness.

At any age, something may happen and this belief is embedded, *"I will never let this happen again"* as protection. We are often unconscious of the lingering *fear* of a recurrence of a similar situation, of being "violated" again.

The *memory* of the violation may be conscious or not; it may be childhood abandonment; abuse; deep seated fears of unworthiness; of not being lovable – only you will know. We store them as beliefs.

We unconsciously relive these toxic memories and images; we keep repeating all the language that continues to incite us; we keep watching the "horror" movies in our memories, and fan the flames of anger, outrage, hurt, pain, fear, disappointment and other negative, destructive emotions.

We need to deal with these fears. It may take some time for the toxicity of a "fresh" emotional violation to go, *but we need to let it go.* Of course forgiveness is made more difficult if it's a physical violation we've suffered, because the scarring occurs in a different way. It remains as a physical reminder of our pain.

Our life path is often changed as a result, and we must rise to the occasion, overcome, and *hold onto the faith that there is spiritual wisdom at work* and somehow good will come of it. Remember you are a part of some community somewhere, so connect with them. If at all possible, *allow others to help,* since they will grow through the process, too.

The Alchemy Of The Heart

Alchemy was the birth of chemistry and originally, it was a highly spiritual profession. It's believed that alchemists did the work of transmutation - taking base metals and turning them into gold – literally. Alchemy also had significant metaphorical and spiritual implications.

The heart will transmute your emotions and turn the base metals of anger, resentment, fear and pain into the gold of forgiveness, love and freedom. Find your way into your heart, put the other person and yourself there, and stay for a while. Love will heal the hurts, help you feel forgiveness, and change your spirit.

Your work is *to make the decision to forgive* and then be conscious of what, and who, you need to put into your heart.

HOW DO YOU FORGIVE – WITH ZOOTS!

Drop to Your Heart

So how do we find our way to our heart? *By using our imagination and conscious effort.* Earlier, I mentioned the habit of "dropping to your heart". This is similar.

Close your eyes and sit somewhere quietly. Focus your attention on your heart area. Now try to be inside, or put your attention on what you feel is your heart space, which may be the interior of your physical heart, our heart chakra, or the spiritual space our hearts occupy.

The first time I tried to do this, at the class I mentioned earlier called Sacred Service (www.spiritualschool.org), I was in awe of how large my inner heart space seemed to be! I had no idea what to expect; I just did the exercise - which was to *"put your attention inside your heart."*

As I sat quietly and focused on the heart area, I became aware of deep silence and a vastness of space - like illuminated black velvet. I know this might sound weird but it felt great and I wanted to stay there! We all seemed to have different experiences when we did this, but we all had a sense of calm, and felt peace and love that stayed afterwards.

Put yourself and your own "forgivees" into your heart space and ask God, Spirit, the Universe, Source or Love to help you.

I imagine when I do this that a beautiful golden, white light wraps itself around both of us (or all of us if there are more!) and I stay there until I sense peace or "nothingness." It feels like everything dissolves away and all that's left is space, peace, silence and light.

This is not always easy. *It takes a considerable amount of conscious effort to keep attention focused in the heart.* We have to learn to "hold" ourselves, and the others in our heart while the alchemy takes place.

Zoots

When my stepfather died, my Mum was devastated. Things happened that made her not only very sad, but also angry. I knew that if we didn't help her get past that anger, she too would become ill.

Research has shown that it's not at a period of intense stress or negative emotions that we become ill, it's about 18 months to two years after the intense experience. That's when we develop things like cancer, rheumatoid arthritis, multiple sclerosis or heart attacks.

If we don't deal with our anger/hostility/grief at the time, a seed is planted. Over the next 18 months to two years, roots and branches grow and "suddenly," there is a full-fledged disease manifested in the body from the festering and unresolved emotions or unforgiveness.

Ask people who have had a significant life-threatening event and see how many can immediately recall the prior stressful event in their lives. *Un-forgiveness has been linked with many diseases - of the body, the psyche and the spirit.*

There is a great quote that says, *"Un-forgiveness is like drinking poison yourself, and waiting for the other person to die!"* If you know the original source for this piece of wisdom please let me know. I knew we had to do something for Mama, but I didn't know what until I met Dr. Paul Pearsall, who wrote a great book called *"The Heart's Code"*.

He taught me that when we send loving thoughts to another person, not only do we boost *our* immune system, but we also boost *theirs*. This made me think about the word, and work of, forgiving. *The word is for-giving.* If we are going to for-give someone, we need to *give* that person love. And if we can't bring ourselves to do it, we can ask God to do it because he loves all of us and it's easier for him! That's my belief anyway!

So I raced home to tell Mum about sending love. She was staying with me for about six weeks after my step dad's death. I said, *"Mum, we need to send love!"* She, being used to me, said, *"What do you mean, send love?"* I said, *"I don't know!"* because back then, I had no clue of what to do or how to do it!

We didn't talk about it any more until it was time for her to go. I had taken her to the airport and when I arrived home, I found a note on my pillow from Mama. She wrote how much she loved me, and what a special daughter I was and wrote of many moments we had shared together. It was a wonderful note and, of course, before I had even finished reading it, I was a sobbing mess!

I was full of love for my precious Mum, and feeling guilty because prior to reading it, I had been feeling relief that she was gone! Sorry Mama! At the very bottom of the note, she had drawn a great big heart on one side and great big heart on the opposite side, and a whole lot of little hearts in between.

This was my Mama's way of sending me love. And you can do that too*! Imagine little hearts going from your heart to another's.* I teach audiences to do this - and we make a gesture that consists of our hands gently bouncing through the air from our heart to another's and we say the words *"zoot, zoot, zoot"!*

Each zoot is a little heart! So that's my Mum's version of how we forgive, and how we can send love - we send zoots! She was very wise; *she knew forgiveness happened in the heart and travels from one heart to another.* Actually, for special people she sent "zooties"!

Please teach your children this. Many people have, and their children continue doing it until they have their own children and in turn, teach them! It has reconnected many parents with their teenagers! It's a fun way to introduce what forgiveness really means and a game they love to play. You will be surprised at how toddlers love to zoot!

If you can't send someone "out loud" zoots, send them silently. It really does work - mostly because you are changing yourself! *Zoots are alchemical.* But then *real love is* alchemical*!*

FORGIVENESS AND TOLERANCE

Setting Boundaries

Forgive, but don't tolerate unacceptable actions.

Forgiveness is so poorly understood yet seems so simple that many people think they should just tolerate any kind of behavior or activity and keep forgiving. *Tolerating unacceptable behavior can hurt everyone.*

Staying in a family situation that is abusive, or filled with pain and anger, is more likely to hurt everyone involved. How can children not be affected since *every soul and spirit is connected.* Unconditionally accepting everyone does not mean having to put up with unacceptable behavior. Accept who they are, be discerning and set boundaries – but avoid judging and labeling.

We need to remove our selves from unacceptable behavior, or do something about it - make a stand, set limits, fight it, protest against it, and stop it from hurting us, and others. *This is called setting boundaries!* We, with faith and being strong in our hearts, can then ultimately forgive those who inflicted it - but *we must not tolerate it.*

A great friend of mine has learned this lesson the hard way. She is the most loving, kind person and a wonderful mother and friend. Sadly, her young adult daughter has treated her with disrespect and dishonor for a long time in many ways, but primarily by being emotionally abusive.

The daughter would not control her foul temper and spoke in an extremely offensive way to her parents. They have forgiven her repeatedly and then become resigned to the fact that this was just her, which of course allowed the daughter to continue this unacceptable behavior.

After a while, emotional abuse can wear people down so they tolerate any behavior - but not without cost to themselves and others. Every time this girl screams abuse at them, scoffs at them, or treats them in some other disrespectful way, she harms their spirit. And hers is harmed in some way.

They need to take a stand, not just for themselves but also for their daughter and other children. This "tough love" might be the hardest thing they have had to do, but it's important in order for everyone to move forwards. *Forgive, but don't tolerate unacceptable actions.*

PEOPLE DON'T KNOW WHAT THEY ARE DOING

> *"Father, forgive them for they know not what they do."*
> *Jesus Christ*

Discernment

For minor "misdemeanors" (not unacceptable actions), always give someone the benefit of the doubt - especially in loving relationships, unless they have given you a reason not to trust them. It is amazing how often we automatically assume (which makes an "ASS out of U and ME") negative or harmful intentions in another.

Examine your thoughts and see how often you are *imagining, expecting or judging,* that someone else is doing something *on purpose* to harm, annoy or bother you, particularly if they have not demonstrated their lack of trustworthiness in the past.

When you first meet someone, stay neutral - that is, *leave expectations behind,* and avoid looking for good *or* bad. People don't usually wake up and decide to offend everyone they meet that day! Take time and get to know who they really are, and what their intentions might be. *Our brains judge but our hearts discern and use wisdom.*

The difference between discerning and judging is staying neutral until you are given a clear picture of what the entire situation is and what sort of person you are facing.

When we deal with people at a heart level, we try to trust and give them the benefit of the doubt, but it's dangerous to give a person who has bad intentions or is self-seeking the benefit of the doubt. It opens the door for their attack. *That's why discerning is so important* – it allows us to receive information about their intentions, and who they really are.

Discernment is insight from your connected higher self. The heart has the capacity to see another person clearly; it uses wisdom and discernment but it doesn't judge them.

Being cynical, judgmental, skeptical or disbelieving is not the same as discernment! *With discernment, we see things as they really are. We see the whole.* Judging others is a selfish act and unnecessary. *We only see a part of the whole when we are judging.*

Judgments justify manipulation of others to do our will, our way, or putting someone down to make our selves feel or seem smarter or better. *Using* judgment is wise. *Making* judgment is self-seeking.

Taking Offense

Lets explore the phrase "taking" offense a little more. Are you someone who is offended easily - do you "take" offense at what people say or do? In that case, it's time to rethink.

Remember, with discernment, we see things as they *really* are and when we judge we only see a part of the whole picture. What's the difference between you and someone who sees things in a different way? *It's always our perceptions - the story we tell ourselves.* This has been mentioned before but it's so important it's worth exploring further!

What are you are telling yourself about the intention of the other person? Do you "see" them in a positive or negative light – i.e. tell yourself a positive or negative *story* about them? What do you tell yourself about *yourself*? These stories originate in our beliefs and reinforce our beliefs.

These are all STORIES! Based on perceptions – not reality. You can *choose* to tell yourself a different story! *Someone who is easily offended is usually a person who is fear filled.*

Unless a person is directly abusive, we would most likely "take" offense if we *believed* them to have negative or hurtful intentions. And we are more likely to assume everyone has those intentions *if we have them ourselves!*

Oh Well...

My friend Kathy says to herself *"Oh well,"* and moves on instead of staying hurt or angry. *"Oh well"* is a great phrase!

Feel the initial emotions, examine their origin (the story), learn and discern, then say, *"Oh well"* and follow it with, *"Forgive them, for they know not what they do."* Then move on.

It makes life so much more joyful than being ambushed, kidnapped and trapped by nasty, bitter, angry, suspicious, vengeful thoughts and beliefs. *Your* thoughts and beliefs based on (most likely) inaccurate *perceptions*!

FORGIVE AND FORGET?
OR FORGIVE AND LET GO?

> *"I can forgive, but I cannot forget,*
> *is only another way of saying, I will not forgive."*
> Henry Ward Beecher

Much has been written on forgiving and not forgetting, but it doesn't make sense to me. Should we forget? We can't just obliterate something from our memory totally – it's there in our cellular memory, but *we can do our best not to think about it or dwell on it.*

As long as the offense is not continuing, when I hear people say, *"I have forgiven but not forgotten,"* it has a quality of *"I have not really forgiven as I am still grieved by it, unhappy over it and dwell on it a lot."* This thinking is like continuously *replaying a videotape of the offending act.* I believe it's better to forgive *and let go.*

When unforgiving thoughts come into your mind, move them, or the person, repeatedly into the forgiving space of your heart, so that they can be transformed and you can *truly* let go. Say *"oh well"* and let go!

I have had many opportunities to practice forgiveness in my life! And I have come to look at those instances, in hindsight, as lessons that I needed to learn, and that the people involved were just messengers.

Some of them did their job very well and I am very grateful they were so diligent! *That's the story I now choose to tell myself.* It took me some time to find this *genuine* gratitude and the right words! It's very different language from that which I first used.

Build A Bridge And Get Over It!

In one particular instance, I spent a year telling everyone about a difficult and challenging experience I had, but each time I told the story, it stirred up pain. I finally realized that I needed *to stop talking about it altogether.* That was when I really became conscious of the need to work on moving things to my heart, so I could forgive, accept the lesson and *let go.*

Does your *language* (inner and outer) keep you trapped in offense, anger and pain? Or does it release you? Can you speak of past events in a way that brings out the blessings they ultimately brought? Or can you laugh about it? *Can you see the part you played in it?* Can you see the others involved in the way that's full of love, compassion and grace?

I have worked consciously on forgiveness, and when bad memories do enter my mind periodically, I use them as a reminder to work on forgiveness a little more, and spend more time in my heart with those people!

I was walking down a street in New Zealand one day and a 16 year old girl and her mother were in front of me. All of a sudden, the girl stopped, looked at her mother and said *"Oh Mum, build a bridge and get over it!"* I thought she was very rude, but I also think it was a great phrase – and perhaps one that would be useful here!

We need to *feel* the emotion, and *at the right time*, make the decision to forgive; then forgive and *build a bridge and get over it*. After all, it is the *past*. Done. Gone. Can't be un done or redone! Time to build a bridge and move on to a new land past the "angry" river!

FORGIVING YOURSELF – "THE BIGGIE"!

F.O.W.O.T.!

I saved the best till last! We have talked a lot about forgiving others and how healing it is. *Imagine if we could unconditionally accept and forgive ourselves,* as well. I am so blessed that Mum taught me to not really care what other people think of me. That self judgment creates a lot of "beat yourself up" opportunities!

Of course, we were taught to be respectful and do the right thing, but *we were not limited by embarrassment.* I think embarrassment is a huge fear based, toxic emotion that pollutes your liver, shuts your soul down, and shrinks your light-filled spirit! *It's FOWOT – fear of what others think!*

Everyone in my family was rather eccentric. For me, it was just a way of life to be "different" from others. I have never felt I had to have a big fancy car or house to keep up with anyone else or prove I was as good as someone else.

I bought all my furniture at the Salvation Army when I arrived in the U.S.A. and I was so proud! I felt like was doing good while furnishing my apartment. Some people I knew were horrified, but I loved what I bought and felt good about supporting that wonderful organization.

I gave up worrying about how I looked when I was young - I had an extraordinarily beautiful and glamorous mother, as you will see from the photos; an equally beautiful sister, and my brother was the male version of that beauty. I was told from a very young age, *"Never mind dear - you have the personality"!* Honestly! (Not from my Mum of course, who always thought I was beautiful!)

After that, I just never worried about fussing over how good I looked. It was a real blessing! I just did my best and wore what was comfortable! That's why Vermont was so perfect for me! No makeup, comfy clothes and tons of organic foods. Heaven!

Sadly, I have learned not many people were blessed with the self-confidence Mama instilled into the three of us. If we made mistakes, we learned from them and didn't beat ourselves up for being stupid. (Well, not for long anyway.) It made us very resourceful and resilient.

And if we had moments of embarrassment, that's all they were, *moments*, followed by laughter. Our behavior was not *controlled* by the fear and handicap of embarrassment.

Guilt

Guilt was not a big issue in our family, either. Rarely do humans take time to think about concepts like guilt and their usefulness! I don't mean guilt over huge issues like crime, but guilt over our silly "daily life learning curves," commonly known as mistakes.

Sometimes, *our mistaken perceptions* cause us to feel guilty, so we need to examine the stories we are telling ourselves and compare them with truth or reality. If we have done something to hurt or upset another person, or done something silly that has caused them difficulty, guilt can make us apologize. That's good, but then we need to *let go.*

Guilt needs to be a gateway to responsible behavior. Carrying guilt and embarrassment around and *not doing anything to deal with them* is as damaging as carrying around un-forgiveness.

Not accepting yourself – warts and all – falls into the same category. Self-hatred is worse, and so are all the negative thoughts we have about ourselves - *"I'm a loser"; "I can't do anything right"; "I am stupid"*, and so on.

These are very victim-like stories *that are not true*, no matter what you say to yourself. You *are* worth loving. Always.

Challenge negative phrases or stories you repeat and *believe* about yourself; *they are rarely kind, compassionate or true.* Take time to put *yourself* in your heart, and sit there bathed in love.

Pray for help to love and accept yourself. I repeat – you *are* good enough; you *are* worth loving! You are loved and accepted by the Spiritual realms and lots of people, so why should you not love yourself, warts and all? *Send zoots to yourself!*

Learn from life's lessons and let go. I love this quote from the Catholic monk Thomas A. Kempis: *"Be assured that if you knew all, you would pardon all."* We have no idea of the vast spirit of wisdom that goes on behind everything! If we did, we would be much kinder to ourselves, and others! Forgive yourself. As you do, joy will magically be with you and in you.

FORGIVENESS JOY-ERCISE 1:
FORGIVE THEM FOR THEY KNOW NOT
WHAT THEY DO

> *"After all this is over, all that will really have mattered*
> *is how we treated each other."*
> *Anonymous*

Today is the way into your future. You are leaving the past behind and forging ahead with forgiveness as a way of living, as a spiritual path.

If anyone does anything that offends you, hurts you, disappoints you or makes you angry, think of the spiritual implications for both of you, and use your newfound forgiveness way of living. Say *"Forgive them for they know not what they do"* to yourself; *breathe* deeply; immediately put them in your heart - and *hold them there until you feel peace*. Even if it takes all day!

If someone hurts you physically or is abusive, find help and if you can, make plans to escape from this situation as soon as you can. It is unacceptable and intolerable. Then *once you are safe*, you can heal and work on forgiveness.

It's important to consider the right timing for forgiveness. Do it too quickly and you may not process the emotions adequately. If you wait too long, however, those toxic emotions will settle in and be poisoning your liver and soul.

There will be ample opportunities today and from now on for you to forgive. Your partner in life or your children will give you many reasons today to practice immediate forgiveness - or better still - non-reaction! If you respond maturely and don't react with anger, impatience or irritation, there is nothing to forgive in yourself - or them.

Today, *nothing is going to offend you, upset you or push your buttons*. You are going to breathe, stay balanced, and in a state of inner peace, and be compassionate and kind.

If you slip and find you are reacting, quickly move into your heart and forgive or at least feel peace, then let it go. Your new mantra is, *"drop to my heart, forgive, let go, send love and move on."* That way you are always bringing light into the world.

FORGIVENESS JOY-ERCISE 2 :
PRACTICE BREAKING THE BONDS

*"When you hold resentment toward another, you are bound to that person
or condition by an emotional link that is stronger than steel.
Forgiveness is the only way to dissolve that link and get free."*
Catherine Ponder

In your seven minutes, you reflected on how you feel about all those
who have "done you wrong." When you cling to those negative
feelings, whose heart, soul and spirit are being damaged? Yours!

*You are, however, connected to them with a "stronger than steel" bond while you
hold un-forgiveness.* While we carry grudges, resentment, anger, guilt
or shame towards anyone, they are living with us, inside us every
moment of every day!

Today your mission is to forgive these people. Sit quietly by yourself
somewhere, make a list of them, then look at each name.

Try to connect with the soul or spirit of that person - not their
personality. If we can look past a personality and see more deeply into
their spirit being and soul, we see a very different picture. We sense
their true nature, and not the selfish, egotistical, win at all costs, often
misguided "human" personality. *Try to see what God sees.*

After you have thought about this person, and realized they did not
know what they were doing, give them grace and hold them in your
heart. Try to do this for at least a minute - a minute is a long time
when you are doing this! Then let them dissolve into the light.

Stop, breathe deeply a few times, notice how you feel, and place the
next person into your heart. When you have finished, *send all of these
people zoots.* Try to see little zoots going from your heart to theirs.

If you can't do that, ask God, your Guardian Angel, Spirit, Love or
Source to sit with you and the other person and bathe you both in
light and love. Maybe they can go to the other person's Guardian
Angel and the two of them can work out a resolution. Seriously!

Sometimes it's easier to resolve these things at a soul to soul or spirit to
spirit level – we mere humans struggle at times to see the whole truth!
If this sounds a little "out there" for you, try it anyway - you may be
surprised!

FORGIVENESS JOY-ERCISE 3: THE OTHER PERSONS RESPONSE

The other person's response doesn't matter! Forgive them whether they know you have done it or not. When we forgive others, we need to be completely unattached to the other person's response or reaction to our forgiving them.

If we forgive someone else and *expect* some change from him or her, *it's not real forgiveness!* Are we forgiving for the right reason – or to see some response? *Our forgiveness must be unconditional.*

If you have made a choice to live a life of forgiveness, no matter what anyone else does, or doesn't do, or how they respond to our forgiving them, you will be more joyful. You have already had a couple of days to practice forgiveness!

Today, *check* to see if you are able to forgive *without any expectation* of what another person should or should not do. Be honest. If you are expecting something from them - stop now! *Forgiveness is not true forgiveness if you expect something in return.*

What is important is that *you* know you have forgiven them - and God knows you have forgiven them! It's all that matters.

Your changed behavior and calmer nature can tell the rest of the world! And you can move on. Ta-Da!

FORGIVENESS JOY-ERCISE 4: PRACTICE ASKING FOR FORGIVENESS

> *"Finally, brethren, whatever is true, whatever is honorable, whatever is right, whatever is pure, whatever is lovely, whatever is of good repute, if there is any excellence, if anything worthy of praise, dwell on these things."*
> *Philippians 4:8*

Ask for forgiveness – whether you did anything wrong or not!

There is an ancient Hawaiian problem-solving, healing process called Ho'oponopono which has had miraculous results. It means to make right or correct an error. It helps *you* acknowledge and be responsible for *your* thoughts, deeds and actions.

This process works through love. You are working on your*self*! *Which changes everything and everyone* else. It helps to release old memories that are controlling your life, and separating you from your divine self.

Practitioners connect with the original source of love, to heal the erroneous thoughts within themselves that *create* problems for themselves, *and others.* They take *full responsibility* for every aspect of their lives – and the impact on others.

There are four elements – *I love you, I am sorry, please forgive me* and *thank you.* They repeat those phrases or say something like: *"I am truly sorry for the erroneous thoughts I have had that have caused this problem in you and in me. Please forgive me. These thoughts that need to be forgiven are out of alignment with the principle of Oneness and Love. I love you. Thank you."*

They say this to themselves repeatedly – *meaning and feeling* it! I was fascinated and tried it. It appears simple – to do it properly is challenging but the results profound!

You have to really enter into the "field" of love and the feeling has to come from deep inside your heart, believing *we are all one*, connected at all levels, and that what I am thinking affects you and vice versa.

Soon after learning about this process, my husband Ken and I were driving and having a fight over navigation (as men and women in cars do!). I remembered this technique and for two hours, I repeated the above phrases. But I did it with an angry heart. I was snarling the words inside my head initially! Needless to say, that didn't work - but it was a great lesson.

Once I realized what I was doing, I dropped to my heart. I could *feel* the difference, saying the words *sincerely* from a place of *real love,* not from negative emotions and memories. *It was all about me anyway* – it was *my* self talk and *my* stories and memories that were triggering *my* angry reactions. *I was the only one who could address those.*

Now You Do It!

Think about the people *you believe* have "wronged" you in the past. Remember, it's all about *your* perceptions and stories! Now ask for their forgiveness! I *know*…you have not done anything wrong - but *were you really totally innocent*? Were you pure in all your thoughts and actions with them? Did you do nothing that could do with a little forgiveness? Hmmm? Be honest now.

And even if you were, and are, completely innocent, still ask for their forgiveness. It's part of the healing process. You don't have to ask for it out loud or in person. You can ask at a heart level as they do in Ho'oponopono. It may help to sit quietly somewhere and maybe have a picture of the person in front of you.

First, connect with the original source of love and drop to your heart, do nothing else until you feel the presence of love. Once you are in your heart and can really feel love, then think of the person and say, *"I am truly sorry for the wrong or negative thoughts I have had that have caused or contributed to this problem in you, and between us. Please forgive me. I love you. Thank you."* If you feel resistance to this, there is still a lingering part of you that does not want to forgive or take responsibility for the part you played!

Or just say: *"I am sorry. Please forgive me. I love you. Thank you"* from your heart and *genuinely feel* it. It only works, as I learned, if you *really* come from love and are sincere in your desire to take responsibility for your actions and the life you are creating. Keep saying it until you feel different!

Kahuna Morrnah Simeona gives this prayer to clear and free old memories, reconnect you with the Divine, and allow inspiration to flow. *"Spirit, Superconscious, please locate the origin of my feelings - thoughts of* (fill in the blank with your belief, feeling, thoughts).

Take each and every level, layer, area and aspect of my being to this origin. Analyze it and resolve it perfectly with God's truth.

Come through all generations of time and eternity. Healing every incident and its appendages based on the origin.

Please do it according to God's will until I am at the present, filled with light and truth; God's peace and love; forgiveness of myself for my incorrect perceptions; and forgiveness of every person, place, circumstances and event, which contributed to this, these feelings and thoughts.

With total forgiveness and unconditional love I allow every physical, mental, emotional spiritual problem and inappropriate behavior, based on the negative origin recorded in my DNA to transform.

I choose being (insert the opposite belief/ feeling/thought from above e.g. kind); I feel (same feeling). I am (same feeling). It is done. It is healed. . It is accomplished now. Thank you Spirit for coming to my aid, to realize the full measure of my creation. Thank you. I love you. Praise God from whom all blessings flow."

There is a pretty song of the simple version on http://www.ho-opoonopono.org, and a lot more valuable information.

Or Ask In Person!

The other obvious alternative is to gather up your courage and character, and go up to the person and actually ask them to forgive you. Be sincere! Or write them a note. This is also a very effective technique in most cases, but I gave you the easier way first!

FORGIVENESS JOY-ERCISE 5: PRACTICE LETTING GO OF EMBARRASSMENT AND SHAME

> *"The world, I found, has a way of taking a man pretty much at his own rating. If he permits his loss to make him embarrassed and apologetic, he will draw embarrassment from others. But if he gains his own respect, the respect of those around him comes easily."*
> Alexander de Seversky

Embarrassment comes from being worried about what *you imagine* other people might think of you. It's FOWOT! Fear of what others think.

And is often defined as "the shame you feel when *your* inadequacy or guilt is made public." Note the word "your." *What you believe* to be an inadequacy or guilt is very important. It's *your fear of other people's perceptions or judgments* of you and what you do or have done. *But really, you are judging yourself!*

The "shame" of "not being good enough" or "as good as" someone else can control our lives. It's most likely based on a false or misguided perception, and story; the seeds of which can be planted by unwitting parents, siblings, teachers or friends. Or by ourselves - *comparing* our selves with others.

We are ashamed of our bodies, or position in life or quality of car, but by *whose standards* are we *judging ourselves*? *Shame closes us down – it blocks our spiritual progress.* If you have respect for yourself, accept yourself and know you are doing your best, with pure and honest motivations and intentions, why be worried what others will think?

Explore yourself – *use shame as a doorway* for looking inside at your deep fears and beliefs. (You ARE worth loving!) If you know you did your best there is no need for shame, take comfort in that. You may identify areas in which you need growth – but that's positive! It's progress, not shameful!

Words listed as synonyms with embarrassment are chagrin, mortification, humiliation, self-consciousness, shame, being disconcerted and uncomfortable. All in all, as an emotion, this doesn't seem very useful!

Recall And Reframe!

Today is the day for you to recall embarrassing moments and find a way to laugh at them! Explore your thinking at the time. What specifically made it "embarrassing"? Was it FOWOT?

Transform the memories with your heart - from chagrin and shame to joy in your heart. Laugh at yourself and *with* others! Remember – you were doing your best at the time! Listen to the *story* you tell yourself about those events. Is it valuable? Or does it make you relive the discomfort?

My Most Embarrassing Moment

One of the few truly embarrassing moments of my life was when I had just graduated from University and moved to Tasmania. I moved from home and shared a house with 4 others! My housemates decided they would play a prank on me as they suspected I had a crush on one of them – which I did!

It's a long story but they basically bought me a cheap supermarket ring, had 18 carat engraved inside it and told me George (name changed!) has asked them to give it to me! I believed them – sort of. I was young and naive!

They were very convincing and played all sorts of tricks to prove to me they were sincere. They managed to drag it out for hours before telling me the truth! At the time it was mortifying. In retrospect, it has become one of my funniest stories!

Note the word *story*! It is the stories we tell ourselves *after* these events that keep our cheeks burning red with embarrassment. We can change the story any time we like – after all we are the ones telling it! Not only is mine now funny, but I use it as a lesson for others to help them see how they can avoid becoming cynical! I *chose* to stay naïve after that experience. I could have misbelieved anything they said, but because they saw it didn't have a huge impact on me – they didn't do it again! I didn't react in a way that gave them satisfaction! *So change your language, change your story and consciously look for the funny side.*

Too many people waste decades being embarrassed or filled with shame - it peaks during the teenage years and some of us just don't un-peak! In my opinion, it's an unproductive use of time and energy, and means *your* fear of other peoples' thoughts will rule your life.

Live Out Loud

My adored niece, Clelia, when she was seven, competed in a gymnastics competition. Since I have always been an enthusiastic person, she didn't have to do much and I would clap, cheer and jump up and down. She did her best to avoid eye contact with me and the rest of the family stayed as far away from me as possible, but that didn't stop me!

And then I overheard her say to a little friend, *"She's not my Mum; she's only my aunt!"* I have lived off that story for years! My desire was to encourage her, and show her how proud I was, *out loud*, and it was all done with a sincere heart.

I figured it was good for her to see that behavior modeled, so she may  feel free to do that with her own children one day. And she still loves me, which is most important! Of course, I am not invited to events with her any more! Just joking! *Go on - be yourself - live out loud!*

Stop allowing your negative thoughts and the fear of what other people think, or might have thought in the past, to rule your behavior and life now. That is what shame and embarrassment are – judging and belittling yourself; shutting down your spiritual growth and letting what others think of you rule what you do, how you behave, or how you live.

If you are enthusiastic or passionate about something, show it! If you dress differently, or look at things differently from others, don't shove it down their throats, but don't deny your way of looking at the world. *Whose life is it anyway?*

After you have laughed at the past, make a commitment to stop your own critical, denigrating thoughts about yourself, and *never let FOWOT change or stop you being the real you!*

FORGIVENESS JOY-ERCISE 6: PRACTICE FORGIVING YOURSELF

> *"The day the child realizes that all adults are imperfect,*
> *he becomes an adolescent;*
> *the day he forgives them, he becomes an adult;*
> *the day he forgives himself, he becomes wise."*
> Alden Nowlan

You have read a lot on forgiving yourself. *Now is the day to do it.* Forgiving, unconditionally accepting and loving yourself are pretty much one and the same.

Remember that you were doing the best you could at the time, with the level of skills and knowledge you had. You didn't know any better, and if you had known better, you would have done something different. Give *yourself* the *love, understanding and compassion* you wish *others* were giving you.

Imagine you are speaking to the little child that lives inside most of us - how would you forgive that little child? You would say to them, in a very loving way, *"I know you didn't mean any harm,"* or *"You made a mistake - that's all", "You tried your best", or "It was not your fault".*

Whatever happened to you as a little child – *was not your fault. You were a little child.* You had no control. Remember that, as you talk to the frightened child that lives inside you.

Speak soothing and understanding *heartfelt* words. Say those things to yourself *now*. Ask for inspiration that lets you see the spiritual truth. Put yourself in your heart and *stay there, wait* until the alchemical work is done.

Another Approach

Continue to work on forgiving yourself and if you can't, right a wrong elsewhere to make up for it. Sometimes to forgive ourselves, we have to make something right. If you can't make things right with the person you have in mind, then right a wrong somewhere else! In some strange way, it works.

At the end of today, your goal is to have released un-forgiven moments from the past, given yourself a lot of grace and love, changed your stories and *set yourself free to move into the future.*

P.S. And when we forgive ourselves, *we need to do it whether another person has forgiven us or not.* What the other person feels is of no consequence for you to forgive yourself. You can only ask them through your heart to forgive you, then let go of whether they do or not.

FORGIVENESS JOY-ERCISE 7: PRACTICE APOLOGIZING

> *"Never ruin an apology with an excuse."*
> Kimberly Johnson

Gulp! Apologize? Do I have to? Well, yes, if you did something that intentionally - or *unintentionally* - hurt or harmed someone else. And as Ms. Johnson says above - *never ruin it with an excuse.*

If you say "I am sorry *but….*", you are about to make an excuse, and you know you are not in your heart, taking responsibility. It doesn't really matter *why* we did what we did. The outcome was pain to another. By making an excuse, we are trying to *justify* our behavior.

We are really saying with words that sound like an apology, *"You deserved this!"* Or *"I am not a bad person - listen to this really strong reason for my behavior that hurt you."* *"It's not my fault really."* But it *might be* our fault!

We need to accept responsibility. We *always* make choices in how to behave and perhaps we chose poorly at that one point in time. We may have been tired, or there may have been other extenuating circumstances, but we don't need to share them. *Apologize and mean it.* Do not justify, excuse or explain. Just Apologize. Sincerely. *And avoid hurting them again.*

To apologize sincerely is to feel it in your heart first. Then, and only *when*, you feel true sorrow at what has happened, do you say, *"I am truly sorry for what I did/has happened/my behavior/the pain I have caused you. Please forgive me. I will not do it again." And then don't do it again! This is critical.*

So many people apologize *just to appease* another person. Or they apologize for *someone else* feeling something. *("I'm sorry you feel that way.")* You have to apologize for *your* contribution!

If you don't really feel it in your heart, you will continue repeating offending actions. After this has happened a few times, *an apology means nothing to the other person*

He Who Forgives First Has More Joy!

Friends of mine in Australia have a big sign above their bedroom door saying, *"He who forgives first, wins!"* Isn't that a great idea? Make it a family activity today to create and decorate several banners that say *"He who forgives first, has more joy!"* and then put them in prominent places in your home.

It is a fun reminder of the necessity to live in a state of forgiving. Playing games with our children like this is an opportunity to teach them and helps them *comprehend* what forgiveness really means.

Imagine if you had learned at an early age how harmful anger and hostility are, and how futile and damaging revenge, resentment and grudges are. Would your life have been different if you had learned back then how spectacular true forgiveness is?

Today is the day for finding those to whom you need to sincerely apologize, and doing it. Take a big breath: You will be amazed at how much better you feel at the end of the day once you have relieved your soul of these burdens you have been carrying!

If They Need To Apologize to You

What if *you* feel another person needs to apologize to you? As television personality Robin Quivers once said, *"An apology might help, but you can change your life without one."* No matter how much you want (or think you need) an apology from another person, you will live without it!

I had an experience of this recently, where I felt someone should apologize. It has not happened, and it will not happen, I suspect, but I forgave anyway. So how did I handle that? I asked for their forgiveness (at a heart-to-heart level - not out loud!) for my part in what had happened, even though I felt an innocent bystander.

I *believed* I must have had *some* part to play, and was sincere when I asked at that soul level for forgiveness. I then gave forgiveness at the soul level. I am still working on that one to turn it from forgiveness to real love.

I have held them in my heart for at least a minute, many times, and I do feel that is working. I have asked God to help me. Once I have done the holding in my heart exercise, *I leave it alone and move on.* After you have apologized to all those you feel you want to today, *let go of any "needs" you have to hear an apology from them!* This will be a very freeing day!

Joy Secret #7

Energy and Vitality

Your Seven Minutes

> *"Aliveness is energy. It's the juice, the vitality, and the passion that wakes up our cells every morning. It's what makes us want to dance. Everything is of interest to a person who is truly alive, whether it's a challenge, a loving moment, a bucket of grief, or a glimpse of beauty."* [1]
> Daphne Rose Kingma

- Do you wake up every morning full of energy and vitality?
- Do you go home every night full of energy and vitality?
- Or do you just want to remember what it felt like to have energy and vitality?

I ask lots of audiences these questions and they all raise their hand at the end! Most of us are walking around exhausted, overwhelmed and feel half dead rather than really alive! Lets start changing that today!

Reflect on all the things that give you energy and make you feel alive:

- Are they things like exercise, sleep, relaxing, learning and laughing, or spending time doing something you love?
- Are there certain people who are energizing?
- What or who seems to drain your energy?
- At what time in your life did you have a lot of energy and vitality?
- What was your joy level at the time?
- Was it a time when you had a sense of purpose and meaning; you felt you were making a worthwhile contribution?
- Do you feel like that now?

- Does your job give you a sense of purpose and meaning? If not, how can you change what you do, so work becomes a "thank God it's Monday" experience not and "thank God it's Friday!"?

AMANDA'S TAKE: OUR TRUE SENSE OF ENERGY AND VITALITY

> *"You only lose energy when life becomes dull in your mind.*
> *Your mind becomes bored and therefore tired of doing nothing.*
> *Get interested in something!*
> *Get absolutely enthralled in something!*
> *Get out of yourself! Be somebody! Do something."*
> *Norman Vincent Peale*

Energy and vitality are signs of *total* wellness. When we are connected to our life forces and they are flowing freely, our whole being feels really alive - vibrant, or vibrating with, unconditional love. *Energy and vitality reflect a more spiritual quality than physical.*

Anything that brings us closer to our spiritual nature, brings us joy and makes us feel alive and full of energy. How many times have you felt exhausted and drained, and then found new energy doing something fun, meaningful or that you love?

The spirit in which we act affects our vitality levels; a positive and enthusiastic spirit charges us with light and life forces. So even in a busy, rushed lifestyle, we can find joy if we have the right spirit.

We can drain, depress or exhaust ourselves by dwelling on all sorts of negative things, or *we can choose* to remind ourselves that all is perfect *in the Divine plan* and that although this seems like a glitch – perhaps a *big* glitch - there must be a reason!

When we change from being stressed, tense and anxious to peaceful; when we accept that somehow everything is a good thing; and adopt a sense of surrender and receptivity to wisdom, we stop ourselves

0 — -10
Death.   Bursting with energy
                                    and vitality and joy of life.

becoming victims, wallowing in resignation, resentment, low energy and misery!

If we are exhausted or disconnected from our hearts, it's difficult to find moments of joy from anything - a beautiful scene, a child who hugs us, a partner who reassures us, but *maintaining* a feeling of joy is even more difficult in that state. Fatigue is a hint! *If you are exhausted, check to see if you are disconnected from your spiritual source and do something to reconnect* – quickly!

We are spiritual beings in a human body. Our body is the "temple" for our spirit (or the Holy Spirit as the Bible says) and our responsibility is to take care of the temple. We need to be conscious of how we treat our physical body, as well as our spiritual health. This chapter is specifically focused on physical energy, and has many lessons from my own experiences when my "temple" was in bad shape.

If you are not as well as you wish to be, I would encourage you to explore what has *really* robbed you of your vitality or brought ill health - whether it is physical, emotional, psychological or spiritual.

WHY MONEY DOESN'T BUY YOU JOY BUT HORMONES MIGHT!

I am not physician or an expert on hormones but I would like to share with you my personal experience, because it has made such a difference to my life!

I have met two doctors (in Australia) and two naturopaths (one in Australia and one the USA) who are also authors and wonderful at helping in this area: Dr. Greg Emerson (www.drgregemerson.com), Dr. Graeme Williams (www.drgraemewilliams.com), Dr Wayne Pickstone (www.uniquehealthandwellness.com.au) and Sherrill Sellman (www.whatwomenmustknow.com).

They all understand bio-identical hormones and have helped me deal with menopause. Dr. Williams specializes also in how hormones affect obesity, longevity, cancer and diabetes. Learning from them has reinforced for me just how important hormones are for our joy, energy and vitality levels.

People think money will make them happy - but as the studies show - it won't! But your hormones really *can* make you happy - or miserable! You might like to read their books and educate yourself, as I can't tell you everything in this section but am hoping to give you enough to know you should read them and be in charge of your vitality!

For the *men and young women* reading this – *keep reading!* This affects you as much as we menopausal women! This information may change your life!

WHY MANY OF US GET FAT AND GRUMPY AS WE AGE.

According to Dr. Williams, it seems one of the main reasons we become grumpy and fat is too much estrogen; we don't have enough progesterone and/or testosterone. Menopausal women, *men and young women* on the pill or with IUDs - are usually estrogen dominant. If you fit into one of these categories, keep reading!

ESTROGEN DOMINANCE
– it matters for men and women of all ages!

Here are some typical symptoms of too much estrogen in your body – straight from Dr. William's scientifically validated book:

FOR WOMEN:
- weight gain - resistant to exercise and diet
- breast tenderness and headaches
- anxiety, mood swings and tearfulness
- hot flushes and insomnia
- foggy thinking
- decreased libido
- fatigue and depression
- endometriosis is more common
- increases the risk of breast cancer, fibrocystic breasts
- osteoporosis is more likely with low progesterone. Testosterone grows bone in women and progesterone is converted into testosterone in women. When she stops ovulating, she stops producing progesterone, so she stops making bone growing, energy producing, libido driving, fat burning testosterone!

AND FOR MEN OVER 30:

The above - plus research shows *all* men have a progressive loss of testosterone from age 30 and about 2/3 have raised estrogen levels causing men to:

- feel tired, become overweight - and lose their "mojo"
- develop breasts and put on abdominal fat
- be more susceptible to heart disease and diabetes
- create.prostate problems
- become intolerant ("grumpy old man syndrome!") and irritable
- develop "fall asleep in front of the TV" syndrome!
- increase frequency and urgency to urinate
- increase the need to urinate *at night*
- feel abdominal bloating

SYMPTOMS OF LOW TESTOSTERONE IN MEN

But wait – there's more. Low testosterone causes things like:

- reduced energy and strength
- softer erections
- decreased enthusiasm
- decreased sex drive
- loss of muscle mass
- osteoporosis
- depression and
- fatigue

Low Sex Drive Isn't a Sign!

Once a man has a "gut" or is overweight, that fat produces more estrogen, which produces more fat, which produces more estrogen and so on in a vicious cycle. *Sex drive in a man*, according to Dr. Williams, *is the last thing to go* – so don't be fooled if you have a healthy sex drive but many of the others symptoms! Be tested!

Women on the Pill

"The use of oral contraceptives (the pill) has been proven to produce a significant increase in the risk of breast cancer during use." (From Dr. William's book). When you take the pill you are taking artificial estrogen, and not ovulating and therefore not producing progesterone. Progesterone counters the effects of estrogen.

Dr. John Lees (Author of "*What your Doctor May Not Tell You About*

Menopause"), is the first doctor who made the world aware of the importance of *bio-identical* progesterone said..."*estrogen tells the cells in the body to multiply, multiply. Progesterone moderates that and tells the body to stop!"* In Dr. William's book, I was stunned to learn (there is sound science to back this information up) that women on the pill *"consume 16,500 times more active estradiol (artificial estrogen) than their body would normally make in one day."* *(Pugh and Moore).*

He points out that the pill gives you more of the same artificial estrogen found in HRT - and there is evidence that HRT increases the risk of breast cancer. If you find this hard to believe - get the book and research the articles yourself!

How To Be Joy Filled With Hormones!

The secret is finding a Doctor who knows about *bio identical* progesterone (the "anti estrogen") and the critical importance of bio identical testosterone for men (and women). The list of side effects from FDA approved *artificial* (not bio identical) progesterone is scary and listed on page 80 of Dr. William's book.

If you feel exhausted. "flat", depressed or other than joyful, find the cause. Find someone who will thoroughly check your hormones, adrenals and thyroid glands at least.

Bio-identical hormones have exactly the same molecular shape found in humans – unlike the artificially manufactured versions. They are derived from plants like sarsaparilla, Mexican yam or soy bean. The molecules of these plants can be transformed into the same active molecule as human progesterone. (Btw: yam cream is not the same as the bio-identical progesterone.) If you would like to pursue this further, do your own research by reading the books I have recommended.

One week after I started using my individually prepared cream from Dr. Williams, my moods were more stable and within 3 weeks there were changes in my hot flashes and many of the symptoms I had been experiencing. Dr. Greg Emerson helped me enormously when he checked out my health in many other areas, as well as hormones.

My husband (61) then decided he would be tested. He went on the cream and his moods changed within a couple of weeks - he felt calmer and less irritable. He didn't fall asleep at 8.00 pm any more!

Regular monitoring is critical when you are on any of these protocols. We need to pay attention to our diet and stress levels as well – they have a huge impact on our hormones!

To be as joyful as you can, your hormones need to be balanced, no matter what your age or sex. Do yourself a favor and educate yourself by visiting their websites or finding other experts in these areas.

DEPRESSION AND EXHAUSTION – OR LYME DISEASE?

I used to have incredibly high energy levels. I would make people exhausted just describing what I did during a day - but I had fun! Then I spent four years still doing a lot, but feeling exhausted most of the time. I looked okay - tired but okay. I was crabby, depressed and if I didn't sleep 10 hours a night, I had no energy. My relationship suffered because there was nothing left for my long-suffering husband at the end of dragging myself through one of my busy days.

As many doctors I visited told me, I had plenty of reasons to be tired. I traveled weekly and had been through a very stressful event before I left Australia. My mother was ill; I was away from her, and unable to help much. I was living in a new country where I knew very few people. All in all, it was easy and accurate for doctors to tell me my adrenals were exhausted. *But that was not the whole story.*

Adrenal Exhaustion

The adrenal glands sit on top of the kidneys and secrete stress-related hormones. When we stay under stress for long periods, they fatigue, cannot function properly and basically, interfere with most of our body physiology, balance and functioning.

There are many books written on this topic because so many women (and these days, men) have problems with their adrenal functioning. The treatment is to relax, slow down, do less, eat better, sleep and all those lifestyle things that you would be doing if you had time!

But since we can't (or don't) stop our lives to that degree, the condition worsens. I did as much as I could, and it made no difference. I found a fabulous naturopathic doctor in Dallas who believed I did have adrenal exhaustion, but *saw it as a symptom and not the cause* of my rundown state.

Lyme Disease - A Clever Super Bug

The real cause of the problem was Lyme disease, which comes from a bacteria most commonly transmitted by ticks, fleas and mosquitoes (and humans I found out!).

It's common to have Lyme disease in combination with Epstein Barr, the type of virus that causes infectious mononucleosis (glandular fever) for many adolescents and young adults, or other co infections. These two conditions combined had led to all my other problems.

I am not a physician or an expert, but I can share with you my personal experiences. Through working with a naturopathic doctor and a master herbalist, I became an expert on Lyme disease! I realized just how many symptoms I had experienced over the years that now made sense - jaw pain, back pain, irritability, shoulder pain, loss of memory, failing eyesight, very dry skin, depression, zero libido, and exhaustion, to name a few!

The best book I have found on this subject is *"Healing Lyme,"* by Stephen Harrod Buhner. Following Buhner's protocol, and the wonderful advice and treatment of Dr. Jim and Mary, had me feeling 200% better!

It Mimics 300 Other Diseases!

I learned that Lyme disease can mimic about 300 other diseases, many of them neurological, and it affects a huge number of people in the world today. See the link for Channel 7, Sunday program "Lyme disease outbreak", at the back of this book for proof it not only exists, but is also debilitating people in Australia, USA and other countries.

Unfortunately, it's not easily recognized because it mimics all those other diseases and is misdiagnosed. Symptoms can affect any tissue, organ or joint in the body. It can make you depressed if it gets into your brain – I had no memory either!

Lyme spirochetes are clever little spiral-shaped bacteria that don't just live in the blood - *they burrow into individual cells.* They get into *every* type of tissue in our bodies. I had them in my eyes, bladder, brain, skin, uterus, nervous system, joints and probably everywhere else.

In retrospect, I actually don't know how I kept going. Those who are doing the research into Lyme disease claim it is at epidemic proportions in the U.S. and rapidly spreading globally. Some believe it's the fastest growing sexually transmitted disease on the planet.

How It Spreads

Lyme disease is not just spread by ticks apparently, but by mosquitoes and fleas, and some people believe it can be spread person to person. Fibromyalgia, lupus, chronic fatigue, multiple sclerosis, and ALS are just some of the diseases that some experts believe Lyme can mimic.

If you feel unwell, and in your heart you think you have not discovered the true cause of your symptoms, have a test for Lyme disease. It is quite difficult to test definitively for Lyme, but I found one place that I believe really gives you the best chance of finding it. They actually test your DNA so you can send them samples from all over the world.

It is in Sydney, Australia. A company called Australian Biologics Testing Services Pty Ltd. I know the woman who began this company many years ago and she is amazing. A pioneer and tireless fighter for wellness and health, she has created this test that can definitively tell you if you have Lyme disease.

If you want to do some of your own research on this subject, visit www.samento.com and www.klinghardtacademy.com/Lyme-Disease, for information from Dr. Deitrich Klinghardt, who is an M.D., Ph. D., and board-certified in neurological and orthopedic medicine. In fact, he thinks Lyme disease may be the way many other infections enter the body.

The Latest Findings

Some of the latest findings are that 90% of chronic fatigue patients are Lyme positive; many patients with arthritis have Lyme disease. Our inability to fight chronic, low grade infections like Lyme disease predisposes us to many other conditions that cause early death, and the spirochetes fill us with neurological toxins on the way.

Remember – there are indications it is not *only* caused by tick bites! *I was not bitten by a tick.* See back of book for more resources and sites.

GLUTEN AND YOU

I believe it's more difficult for us to feel joy if we are permanently exhausted, so I'd like to discuss gluten. Again, I am not an expert on this but have studied it a lot – and would like to share some of what I have learned.

Gluten is a huge (in molecular terms) protein that is in wheat and many grain products. It is in almost every processed product you buy in a supermarket – unless it says gluten free. Celiac disease is an inability to produce the enzymes to digest gluten. Gluten is actually dangerous for these people.

Many people in westernized countries develop a *sensitivity* to gluten, because we eat so much of it. *"Dangerous Grains"* a book by Braly and Hoggin discusses just how many people became allergic to grains and pasteurized dairy products. It may include you!

Once again, like Lyme, the symptoms of celiac disease or sensitivity to gluten are many and varied, but all result in your digestion and intestines being severely damaged, which then links to many other disorders, physical or psychological. (See the book "Gut and Psychology Syndrome".)

Many celiacs don't have the enzymes to digest casein, either, which is the *protein in dairy products.* As a result of the lack of these enzymes or being allergic to them, the "large" protein molecules "burst" through the gut walls into the blood. This continual leaking eventually destroys the gut lining, with potentially serious health consequences.

The large proteins floating around in the blood are seen as foreign invaders and our immune systems attack them. This can lead to many

other problems, auto-immune disorders and symptoms that mimic many other diseases.

Gluten sensitivity can cause an array of symptoms such as irritable bowel syndrome, gas, bloating, pain in the stomach, aches and pains, malnutrition, mood swings, aggression, depression, anxiety *(very common)*, autoimmune disorders and mental illness.

Some believe there are genetic factors that predispose a person to celiac allergy, so if your baby does not respond well to flour and products with gluten in them, it would be worth checking to see if they lack the necessary enzymes - or if they are just sensitive to it.

There are definitive tests available now that will tell you quickly if you are allergic to gluten and casein - you may need to ask your doctor to have them done. And sometimes blood tests don't tell you! You may have a sensitivity that is not clinically detected, but still causes symptoms.

One of the simplest ways you may be able to test for this is an elimination diet, which means you stop eating all gluten and dairy for a month or so. You will notice rapid changes in how you feel if there is a gluten issue.

Go off every little bit of those proteins for at least a month and then test yourself - eat some gluten and see what happens. Gluten is in all products containing wheat and is in oats, rye and barley.

To be gluten free, you cannot eat breads, cookies, muffins, wheat pasta, cereals or anything else made with those products - unless it says gluten-free. Be careful with sauces, relishes, condiments and soups as well. *Read all the labels.* Luckily there are now many books written on gluten-free cooking, and more products are available in health-oriented supermarkets.

It is believed that there is no safe level of gluten if you are a coeliac or allergic to it. Not only can it rob you of your energy and vitality, but it actually can do harm to keep eating gluten.

THE STORIES YOU TELL YOURSELF

So, onto other things that may sap your energy and vitality. You already know many of them, which is why I am sharing what you may not know!

We all know that exercise, sleep, healthy food, good eating habits, balanced lifestyles, rhythms and routines are all critical for energy and vitality. We just don't do them! We work too much; travel too often; rush; do other things when we eat; don't balance work with play; are too stressed and we wonder why we don't feel good!

What Is It That Stops Us Doing What We *Know* We Need To Do?

Why do we keep harming ourselves? What story are we telling ourselves about the activities? This is the time to FARC - to rewire the brain. (Focus, Awareness, Repetition, Celebration).

Lets *focus* on what it is you want to do, and become *aware* of what stops you, including the story you are telling yourself (or excuse!).

One of the newly discovered critical factors continuing our bad habits, (which are really physical brain loops), is that when we avoid the healthy behavior and give in to the old habit, our brains release a bit of dopamine, which makes us feel good!

Sadly, this is a reward for us and reinforces the old pattern. To make the changes, we have to *repeat* the new behaviors. It is hard FARC-ing for a few weeks – but well worth the effort. We need to *celebrate* changes along the way.

Creating A New Habit – What Fears Are Stopping You?

Lets choose one. Exercise. What story do you tell yourself about exercise if you are not doing it on a regular basis? I don't have time. It's too hard. I hate exercise. It hurts. It doesn't work. I hate sweating. I am too fat to do it. I don't want anyone else to see my body.

The list is endless! What are your fears around exercise? Only you can search your heart, mind and the stories you are telling yourself and decide if they are actually true!

What about meditation? We tell ourselves we don't have time; we don't know how to do it; we must do it one day but not today; or things like *"I tried it and I can't do it"*! That's precisely why you need to practice!

We are masters at convincing ourselves that our excuses (stories) are valid. And in some cases they are, but most of the time they're not. They're easily challenged! Often it's fear of what others think (FOWOT) that stops us embarking on a new path.

Or we start with too big a step – for example, did you know that walking for 10 minutes a day has enormous health benefits to a very unhealthy person? Just 10 minutes. That's not hard! But if we tell ourselves we must run for 30 minutes each day – it's just too much to even begin. Sometimes we just ignore the reality of how unhealthy we really are and how desperately we need to do something!

What Really Stops Us?

But those are all relatively superficial things – what is it that *really* stops us doing what we know we need to be doing? I believe it's *lack of prioritizing and consciousness!* That's why the A in FARC is so important – most of us are totally unaware, unconscious of, or oblivious to, our real state of health and the stories that drive our behavior.

Jim Rohn said *"take care of your body. It's the only place you have to live."* Seriously, think about it. Your body is the only place *you* have to live!

We are all so busy and time poor these days that we think our bodies will just keep going forever but they can't. They just can't! They do really well and try very hard, but at some stage, some part of the body says "enough" and then we are in trouble! Joints stop moving; muscles tear or don't work; arthritis sets in; hearts stop working; stress takes its toll; cholesterol builds up – all the *lifestyle* diseases we suffer from today emerge.

Did you know that people who live sedentary lifestyles – and sit for more than 50% of their days have a 60% higher chance of developing bowel cancer? *All you have to do is get up and move more* - be more active and that lessens your risks enormously! And yet we just keep sitting for longer periods! Set a timer. It's cheap, easy and effective. Note: What did you just say to yourself – your story - when you imagined doing it?

I remember working in the Brompton Chest Hospital in London and the saddest thing I ever saw were people who had emphysema. They had good brains, and bodies that would still work well but they could not do anything because they had no oxygen or breath to do it. They were "trapped" inside their bodies.

Many of us are "trapped" by our minds: *By what we tell ourselves – the stories or false beliefs:* By what we say about how healthy we really are and our need to exercise, rest, sleep or eat properly.

Rhythm And Flow or Rush And Stress?

"*Go placidly amid the noise and haste,*
And remember what peace there may be in silence."
"*Desiderata*" Max Ehemann

There is something really relaxing for me about a walk on the beach – if I am having a leisurely walk! Today, after what seemed like months of rain, I made it to the beach. It was wonderful to smell the ocean and hear the waves; to feel the sun on my skin and to have time to sit and watch the rhythm of the waves.

There is something very soothing about that rhythm. Most people in western cultures *rush* even when it's not necessary. Often out of habit.

A young man found himself rushing his toddler to be "ready" and dressed, until the wise little soul said *"Daddy, why do I have to go faster?"* It stopped him in his tracks because he realized there was no reason. It was a Saturday. *He was in the habit of rushing* – not tuning into the present or the rhythm of the baby, or a Saturday!

Rushing is our new normal – it's not really a rhythm in harmony with nature or joy. We rush to deliver children to birthday parties, sporting events, school, and extra lessons with which we crowd their lives. But we don't sit about with them relaxing, laughing, being present, just loving them.

We race to beat traffic; we race home and immediately start cooking dinner whilst a load of washing is on; we listen with one ear to our partner or children; at the same time we are thinking about what needs to be done tomorrow. Then we answer three text messages and four phone calls! *We multitask and rush ourselves into exhaustion!*

We Cannot Multitask Effectively

Neuroscience is proving that we cannot multitask and maintain performance. We *can* do several mental tasks at once *but* performance and accuracy diminishes quickly.

Linda Stone, a former VP from Microsoft is quoted in *"Your Brain at Work"*, an excellent book by David Rock, as creating the phrase "continuous partial attention" in 1998.

It means that people focus on a number of different things at once – and keep scanning the environment in case there is something more important happening. It leads to "constant and intense mental exhaustion"!

It reminds me of talking to someone at a party and they're not really listening – they're constantly scanning the room to see if there is anyone or anything more interesting or important! If you've ever done this, it's exhausting – and rather unpleasant for the person you are only half listening to!

The research in Rock's book suggests that we focus on only one conscious task at a time especially *if accuracy and performance matter.* If you are performing *automatic* tasks like chewing or typing, you can multitask more easily, but it's not as good as focused concentration.

Flow

The opposite of multitasking and a source of great energy and vitality is being in flow – as described by Mihaly Csikszentmihalyi. (Don't try to pronounce it!)

Flow is that state athletes call in the zone; it's when you find yourself so absorbed with a task or activity that hours have passed in what seems like minutes. At the end you are energized and feeling alive!

In his many wonderful books on the topic, he lists the criteria to enter a state of flow:

1. Begin a task we have a chance of completing; it's a challenging activity that requires skill

2. Concentrate on what we are doing

3. Have clear goals and a chance for immediate feedback

4. Be so involved we forget our stresses and worries, but it's effortless

5. Have a sense of control over our actions

6. Experience a loss of self consciousness and a sense of oneness

Flow is basically a state of being in rhythm with our skills and abilities, and what we are doing. We can change time and find more if we want to! Breathe, be present to and feel the flow and rhythm of nature. Go with it.

ENERGY AND VITALITY JOY-ERCISE 1: SPIRITUALLY RE-ENERGIZE

> *"The more you lose yourself in something bigger than yourself,*
> *the more energy you will have"*
> *Norman Vincent Peale*

This is the day to tap into the giant "battery" in the sky or all around you. Make a commitment to find your spiritual renewal center today – *remember joy is an inside job*! Be quiet and spend time with God, or whatever spiritual source resonates with you, or be in nature.

Spend time with children - yours or someone else's!

Whenever my husband and I play with our God-children, grandchildren, nieces or nephews, we go home physically tired, but spiritually renewed and energized. We love spending time with them.

Contemplate, meditate, sit in silence and allow the silence to gently seep into your soul. Try talking to God like He's a person sitting with you - He really is! Or imagine your angels or guides are there with you - they are as well!

If you don't know how to meditate, you can simply sit and pray. Kneeling while you pray is even better! Or sit in a quiet spot on your own and focus on nothing but your breathing. *Imagine your breath flowing in and out of your heart area.* Instead of focusing on your breathing, you can find a sound that relaxes you. Perhaps ahhhh or ommmm or whatever sound you like that works for you.

Your mind will wander to other thoughts but just *gently* bring it back to your focus. Remind it that now is not the time for thinking – it's the time for silence and focusing on reconnection.

Your Mind Is Designed To Think!

Be kind to your mind – it's just doing its job! It's designed to think, so it's almost impossible to stop it. However we can train it to rest every so often! Meditation is an exercise to improve your mind control.

Persevere if you find this initially difficult. Many of us are so used to having our minds work at a million miles an hour, that it takes time and *regular* practice to train it to slow down or stop. Men often find this easier because they actually can think nothing! True! Science has shown it. Whereas women's brains never stop firing a million miles an hour! So keep practicing this new habit.

Even if you think your quiet session achieved nothing because you could not stop your mind racing – there are *still huge physiological benefits from what you did*! Do this for five, ten or twenty minutes *at the same time* every day. Some days you may need longer than others.

The Same Time Each Day

Doing it at the same time is important as I truly believe we make "appointments" with our spiritual guides. If they know we will be quiet and meditating at the same time each day – they can connect with us. I bet they have busy schedules as well and appreciate our consideration! *Remember to ask* them to meet with you!

For me, slowing down and truly feeling silence and is what really recharges, centers and grounds me. I can't always do it, but I practice regularly. More often, I find the silence, and just sit in it. Robert Sardello's book, *"Silence"* might help you with this - it did for me! Another resource is www.beyondthemind.com where there is an easy and free series of short meditations that really work: And a book called *Silence Your Mind.*

Take the time today, and each day, to do something that lets your soul rest and your spirit renew. Stop rushing; be present to the peace, and enjoy the renewed sense of vibrant energy that comes to you.

ENERGY AND VITALITY JOY-ERCISE 2: PRACTICE JOYFUL EATING HABITS

"The secret of your future is hidden in your daily routine."
Mike Murdoch

You become what you eat or drink! *Read the labels!* Your body renews itself on a regular basis using building materials directly derived from what you put into it. Select carefully - *it will become part of you soon!*

If you buy a lot of processed foods, you may be compromising your health every time you eat them. You will have heard of the dangers of trans fatty acids, excessive sugars and salts in most processed foods.

High fructose corn syrup (HFCS), which is in almost all processed foods, is potentially horrible for your health! Avoid it like the plague as well as anything that has hydrogenated, or partially hydrogenated fats.

Check the web for sites that educate you about healthy and safe food ingredients and additives – and in your makeup as well. The skin absorbs every ingredient you put on it – and your liver has to deal with any toxic chemicals.

You may have seen articles on artificial sweeteners, diet products, flavors, colors, and what they do to us. They can *increase* obesity! Pay attention to these warnings - they are not written by people who want to mislead you. They want to educate you and change your habit of eating and drinking substances that may harm you.

Read every ingredient label on all the food you buy! I use a great app called *"The Chemical Maze"* by Bill Stratham when I shop. It tells me what all the numbers mean and how safe, or not, they are.

Watch This DVD

A young couple created a company from their passion to cure a relative of illness - nutritionally. Their extraordinary DVDs - *"Food Matters"* and *"Hungry For Change"* are changing the world! Visit their site *www.foodmatters.tv* and you will be in awe of what you learn.

Examine Your Shopping Habits

Today is the day to observe your eating, shopping and drinking patterns and routines. Where do you shop? Do they have good, fresh foods? Do you look at the ingredient list on every processed item you buy? Do you prepare and cook food yourself or just buy it all pre-prepared?

Do you buy organic or local fresh food when you can? Organic foods are grown without pesticides. Most pesticides, herbicides and fungicides have toxins and fake estrogen in them so they may affect your hormone balance as well as increase your toxic chemical levels! *Scrub all your fruit and veggies before you eat them.*

Root vegetables, onions and potatoes absorb pesticides in the soil so try to *at least buy organic potatoes and root vegetables this week*, and from now on if you can. If you live largely on processed foods bought from supermarket shelves, try to change this pattern.

It may take a little more time to buy fresh food and cook it, but you will feel better; bond with your family more (especially if you make meal times a family affair!); teach your children how to cook; give them a better start in life, and be planting the seeds for a much healthier old age for them - and you. Let Jamie Oliver guide you with his quick and easy nutritious meal cookbooks or TV shows.

Lunch

Can you find a place that makes healthy salads or sandwiches? In the USA, when you order a sandwich you almost always receive potato crisps. Ask for fruit or salad instead.

Can you make something healthy at home the night before and take leftovers for lunch and save money? There are always healthier options that take only a tiny bit of planning and have huge impacts on your energy levels!

Snacks – If You Must, Choose Wisely!

If you snack during the day - do you really need to? *Is it real hunger or just boredom? Or emotional compensation?* My husband always used to resort to "comfort" foods when he was stressed – until he realized how bad they were for him and decided to call them "crap" foods!

And if you must have a snack, on what do you snack? Do you *choose* fruit or candy, cookies or a protein bar with the least amount of sugar you can find, fresh nuts and seeds (walnuts are great!), or vegetable sticks? Every mouthful you eat can either be beneficial or harmful.

Often, we interpret thirst as hunger! If you are hungry, drink a glass of water first and see if you still need food. These small changes in awareness and choices can dramatically impact how you feel.

How We Eat

How we eat is critical! If you are gulping your food down in a hurry while you're typing, writing or driving, your body cannot really digest it in the optimal way.

We need to have little rituals while we eat: *Stop; sit; bless the food; eat it slowly, and chew each mouthful 30 times.* Yes, 30 times! Try doing that and you'll see how most of us don't really chew our food at all. Most of us are not even aware that we shove our next mouthful in *before* we have even swallowed the previous one!

Chewing 30 times allows the sensory systems set up in the mouth to prepare the stomach and digestive system for the food that is about to arrive - the process triggers the release of the appropriate digestion enzymes.

Ideally, *when we eat, we should just eat*! No speaking, or watching TV! Especially if the show is violent or gruesome, because that is sure to negatively affect our digestion!

Avoid drinking water while you are eating since it dilutes your digestive juices and interferes with healthy digestion. Wait for 30 minutes *after* you eat to drink water. Drinking a glass of water with a tablespoon of organic apple cider vinegar, 20 minutes before you eat, apparently helps digestion – it does for me and I enjoy it in a wineglass!

Many of the bad eating and drinking habits we have are just that - habits. Once we recognize the patterns or rituals we are stuck in, we can change them and create new, digestion and health enhancing rituals and patterns.

Ask yourself, *"Does my stomach want this or my mouth?"* Do you just want the taste of something or are you actually hungry? Very often it's thirst or our taste buds that trigger our desire to eat. Stop and decide whether it's a stomach *need, a mouth need, an emotional need or thirst.* Be conscious of why you want to eat something you know is unhealthy.

Make Eating a Wonderful Experience!

Do something to make your food exciting and create a joyful experience as you eat. Set the table beautifully; present the food so it looks wonderful on the plate; have an excited attitude as you present the food.

When possible, *involve your family* so they enjoy the preparation of the food. Let them contribute to the decision-making process - make it a fun event. *Create a new and much healthier rhythm and routine* of eating and drinking for you and your family.

Remember to *prepare your food with love!* What you are feeling and thinking as you prepare food can make its way into the final product! *Cook with love and be thankful* for the food and the people and plants that provided it.

Say Grace and be thankful for your food and ask for it to be blessed. We may not be able to scientifically prove that these things make a difference yet, but I bet we will one day!

ENERGY AND VITALITY JOY-ERCISE 3: PRACTICE DRINKING CONSCIOUSLY

Most of us are chronically dehydrated - we need to drink more good, pure water, especially if we live in air conditioning all the time. Put some lemon or lime wedges in it if you want flavor!

Apart from coffee or tea, there are other sources of caffeine like standard sodas and energy bars. Be conscious of how much caffeine you are *actually* consuming. If you go off it and have withdrawal signs - it may be indicating you were having too much!

Squeeze your own juices or visit a juice bar - vegetable juices work wonderfully to renew energy. Water is essential for life. The average adult body is 55% to 75% water. Two-thirds of your body weight is water. Make sure you drink enough *good quality* water! It's amazing how quickly the body can dehydrate.

By the time we actually feel thirsty, we are probably already dehydrated. Most of us are frequently dehydrated and don't even know it. It's better to drink small amounts of water every 30 minutes (apart from when you are eating) instead of drinking a full glass twice a day!

In America and most western countries, tap water is usually germ-free but we do need to consider ways to make water vital, alive and chemical free. Visit the www.miracleproducts.com.au store for good information.

You may want to do a search on the web and read about the potentially harmful effects of long-term *sodium* fluoride (added to water and toothpaste) ingestion. Some people believe *sodium* fluoride *does not protect* your teeth and does not keep your bones strong - and instead that it often has the reverse effect! It's believed that *calcium* fluoride, as it occurs in natural vegetables, like cauliflower, is extremely beneficial to bones and teeth.

Coffee and Sodas Dehydrate!

If you are thinking, *"I drink a lot of sodas and coffee and tea, so I can't be dehydrated,"* you may be wrong! *Caffeine can be dehydrating.* Why do you think people have withdrawal symptoms such as headaches, behavior changes and bad moods when they suddenly stop drinking a lot of caffeine? If you want to drink a lot of something other than water, there are many benefits in organic green or herbal teas.

Do you know that one of main ingredients by far in an average soda is high fructose corn syrup (HFCS)? It is not natural fructose - it is highly processed and comes from corn (often genetically modified).

An average American drinks 52.9 gallons of carbonated soda *(full of high fructose corn syrup (HFCS) or artificial sweeteners)* a year. That might provide liquid but it's not like pure spring water!

Research is showing that high fructose corn syrup is associated with obesity. In an article in the Dec. 4, 2005 Seattle Times, Dr. George Bray was quoted as saying, *"High-fructose corn syrup isn't completely responsible for the nation's 6 million overweight children"* but added, *"it's a big part of the problem."* Do yourself a favor and learn more about HFCS - it's in almost every processed food item you buy.

Please think twice or twenty times before you drink ordinary or diet sodas! Keep them out of your home and teach your children to drink water or natural juices. There are some sodas available at the health food store or in the health section of your supermarket that contain natural fruit juice sweeteners, evaporated cane juice, stevia, or xylitol. The last two are safe artificial sweeteners.

Read your labels carefully - and remember "natural" on the label does not always mean the same natural we are imagining!

Diet Drinks Can Be Worse!

And before you breathe a sigh of relief, thinking, *"I drink diet sodas,"* they are many who believe diet drinks to be equally bad! Diet drinks have artificial sweeteners that are artificial and thought to *cause* obesity!

You may want to read *"Sweet Deception"* by Dr. Joseph Mercola or *"Aspartame Disease - An Ignored Epidemic"* by H.J. Roberts for more scientific details that may convince you to change your habits. Today is the day to start drinking more water and green tea, preferably spring water, structured or filtered tap water - a little every 30 minutes - and blessing it before you drink!

ENERGY AND VITALITY JOY-ERCISE 4: PRACTICE USING IT OR LOSE IT

How Much Do You Move?

We live in a society where people are searching for *artificial* energy boosting substances - *when just doing some physical activity every day* may provide that extra edge to make it through the day!

Go through a typical day in your mind from the minute you wake up to when you go to bed. Is going from chair to chair your primary source of movement? Do you stand on escalators rather than walking?

Do you drive when you could walk; take the elevator when you could use the stairs; send emails to the person across the floor rather than walking to them?

When you arrive home do you engage in active or vigorous housework or have you hired a cleaner and a gardener to save you the effort of moving?

Think about *your posture at work and at home*. Do you slouch over your desk? Do you ever stand and stretch? Do you have pain in your neck, shoulders or low back? These are often caused by, or contributed to, by your posture and lack of movement and are warning signs that you need to move!

In fact, *the real warning signs* of impending damage are *burning, tingling, tightness, stiffness numbness, heaviness, dragging, discomfort, and pulling*! Pain is felt when the damage is already done! *Move* every time you feel a warning sign – preferably in the direction opposite to that in which you have been stuck! Think very honestly about your movement levels during the day - it may save you years of pain later.

And how long have you had this pain....?

We Must Keep Moving

The vast majority of us have become sedentary in our lifestyles. Are you guilty of texting or calling someone in the same house? *The human body must* keep moving. *Everything* stops working well when we stop moving. You only have to see the effect paralysis has on muscles, digestion, metabolism and joints to understand that.

Movement to joints is like spraying the lubricant WD-40 into them! If we don't stretch and use our muscles, we end up old, stiff and stuck when we are young. I am 59 and my joints are more flexible than when I was 20 - and that's the way it can be! I don't have a special body that is more elastic than everyone else's. I have just kept mine moving.

I have done yoga and Qi Gong for years. I stay active and am conscious most of the time of my posture. As a physical therapist, I saw thousands of people with pain - mostly caused by their inactive lifestyles.

Pumping Iron!

People in their 70s and 80s are often frail and fall because their muscles are weak and they shuffle. I am on a campaign to keep everyone strong before shuffling sets in!

Our former neighbor in Dallas was a lovely, active 83 year old. She lived on her own. She had to stop walking on her beloved bird trails because of pain in her knee. Out of desperation, she started going to aerobics and weights classes. She became a new woman! She was amazed at how much better she felt with no pain and a new lease on life.

That's what exercise and strengthening work does - at any age. Of course, you need to check with your doctor before you embark on any exercise program. From the age of 45, we really need to be building up our muscles as well as aerobic exercise.

Check out www.powerplate.com for a brilliant, easy way to become fit, strong, flexible and thin! I believe this machine will change the way we age – I love it so much I bought one! And I don't have shares in the company!

Make Movement A Habit – Set Timers!

We need to build movement into our daily lives at the very least. I sit on a big exercise ball when I work because it makes me move more than a chair. If you decide to do this make sure the ball is secure! I make sure I stand and stretch every 30 minutes. We set timers in our office!

Just stand up and stretch as much as you comfortably can –for a minute - that's all. Or less. That short time still has a great effect on your body and your energy levels.

Use the stairs at work instead of the elevator or escalator. Park the car further away and walk if it's safe. Go for a walk at lunchtime instead of swapping one seat for another when you eat. Play a game with your children instead of sitting in front of a television.

Walk daily if your neighborhood is safe. If not, run up and down your stairs at home for 20 minutes. (Check with the doctor before you start if you are not used to exercise!) Buy a Powerplate, (www.powerplate.com, www.fitensspersonally.com for cheaper powerplates and information) a treadmill, or clean the bathroom or kitchen vigorously.

There are many ways to bring movement into your home and workplace. Be creative and find as many as you can. Your energy levels will skyrocket if you make movement and exercise a part of your daily - or even weekly - routine.

Exercise Busts Your Stress!

But wait, there's more! Exercise is also the best way to bust stress, not just pain! Exercising is a proven anti depressant; it helps you lose weight and it is one of the best psychological and physical stress busters known.

Children are always moving and playing- they never sit still – unless we mesmerize them in front of the TV! *Limit the time your children spend in front of the television or the computer* - they are things that can stop a child doing what they innately know is critical - moving!

Today is the day to make movement and exercise a regular routine in your life and that of your family. Maybe you can all take up dancing or *do joy jigs every day*!

ENERGY AND VITALITY JOY-ERCISE 5: SLEEP AND ENERGY

"Lack of sleep disrupts every physiologic function in the body.
We have nothing in our biology that allows us to adapt to this behavior." [2]
Eve Van Cauter

" People who are sleep deprived have elevated levels
of substances in the blood that indicate a heightened state
of inflammation in the body, which has recently emerged as a major risk factor
for heart disease, stroke, cancer and diabetes." [3]
Dr Sanjoy R. Patel

Exercise is critical for us to have health, energy and vitality, and so is sleep. While we sleep, we heal and recharge our batteries, yet gazillions of people are not sleeping well, partly because we are not exercising enough to make us physically tired!

Instead, we exercise our minds all the time, feel "fried", and constantly feel over-whelmed. That means we go to sleep exhausted, and either can't fall asleep or find ourselves wide awake at 3 a.m.! How are your sleep patterns? Generally, to be well, we need about seven hours of sleep a night. Hard if you have babies, I know!

Do you wake up refreshed and alert? If not, try these:

Exercise sometime during the day so you have some real physical fatigue - not just mental exhaustion. If you are going to exercise at night, do it before dinner so that you are not energized just before you go to sleep.

Do not take your laptop or any work to bed! That will probably make you stay up much later than you planned and stimulate your mind just before sleeping.

Avoid watching television in bed. Watching anything other than a meditation channel with soft music and beautiful scenes is unlikely to help you sleep!

Listen to beautiful, relaxing music just before you sleep or as you are falling asleep.

Listen to a meditation track or music designed to make you sleep - there are many available. Try to make the room as dark as possible and as quiet as possible.

Quietly reflect on the day and focus *only* on things for which you are *grateful*. Write in your gratitude journal each night, in bed.

Always have a notepad and pen by your bed. Often when we wake up and can't go back to sleep, it's because we think of some brilliant idea and we stay awake (even unconsciously), because we might forget our idea. Write the idea down. If you wake and think of some problem, write it down, and tell yourself you will worry about it tomorrow at a better time. That often lets you go back to sleep.

Sometimes before we go to bed, *making a list of all the things we have to do the next day helps our mind shut off* and lets peaceful sleep drift in. Actually, doing this just before you leave work is better timing!

If you write down a problem before you go to sleep, and ask the spiritual realms to provide you with a solution, you might be amazed at how the answer is just there when you wake up. Or it may come to you in the shower. It's wonderful how often this works, as long as you let the problem go once you have written it down, and trust the answer will come.

Focus on your breathing. Just imagine the breath flowing in and out of your lungs or heart area gently and rhythmically.

Give it a color. *Create the feeling that you are floating on a huge, very still lake* - you are safe, protected and fully supported as you completely relax into the feeling of lying on this lake.

Set Up Rhythms And Rituals

If possible, try to set up a rhythm, and a set of rituals for going to bed. Aim to go to bed *at the same time each night* - the earlier the better. Some people say that every hour of sleep before midnight is worth two after!

Perhaps you can have a *warm bath or shower* as part of the ritual before you go to bed. Talk and think only about *positive* things - not about all your worries and problems. Focus on things for which you are *grateful*.

Maybe you and your partner can give each other a *massage* once a week. You may wish to *pray* (on your knees or not) for a few minutes each night just before you sleep. Allow yourself to be comforted and held by your higher wisdom. Praying for those you love, counting your blessings, and dwelling on gratitude are the best ways I know to go to sleep!

Sleep Foods!

Sometimes what we eat before we sleep can make a difference.

Bananas have magnesium and serotonin; chamomile tea has a mild sedative effect; warm milk, almonds, and slices of whole wheat toast actually contain tryptophan, which relaxes us; and a tiny bit of *raw* honey can help too.

Small Changes: Wake Up Refreshed!

Li*stening to what we say to ourselves* as we go to sleep, and staying away from the television and computer for at least an hour before bed may be the only things we need to do to transform our sleep, and allow us to wake up feeling refreshed and alert.

And speaking of waking up - try to find an alarm that doesn't make you to sit bolt upright in bed with terror! Something that welcomes you gently into the day is a much better way to start than the sudden jarring that many alarms provide.

Today - plan to sleep well and make this your new rhythm.

ENERGY AND VITALITY JOY-ERCISE 6: PRACTICE STRESS BUSTING

Stress is a fact of life – it doesn't have to be a way of lite!

Stress is probably our greatest zapper of energy and vitality. Constant stress and pressure are exhausting both mentally, and physically. Remember your adrenal glands and how hard they work when you are stressed. Today, *do your best to stay calm and peaceful.*

Watch carefully what you say to yourself as most of our stress comes from our words, perceptions and the *stories* we tell ourselves about what has just happened. *Listen carefully, and be alert to your internal dialogue, self talk or story, and challenge the truth of it.* Remember, it's a *fairy* story!

Events that happen are just events. They are neither good nor bad, but we *perceive and judge* them as good or bad.

For example, if we see a strange look on our boss' face, we suddenly fear we might have done something wrong, when really the boss may have just had a moment of indigestion!

Worry – Is It Valuable?

Think about the value of worrying. Will it change things? Probably not, but you will waste a lot of time. If you are *concerned and take action* to rectify a situation, you won't waste time stewing in inaction and worry.

Worrying is vividly imagining what you don't *want to happen!* We know that vividly imagining what you *do* want to happen works because Olympic athletes use the technique – they call it mental rehearsal.

So if vividly imagining what you do want to happen makes it more likely to happen – why would it be different if you vividly imagined what you *don't* want to happen? *Stop imagining the worst! Now and forever!* Try saying, *"Oh well…"!* I have found many times that if I say, *"Oh well…,"* I breathe again and relax.

Deep Breathing

Which brings me to breathing: deep breathing– probably the greatest weapon against stress! When we feel stressed, our breathing becomes shallow and rapid. There is less oxygen delivered to the brain and we stop thinking clearly.

Notice your breathing today and keep taking *deep, long breaths* in *and out.* It's often the out breath that suffers when you are stressed. Consciously blow out all the bad stuff.

Make a commitment today to *catch yourself* rushing and stop it! *Wake up earlier* if you need more time to do what you need to do. *Leave the house a little earlier,* so you are not driving like a crazy person - creating even more stress for yourself and others.

Breathe deeply, slow down, stop stress inducing stories and you may be surprised at how calm you stay, and how much more alive you feel at the end of the day.

ENERGY AND VITALITY JOY-ERCISE 7: ENERGY SUCKERS AND GIVERS!

> *"Don't hold onto your anger, hurt and pain.*
> *They steal your energy and keep you from love"*
> *Anonymous*

I bet at some stage in your career, you have had someone on your team who was an energy sucker. What was it like when they left? It seemed as if the sun had come out! Everyone was laughing, working well together and happy all of a sudden!

That's the impact an energy sucker can make in your life, at home or work. One energy sucker can destroy a very large team! Typically they are pessimists and cynics, and/or they think they are superior, although inside they are usually feeling insecure. They often put people down to make themselves feel better. *Do everything you can to limit your time and exposure to these people.*

If you have to be around them, try to prepare yourself. Imagine there is a cocoon of light or some impenetrable material around you. You can give energy out of this cocoon, but no one can take it out without your permission. This sounds strange but it is pretty effective! If you live with an energy sucker - try the cocoon!

You can also visit my Youtube channel – *amandagoretv* – and watch clips describing the difference between energy suckers and givers and hopefully the suckers will take note!

Try to counteract the time you have to spend with these energy suckers by hanging around lots of energy givers. Energy givers are happy, optimistic, upbeat, positive people and they always make us feel better. Try to be one as well. *Doing the joy-ercises in this book makes you an energy giver!*

It's A Parents Job To Teach Children Optimism

Because we don't consciously focus on teaching children optimism, we often model energy-sucking ways for them. And then we wonder why some, or all, of our children are little energy suckers!

Be cheerful and focus on helping children (and yourself) *see the bright side of life,* rather than the rush, frustration, anger and disappointment. They will have plenty of time to learn that themselves when they are older.

Today is the day you are to make your home a haven for energy givers. Banish energy suckers! *Be open,* positive, optimistic, play and have fun with your family. *Laugh a lot. Be the CEO - the chief energy officer!*

— Joy Secret #8 —

Listening

"God gave us two ears and one mouth. He was hinting!"
Anonymous

YOUR SEVEN MINUTES

- Are you a good listener?
- Would your family say you are a good listener?
- What would your friends and colleagues say?
- Ask a few people today so you can confirm your thoughts!
- What person in your life listens to you the best?
- What do you experience when they are listening intently?
- How do you feel afterwards?
- What happens during the experience that to make you feel that way?

Think of someone who really doesn't listen at all or interrupts all the time.

- What's it like to be around them? How do you feel?
- Where is that feeling in your body?

AMANDA'S TAKE: LISTENING VS HEARING

"Conversation: a vocal competition
in which
he one who is catching his breath is
called the listener."
Anonymous

Very few people are great listeners let alone *good* listeners!

Listening and hearing are completely different. Most of us can hear - but how many of us *really listen*? When we hear something we forget it in a moment. *When we truly listen, we remember* because we are *totally present –totally mindful.*

Do you remember a song by Mike and the Mechanics called *"In the Living Years"?* It was about the conflicts in communication between a father and his son. The chorus has a line, *"You can listen as well as you hear."* This really struck a chord with me.

Hearing is physiological; *listening is an art.* Dictionary definitions of hearing are mostly linked to the actual physical ability to hear. We are either capable of hearing or not.

We *hear* sounds but we have to *listen* for the *meaning.* More importantly, we *listen* for *feelings.* We sort through the sounds to discover what the person's *soul or heart* is saying.

When we truly listen, we pay attention to far more than just words. We see the body language; we pay attention to the voice tones, which are very powerful, as any husband will tell you! We watch facial movements and expressions, breathing and eye movements. We tune into every little nuance.

We set aside our own thoughts and chatter. *We see the world through the other person's eyes* - and touch their soul.

We can actually understand what they are saying because *we are entering their reality,* rather than experiencing them *though our preconceived ideas and expectations.*

Listening takes work, patience and commitment. Hearing is easy for most of us.

LISTEN WITH YOUR HEART FOR FEELINGS

> *"Words are just words and without heart they have no meaning."*
> Chinese proverb

Listening is a quality of the heart. Hearing is a faculty of biology. That means we must be "in our hearts" to be great listeners. If we are doing other things while someone speaks, we are just hearing sounds.

Unless we are totally focused on them, present and absolutely mindful, we can't enter their reality/world and see things the way they see them, which is the only way we can truly understand how someone else might feel.

Have you ever been driving with a child in the back of the car and they are babbling away about some important story (for them) and we make all sorts of *"Uh-huh"* noises. Finally the little one says, *"Mummy/Daddy, you're not listening to me!"* And they are right! *All* people sense when you are not truly listening, especially children.

Three Dimensions
– Words, Non Verbals, and Heart, Spirit, Soul

When someone speaks - there are the words, and then there are the other dimensions of actual communication. Words can lift up, inspire, enthuse or crush. When people talk, they also use their *faces, bodies, voice tones, breathing, pauses, and other non-verbal qualities.* These *non-verbal cues* are the second dimension of communication and are *more powerful than words.*

The third and probably most important dimension is that which comes from *their heart and soul.* These are much gentler, subtle vibrations and are *the spirit in which the words are said* – love, fear, joy, compassion, frustration, anguish. They can only be picked up with a heart that is tuned in.

Feelings (not emotions) are the language of the spirit and come wrapped in words, tones, actions and non-verbal gestures.

Respond To The Feelings

It's the feeling people want us to respond to, not the words, and yet most of us are oblivious to those wrapped, tender feelings! We hear their *words,* wait for the next gap in the conversation and jump right in with *our own words.*

Our words disguise *our* feelings, which *we* want them to respond to, but the other person doesn't know that so the loop continues. We both end up unheard and unhappy.

Imagine what would happen if every time you listened to someone, your goal was to unwrap the feelings their words were covering. I call that "heart listening" where your spirit connects to theirs and amazing understanding happens.

Listening is very active and takes concentration and effort. You are *constantly hearing, unwrapping, going to your heart, connecting to their spirit and decoding.* There's a lot to do when you truly listen; you can't be busy doing something else or planning your return volley of words.

Stephen R. Covey says in his book, *"The 7 Habits of Highly Effective People,"* that *"Most people do not listen with the intent to understand; they listen with the intent to reply. They are either speaking or preparing to speak."* That leads him to one of his golden rules: *"Seek first to understand, then be understood." When we understand, we fear or judge less* and everyone experiences more joy.

WE CAN'T FAKE LISTENING!

With every conversation, especially important ones, take time to *go into your heart first* so your spirit will convey a true desire *to listen with love.* That way it's easier to understand what the other person, or people, are *really* saying.

They will feel heard and acknowledged. You are a good listener if people always feel heard, acknowledged and validated around you. *It's the number one thing people want in life; it makes them feel special.*

Conversely, they will sense when you are judging, preparing your "defense," or waiting for them to stop speaking so you can burst forth with what you have been preparing to say – while they were speaking!

The Vast Silence In Your Heart

Mother Theresa said, *"We need silence to be able to touch souls."* True listening from that state of silence doesn't just mean no sound coming out of you or anyone else! It means *being in the vast silence within your heart.*

True listening often requires *making noises* that indicate you are following what they are saying and understanding – not necessarily agreeing, but *understanding.*

David Bohm, a famous quantum physicist and colleague of Albert Einstein, once said, *"When you listen to somebody else, whether you like it or not, what they say becomes a part of you."*

Within the universal field as it is called in quantum physics, we create another field between us. *When we bring our Divine selves or love into that field, and remain open, we can be, or are, taught the truth of all things.* As you listen, be in your heart, and focus completely on the other person.

Imagine your heart has ears!

You may or may not look at them - some people feel better heard when you make eye contact with them intermittently and others prefer consistent eye contact. Do nothing else. Plan no reply speech. *Do not rehearse* what you want to say while they are speaking. *Do not judge* what they are saying before or as it comes out of their mouths.

Try and quiet your own inner dialogue and be aware that there is *a big difference* between negative inner dialogue from your ego and intuition or inspiration!

Intuition And Responding

Intuition is the "inner tuition" your heart's wisdom shares – it's usually a *knowing* or a feeling about some action to be taken, or words to be said. *Try to sense the difference.*

When the person finishes speaking, *slowly count to 5 before you say anything. Breathe in and out once before you speak. Respond to, and acknowledge* **how they feel,** not just their words, but be careful to respond - not react.

You may say things like, *"That must have been very frustrating for you"* or *"I imagine you were very disappointed when that happened."* Other responses might be, *"Wow. How did you manage to keep going - that must have been very hard"* or *"I am so sorry you felt I did that; that was not my intention."*

You could also say, *"I am so sorry you perceived it that way and I can see how you could have"* or *"I can see your point of view and that it would have been very... (insert feeling-based word here)."* It's a given that you are *sincere* at this stage! If you're in your heart, you may not speak at all, but *they* will feel heard, deeply understood and safe.

Relax if you don't completely understand the *content.* For that you can ask clarifying questions. *Listening involves more than comprehending what the words mean.* People generally are not interested in our opinions, thoughts or ideas - even if they ask! *They are interested in feeling understood, validated and acknowledged.* That's why our hearts need to have ears and eyes for feelings.

IT'S ABOUT THEM – NOT YOU!

You understand now that communication is not about us; it's about *connecting on a soul level.* Miscommunication is rampant because words at face value do not often convey what people really mean or feel.

Our hearts need to listen, interpret and internally reframe what a person is saying into what they really need or want, and then we respond to that need. Sometimes it's difficult to truly listen, especially when the speaker is highly emotional. If this emotion is directed at us, we may feel defensive, judged or criticized. RTB! Remember To Breathe!

People's language usually communicates more about them, their state and issues than about you, no matter how it sounds or how we perceive it! When we are only hearing words, it's easy to be defensive - and feel we are being judged, criticized or attacked - whether we are or not.

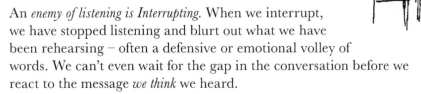

If we remain in our hearts, trying to *understand* what a person is really feeling, we are less likely to be trapped at the surface of words or emotional states. Ask yourself – *"what does this person really want from me?"* When you are good at heart listening, what you communicate will make the other person feel truly understood!

An *enemy of listening is Interrupting.* When we interrupt, we have stopped listening and blurt out what we have been rehearsing – often a defensive or emotional volley of words. We can't even wait for the gap in the conversation before we react to the message *we think* we heard.

When we focus on our own emotions, without remembering that most communication is about the *communicator*, we can miss the point – the soul level - completely. We end up fearful, unhappy, angry, defensive and hostile and feeling "attacked".

The speaker feels totally unheard, dissatisfied, frustrated and disappointed. The issue remains unresolved and the atmosphere tense. Remember, *listening is about them - not about you.*

SPEAKING - CHOOSE YOUR WORDS WISELY

Any chapter on listening needs a section on speaking! You'll probably find you speak much less with this way of listening; however, speaking is part of the connection in communicating. Before you speak, check with your heart *quickly* and ask, *"Will this response be helpful to this person?"*

If your reply is *"no"*, then wait a moment, and if nothing comes, respond in some appropriate way. Make a noise or genuinely be thinking about what they said – or ask them gently to elaborate and help you understand. *Long, awkward pauses can make conversations uncomfortable and difficult. Keep breathing!*

Use *softeners* like *"If I may…."* Or *"help me understand…"* , or *" I can't imagine how you are feeling…"*, or *"tell me more about …"* and so on.

Choosing the right words is important – choosing *the right spirit, way and time to say those words is critical.*

Words can be weapons, and are often used as such. Be very careful – words do hurt people and stay in their cellular memory forever. You might feel better "getting something off your chest" but you may be sending a spear through another person's heart causing a deep, abiding wound that is hard to heal. Be very conscious of the words you choose to use!

If we only spoke from our hearts focusing on the positive and gratitude; on the good in others, or in all situations, and that's all we let come out of our mouths or in our actions, we would be great communicators and connectors. And joyful!

Speaking To A Spiritual Being

Imagine you are listening and speaking to a great Spiritual Being when you are with others. It's a brilliant way to *immediately* transform communication!

You wouldn't dream of speaking to God or some Spiritual presence in a surly, defensive, belligerent, angry, critical, nasty, rude or derisive tone, with resentment and abusive words! Nor would you dream of listening to a Divine source with a mind full of judgment, ridicule and disgust, or of not listening with your total, undivided attention and respect.

As the spark of the Divine lives in all of us, conduct every conversation as if
you are listening and speaking to that part of God or the Divine in everyone –
including ourselves.

LISTENING JOY-ERCISE 1:
PRACTICE LISTENING TO THE DIVINE

"Listening is a creative force that transforms relationships.
Listening is a sacred art. It is an awareness
that not only are we present to each other,
we are present to something that is spiritual, holy, sacred." [1]
Kay Lindahl

Spirit talks to us in many languages. Languages like: *gut feelings,*
instincts, intuition, inspiration or a sense of knowing something is right. Maybe
it's through angels who appear in our lives as people or in dreams;
or books we read; advertisements we see; evangelists or speakers we
watch; children; life dramas; misfortunes and so on.

It has to be this creative and flexible because few of us ever stop to
listen directly! I remember going to church one day, about a year after
I had moved to Dallas from Australia. The pastor at Highland Park
United Methodist Church, Mark Craig, had given another brilliant
sermon. And I was once again crying!

I didn't understand why this happened every time I went to this
church. I would be perfectly okay before I went in, and within
minutes, I would start to cry. It was a different sort of crying from the
usual. Tears would stream out of my eyes, but I wasn't crying like I do
if I am upset.

I started to think there was something wrong with me!

Perhaps I was much more *lonely* than I thought (I just mistyped, "I was
much more *lovely* than I thought." Was it a slip - or was God talking to
me just then? Ha ha!)

After a while, I realized that many times when I went into that
church, a feeling of love enveloped me. I didn't know anyone in this
congregation, and they didn't seem particularly welcoming. It dawned
on me that this was unconditional love I was feeling and I was crying
with joy.

Once I realized that, I felt more sane! I was told once that the Holy Spirit can move people to laughter, dancing or tears - cleansing tears – but I hadn't experienced it before.

What Is Wrong With Me?

But back to the day I was talking about. This particular day, I was sobbing, not just crying. I cried all the way home and thought, *"What is wrong with me?"*

I felt I should read the Bible when I arrived home to see if there were any clues in it, because I had no idea what was wrong! This was pretty unusual, as I did not read the Bible much!

Once home, I could not read as the tears were blurring my vision so badly. So I just had to sit there. God was moving in his mysterious ways! As I sat, I became aware of a feeling of being overwhelmed. I knew I had some big task to do, but I didn't know what it was, and I was sure I was inadequate for it, whatever it was!

After waking up to that, I sensed what I can only describe as a "smiling, loving indulgence". I couldn't see or hear it, but I could sense the smile, and a love like that of an indulgent and patient parent, and I "heard" (but really sensed), *"Do you think God would give you a task to do and not give you all the skills or the help you needed to do it?"*

That was it. I stopped crying instantly. I smiled and thought, *"of course not!"* I continued with my day feeling energized! Have you ever had a similar experience?

Your Task Today - Listening To Your Higher Self

I bet Divine inspiration touches us all the time, but we don't stop long enough to hear - unless we are facing a crisis. Take time to pray, ask and to listen. Ask what we need to do. What is the advice for you? What is the Divine design for your life? Are you on the right path? Importantly, ask how you can be a blessing to others.

Ask for help - and *hold joyful expectation that what you have asked for is already done. Feel as if your prayer is already answered.* For example, if you prayed for rain, feel the rain falling on your face, smell the moist earth, hear the sound of it hitting the roof. This is important!

Be patient with a heart full of hope that the answer will come when the timing is perfect - for you - even though it might not look like it right now. Know your prayer is answered - as long as it is in the highest good of all!

Always have the intention in your heart to be fulfilling your spiritual purpose. Ask Infinite Spirit, *"What do you need? What can I do for you today?"* every morning. Pray all the time, but part of prayer is "listening" to the answers you are sent.

God and the spiritual realms hear every prayer, and send blessings and grace - *so stay open and watch for the miracles.* They may be in things you see or pass by, strangers you meet, your friends or family - you

 never know where the answer will come from so stay awake; be conscious; expect to find the answer somewhere – look for the signs!

The spiritual realms and your higher self always answer. *Always.* Listening to them is your mission for today – should you choose to accept it!

LISTENING JOY-ERCISE 2: PRACTICE LISTENING WITH YOUR HEART FOR FEELINGS

Make Others Feel Safe

When listening, accept people for who they are and try to make them feel safe. A great question to ask yourself when listening to another person is: *"What does this person really need from me right now?"*

Let your heart surround them and quiet your inner dialogue or thoughts. This helps you to more accurately sense their true feelings. Words are "feeling wrappers". *Unwrap them to recognize the essence of what people are saying* - even if they are not conscious of it!

When you are this present with someone, conscious of the whole and sincerely desiring to understand, they feel secure, safe, loved, heard at a soul level, known for whom they truly are, fully accepted and understood!

Think of your best friend - the one who knows you better than anyone and still loves you. They understand your little idiosyncrasies and annoying habits and *still* seek your company! They give you, as you do them, a safe space to be; one that allows interaction without fear of judgment, hidden agendas or confrontation. *Listen to everyone as if he or she were your best friend.* All day, and every day from now on.

On The Phone

When you are on the phone, *stop and do nothing else*! In fact, close your eyes so you can tune into them and the sound of their voice if that helps you. People can sense whether you are being attentive, even if you are not in the same location.

We live in a fast-paced and noisy world, but it is still important to *give the speaker your undivided attention*. Sit in a comfortable chair and listen as if they were sitting across from you. Cell or cordless phones make this much more difficult as we are inevitably doing other things while talking! Use discipline and *stop for important conversations and listen to people's hearts*.

On the phone, we don't have the advantage of body language to help us work out what feelings are present. Although our ears can only use voice tones and breathing patterns to help guide us, *our spirits know no boundaries*.

We can still listen and respond to them using the heart's kindness and wisdom. It may be a little more challenging, but with practice, we are able to listen deeply even over the phone.

When You Are Too Busy To Listen

What about those situations when you don't have time to be present, in your heart and listen from there? I have found that people don't mind if I tell the truth. I say, *"I am really sorry, but I am so busy right now that I cannot give you my full attention. Could we have this conversation in 20 minutes?"*. I always give a set time frame and honor my commitment with that time.

If you are the one needing to talk with someone, and your prospective listener asks if they can have a little time to prepare themselves - *understand and appreciate* that this person genuinely does want to listen with their heart, but cannot do it at this minute.

You will appreciate their honesty and the undivided attention you receive when the conversation *does* take place.

Your mission today: To truly connect with others, do nothing else while you listen; make everyone feel safe by listening from your heart, accepting them and responding to the feelings wrapped in words. Then notice the difference in *your life and their joy!*

LISTENING JOY-ERCISE 3:
WHY AM I BEATING MYSELF UP?

Most of us wouldn't speak to our worst enemy the way we speak to ourselves! Today may be a day of waking up! Have you ever spent a day consciously listening to how you speak to yourself? We often say dreadful things *to* ourselves *about* ourselves. We call ourselves idiots, ridiculous and *judge ourselves constantly.*

Some of us "should" ourselves a lot. We say things like. *"I should have done that better"; "I should have known that"* or *"I can't believe I did that"; "I am so embarrassed; I am so fat; I am such a loser; I suck at relationships."* I could go on for pages and so could you, probably!

Who needs enemies when we judge ourselves like this! This is the day we start treating ourselves kindly, look at ourselves from our heart's perspective and seek to understand ourselves. *The purpose of today is to become conscious of this self-destructive language.*

Firstly, become conscious of *everything* you say to yourself. Track it all day. Stop as soon as you become aware of something negative you said to or about yourself.

Secondly, jot down the most common nasty phrases you use on yourself. Writing them down is important, as they look even more sinister (or silly!) on paper. And you can actually see the phrases you are constantly repeating to yourself.

Be on the alert, since many of us have a nasty inner voice - I call it the "criticizer" - which blocks us from receiving inspirations and truthful insights about ourselves. It appears faster than we can imagine and before we know it, it has stopped any true listening, and triggered a defensive reaction of anger, shame or one of many troubling emotions that create blind spots.

Repetition reinforces belief, so imagine the impact of telling ourselves thousands of times how useless we are, or what losers we are, or any of those other phrases you have written down. Look at the list you have made of the criticizer's favorite lines - and make time during today to *question if they are:*

1. True
2. Useful
3. Judgmental
4. Phrases that our father/mother/ siblings/ teachers/ partners/ friends said to us years ago that stuck in our minds
5. "Stuff" that we took on and made our own even if it was not true or helpful
6. Observations or stories that were true at one time but are no longer

Your most common phrases may highlight the *three core fears in life, which are I am not worth loving- or I am not good enough; I am unsafe in some way; or a fear of death, separation or abandonment.*

This is a fabulous exercise to do with your children - no matter what age. Make sure they feel emotionally safe as you listen and help them. It will be one of the greatest gifts you can give them.

An Easy Way To Change!

Once you make the commitment to change, it takes repeated re-patterning – FARC-ing! – to help silence the criticizer.

This technique helps you FARC! Find a rubber band large enough to be very loose around your wrist. (Keep your circulation going!) Maybe you could use one of those now very common quarter-inch wide bands and write, "worry buster" on it!

When you hear the criticizer, pull the rubber band far enough out from your wrist so that when it snaps back it stings slightly. Don't pull it out so far that it hurts you or draws blood!

Be responsible, sensible and kind to yourself. This is just a *trigger* to help you change your thought patterns! LOL.

The rubber band is just a fun and effective way to reprogram your mind. When used consistently, it really helps to stop negative thoughts or worry!

LISTENING JOY-ERCISE 4:
PRACTICE LISTENING TO YOUR HEART

"As a man thinketh in his heart, so is he."
Christ Jesus

The *pure* heart is not judgmental, it *uses wisdom and is discerning.* Some people choose to hate, trick, lie, steal from or harm people - they don't listen to their pure hearts.

The voice of their conscience becomes fainter and they justify to themselves that they way they live is acceptable or necessary. Discernment keeps us connected to our *conscience* and our *consciousness.*

In the Sermon on the Mount, Christ said, *"For where your treasure is, there will your heart be also."* Thoughts of the pure heart are true, wise and safe. *The treasure a pure heart seeks is connection to the Divine,* and working for the highest good of all.

Is your treasure spiritual connection and doing the right thing or "false gods" such as possessions, control, or power? Which do you long for? It will affect the choices you make, your health and your destiny. Watch a persons behaviors and you will see what they truly treasure.

Today is your day to listen to the *pure* heart's quiet voice. Compare the "voices" of your judgments with those of a pure heart. Which is louder and more insistent? Think about which one rules your behavior.

Most of us are not conscious of the competition inside the heart, choosing between *conscience* and *judgments*. *Judgment often wins, because it's a habit.* We need awareness to short-circuit our negative habits.

Most of us don't even know our heart has a voice. We occasionally notice gut feelings or intuition, or we have a sense or, we just know something is true or right or what we need to do. *These are some of the ways your heart "talks" to you.* Subtle, quiet and clear.

Your Amazing Heart And How to Listen To It

Our hearts generate an electric current that is 60 times more powerful than any other body organ. It creates a doughnut-like electromagnetic field that spreads up to ten feet from the body and can affect another person's brain waves! It connects us with all living beings.

Hearts that are pure, full of appreciation and gratitude change everything! They are so much more than a pump. Visit http://www.heartmath.com to learn more about the incredible nature and power of the heart.

For some people, listening to the heart takes time and is more easily done in silence. Initially you may need to find a quiet spot, but with practice we can tap into the heart's wisdom anywhere, because it's a conscious awareness, a feeling and a state of being.

In this quiet spot, ask for help; quiet all the mental chatter to clearly hear the heart, and be conscious of body sensations - inspirations, gut feelings or a sense that something is right or not. Clear, true hearts know what is best for us - we just have to learn the language. To be awake to that knowing or the way the heart communicates with us takes a conscious effort. Make the time to sit quietly and reflect.

Ask your heart what you need to know. Be prepared for the answers to come in different ways. If the answers are judgmental or nasty - your hearts gentle whispering has been overridden. Start again!

If you feel peace when you have made a decision, it's probably your heart letting you know all is well. If you don't feel peace, better go

back and double check! *Inner peace is the benchmark for a pure heart based decision.* See which makes you feel more peaceful, safer, happier, and feels right - judgment or heart speak! It's a no-brainer!

LISTENING JOY-ERCISE 5:
PRACTICE DISCERNMENT AND SPEAKING ONLY GOOD

> *"Everyone is God speaking.*
> *Why not be polite and listen to Him?"* [2]
> *Hafiz translated by Daniel Ladinsky*

We all have that Divine spark of Love within us. At any moment, *God might be speaking through us to others or through others to us!* Many of us are polite but don't truly listen.

Sometimes in our culture, being polite is merely pretense. My understanding of what Hafiz meant by "polite" is to be *present* and *kind*. It's time to *go forth and see the spirit in everyone – actively look.* Keep reminding yourself as you listen and speak that you are listening and speaking to that Divine spark.

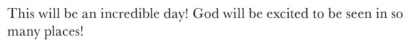

Treat everyone with the deep reverence. Be aware of your voice tones, words, gestures, breathing and patience!

Today's challenge is also to speak only reverent, positive words. Not one negative word is to come out of your mouth or swirl around inside you. See the good in people and situations and say only good things about them. If you can't say anything good, say something neutral or don't say anything at all!

This will be an incredible day! God will be excited to be seen in so many places!

LISTENING JOY-ERCISE 6:
PRACTICE ASKING QUESTIONS

> *"I know that you believe you understand what you think I said,*
> *but I'm not sure you realize that what you heard, is not what I meant."* [3]
> *Robert McCloskey*

My wonderful Aunt Nancy was one of the real eccentrics in the world. She started life in India, had several husbands; maharajas in love with her, and lived an exotic life throughout several countries. I adored her!

She taught me many lessons - the most memorable of which was, *"Darling, if you want someone to think you are interesting, listen to them, then ask questions about what they said. They will think you are fascinating!"*

She has been proved right time and again. People love being around someone who takes a sincere interest in them. *To be interesting, show interest!*

I am naturally curious and much prefer to ask questions - pertinent questions - than speak. *Everyone we meet is fascinating!* They all have rich stories and experiences, and because I truly listen, and genuinely show interest, they think I am fascinating, while I am busy finding them fascinating!

There is so much to learn in life, and most people love to share what they know. My husband is always in awe of what I find out about people, what they tell me, and how quickly I bond with them. I am sure it is largely in part because I do listen, and am *genuinely* interested.

I am never certain what person has been chosen to deliver a message or help me. *It gives meeting everyone and anyone a whole new dimension.* Remember to ask questions that don't just require yes or no answers. Give people a chance to expand and share with you by asking questions that encourage them to give you more detail.

Questions that begin with, *"How did you…"; "What was it that you found so …";"How specifically did the …";"When was the…",* and *"Can you expand on the bit about…"* are always good conversation kick starters.

Pay attention to the answers! And comment on them as well! If you are just asking questions to be polite, they will know and you will both be bored.

Never be frightened of looking or sounding stupid because you ask a question. I am never ashamed of not knowing something - none of us know everything. If I have not had an experience that has taught me about this subject, why would I judge myself badly? I am grateful that this conversation is my chance to find out!

If you are interested, truthful, sensitive, and being guided by the wisdom of your heart, asking a question is rarely offensive or insulting.

A Great Way To Teach Optimism And Open Conversations

To start a conversation, ask, *"What's the best thing that happened to you today?"* I love this one! Try it with your family every day - make it a ritual in the evenings over dinner - and watch the group dynamics change.

It can be transformational when everyone knows you will ask them that question routinely. They come home thinking about the answer because they know you will ask it! This is a small change with a monumental effect. *It teaches children optimism as well!*

Make it the opening ritual at staff meetings. Ask *"what's the best thing that happened to you since we last met?"* to dramatically improve the energy and vitality of your meetings. You can even use it on your voice mail!

Conversations Are Two Way!

Conversations are not a one-way street. If someone seems interested in listening to you and your story, be willing to share it! Michael Grinder is one of my mentors. He is a master of non-verbal communication and an educator's educator.

Visit www.michaelgrinder.com. It's magical to see Michael in action with teachers and corporate groups. I have studied with him for 20 years and wanted to share with you one of his strategies (with his permission) for helping improve our true listening skills. When someone is speaking and they finish, wait. *Do not speak.* As Michael says "WAIT" really stands for, *"Why am I talking?"*

Instead of speaking immediately, nod, look down, and reflect on what the speaker said. (I take this time to unwrap the feelings.) Count to five and if they say nothing more, then you can reply.

It is extraordinary how much more information someone will give you in that short space of silence. It's rare for people to wait five seconds, because they have been rehearsing their reply speech ever since the other person started speaking.

Most of us have already formulated our answer (instead of listening to what was said), and have been waiting impatiently for them to shut up so we can talk!

So ask questions, be interested in the answers, and when the speaker finishes, wait five seconds at least, unwrap the feelings and then - *only then* - talk! Persevere - it sounds easier than it is, but it's worth it!

LISTENING JOY-ERCISE 7: DISGUISES THAT WORDS TAKE ON

Mis-Communication Guru!

When you sense something is wrong and you ask, *"What's wrong?"*- the word, *"nothing"*, takes on a whole new meaning! I have learned so many lessons since I married!

I was 49 and my husband 54. I had been single for about 20 years, and I thought I was Miss Communication guru but marriage has been a humbling experience. I found out how little I really knew!

I was the *mis*-communication guru! It took us two years to really appreciate that what we say is not necessarily what we mean or need!

My husband and I have had a number of "discussions" where there appears to be some specific issue with the cooking, car, house, garden or some tangible physical thing, when really it has nothing to do with those. They were just the words wrapping the feelings! How long it took me to recognize that! And him!

It's incredible how *the need to be acknowledged, feel safe, loved, and understood* are at the bottom of so many silly little "issues" we discuss. Okay, I really mean fights! (See how we use words to disguise things?) Feelings of insecurity, inadequacy or fear appear as arguments about who is going to navigate or do the shopping! Am I the only one, or have you noticed this as well?

I am in awe of how I can be so unaware of my own – and his - feelings at times. For example, I wonder why I am making such a big fuss over money sometimes, when really it was a need to feel secure, safe and appreciated!

AMMY

Our amygdala (AMMY) is part of our old brain, responsible for our survival. It's the source of many of our deep, hidden fears. Our memories of emotional events are stored there and in our cells, and years later, those feelings can surface under very different conditions from those in which they were created.

Under stress the amygdala instantly takes over. *It's interested in our survival not our success.* It sees anything different as dangerous!

Our AMMY takes over so quickly and completely that we usually have no idea of the source of our disproportionate fear, anxiety or anger. We don't know that what appears to be upsetting us about has nothing to do with current reality!

It's from the past and AMMY's survival instinct. *So today is the day to notice the real source of our fears and catch AMMY in action.*

Teenagers

When a teenager says *"I hate you"* - do they really mean it? Or if they say they "hate school," is that the truth? Rarely. Most of the time they are scared about something, and our job is to find that fear and reassure them, or help them face it.

Listen very, very carefully to teenagers - they bring great gifts with their "difficult" years! Apart from the gift of stress wrinkles, they can teach you to be experts at unwrapping feelings!

Projections

When people make judgments about others, it's often a projection of what they believe about *themselves*. For more help in this area in detail, visit www.thework. com. It is Bryon Katie's website and her practical techniques are very useful for helping us see how we cause a lot of our own pain with misperceptions, thoughts, beliefs and stories!

If we are jealous, perhaps we are really telling ourselves nasty things about how unattractive we are, and comparing ourselves with others – highlighting our own insecurities.

Waking up to our responsibilities, being conscious that the emotions of disappointment, anger, frustration and many others are caused by *our thoughts*, allows us to help both ourselves, and others, find joy. Wanting to understand what other people are feeling as they are speaking helps you respond more appropriately.

Sense if they need privacy or if the timing is right for this discussion. Asking the question, *"I'm wondering, what thought is causing you to feel this way" may* improve the other person's insight. Or ask *"help me understand…..what are you saying to yourself about this?"*

Then again, this may just make them angry! It really has to be done with great love, from your heart and with a sincere desire to truly listen and understand, at the right time. Use a gentle voice tone and preface your question with "softeners" like *"If I may…"; "help me understand…"; I'm wondering…"*.

Use the language of the heart, which reassures them and allows others to feel safe. Be wary of taking the meaning of any words literally - especially at times of stress. You will miss the real message being transmitted to you. *Deep listening is a hug you give the other person with your heart!*

Joy Secret #9

Laughter

YOUR SEVEN MINUTES!

Think of the last time you laughed so hard tears ran down your cheeks.

- Can you even remember it?
- Can you remember the last time you just laughed a lot?
- Do you have different sorts of laughter?
- What is the happiest time you can recall?
- Did you laugh a lot then?
- What – and who - makes you laugh?
- When you laugh, how do you feel?
- Where do you feel it?
- When you hear little children laughing, how does it make you feel and do you find yourself smiling or laughing as well?
- Do you laugh enough?
- How can you bring more laughter into your life?

AMANDA'S TAKE:

"What is laughter? What is laughter?
It is God waking up! O it is God waking up!
It is the sun poking its sweet head out
From behind a cloud
You have been carrying too long
Veiling your eyes and heart.

Oh, what is laughter, Hafiz?
What is this precious love and laughter
Budding in our hearts?
It is the glorious sound
Of a soul waking up!" [1]

Hafiz, translated by Daniel Ladinsky

This poem above is from a book I love called *"I Heard God Laughing"* by Daniel Ladinsky. He has translated and interpreted the wonderful writings of Hafiz, one of the best-known Sufi poets from Persia.

The book is so joyful that laughter almost bubbles out of it just as it lies on my desk! And it certainly makes me feel good and touches my heart when I read it. I really believe laughter is *"The sound of a soul waking up."* Listen to a little child laughing hysterically and you will know that it's true! It's the sound of the soul stirring. It bubbles out from and into hearts. How alive do you feel after a great laugh?

Learn Better With Laughter

Early in my speaking career, I worked at making my presentations entertaining because I didn't want people in a coma at the end of an hour! But after 23 years, I am pretty much myself on stage and what I speak about is so loaded with life humor that we all just laugh! I have fun; the audience has fun; and all our souls become happy and connected.

It is the most amazing transformation to see 7,000 (or 70) people light up with laughter. Often they have come from stressful, busy lives burdened by problems, dramas and overwhelmed with all they have to do. They look intense, focused, with furrowed brows.

Most are disconnected from themselves and others; talking fast; unable to really "see" others. But at the end of an hour of laughter, they almost glow and sparkle!

Strangers have arms around each other and relaxed faces. Many have let go of problems they were hanging onto. They have changed their perspective, lightened up, and actually feel more joyful. They have experienced the power of joy and endorphins are racing through their bodies!

Smile - Release Endorphins

Endorphins are the body's natural happy drugs! Joy Germs! They are very powerful hormones - more powerful at pain relief than morphine. They make us feel great - happy, peaceful, relaxed and joyful.

We can't synthetically manufacture anything as powerful as endorphins, but humans can do things to produce them anytime! A simple way to release them is to put a big "silly" grin on our faces – *and include your eyes!*

Seriously! Just put a big smile on your face and make sure your eyes are involved - you will be releasing lots of endorphins! Someone did this as a scientific experiment and it works. I am not kidding! When we fake a grin - *I* know you are not smiling, and *you* know you are not really smiling, but *as long as your "crows feet" muscles around your eyes are active*, our body-mind believes we are genuinely smiling!

Our body senses the muscles moving at either end of our mouths, and our "crows feet" muscles – the muscles at the outside edges of our eyes - which all send messages to the heart, digestive system and hypothalamus, and that tells the rest of our systems, and soul, to release endorphins.

So if you can't laugh, then at least put a big grin on your face, crinkle your eyes and *you will soon start to feel better.* And if you can't make it a huge grin, then just make a small smile and work your way up.

Every morning as soon as you wake up – *make your mouth and eyes smile.* It's a great way to start the day and will put you in a better frame of mind. Or make it a daily ritual to *smile the whole time you have your shower* and see how you feel! If you have three smiles to every one grimace or negative event, your health might improve!

LAUGHTER AND HEALING

We know that *laughter helps healing and boosts the immune system*. Norman Cousins, in his book *"Anatomy of an Illness"*, was the first person to write about how he healed himself from a fatal illness by checking out of hospital, and working with laughter and optimism as his primary method of healing.

Now, laughter therapy is an accepted and valuable form of treatment in hospitals and hospices. Cousins writes *"laughter is a form of internal jogging. It moves your internal organs around. It enhances respiration."* And it does!

Laughing helps you breathe better, and jiggles things around inside, which improves circulation, and gives you an endorphin high! This is not a very scientific way to describe the studies that have actually been done on the health benefits of laughter, but it's true.

If you really want to help someone heal more quickly, *help them laugh.* Keep everyone laughing around them to keep their spirits high. Even if you can make them smile, it will help and they will feel better because endorphins are reducing their pain.

Children laugh about *three hundred* times a day. Guess how often we grouchy old adults laugh? Seventeen! And I bet a lot of us don't even do that most days! Set a new target for yourself – *laugh or smile at least 20 times a day.*

Laughing will keep our hearts healthy, reduce the stress hormones pumping around our bodies, boost our immune systems, keep us younger, help fight off disease and live longer.

Consciously create opportunities to laugh. Watch comedy videos, movies or programs - not dramatic violence or news!

Do you know that for about five hours after you watch a violent movie, your immune system is less robust? Comedy videos actually *boost* the strength of the immune system.

Laughter can even make you fitter! One study has shown that if we laugh 100 times in a day, it is the equivalent of rowing 10 minutes on a rowing machine or spending 15 minutes on an exercise bike. For me, laughing 100 times a day is *way* more fun than 15 minutes on an exercise bike!

NOTICE FUNNY STUFF

A sense of humor and seeing funny things helps us be more creative *and* joyful. *Consciously look for humor* around you each day. It could be in funny street signs, babies laughing, or animals being cute.

Once you *set the intention* to notice funny stuff, you will be surprised at how "suddenly" funny things are everywhere! They have been there all along but we haven't focused on or noticed them before. To help you see all the funny stuff around you, your mission today is to make yourself a set of "funny" glasses!

Not funny looking necessarily, but ones that magically make everything you see through them appear funny. You have to pretend - be creative. They're a symbol remember? Wear them for a while each day so that when you have them on, the whole world is colored "funny!" They act as a constant reminder for us to consciously find humor, fun and joy in everything.

I know it's silly, but try it before you judge it. They might be very useful at work! *To develop in children optimism and a sense of fun, we need to have rituals in our homes to consciously create or notice humor!*

One great ritual to establish is to *ask everyone in the family to take turns at wearing the funny glasses* while they talked about the funniest thing they saw, heard or thought that day. Or to talk about some difficult thing that had happened, and try to see the funny side of it. Imagine the wonderful lessons you would be teaching children - *and the grownups* - if this was a family tradition.

JOY FAIRIES

When I speak about the importance of laughter with groups - there are always a sad few who say, *"Gimme something to laugh about!"* The problem is that there is no fun or joy fairy who flits around, sees us miserable, and then changes everything by waving a magic wand over us! *We have to be our own joy fairies. We* need to be the ones who bring ourselves joy and laughter – remember, joy is an *inside* job!

It seems that many people aspire to be a CEO, CIO, CTO, CSO or

C-something in the corporate world, so as of today, you can become your own official CJF - the *Chief* Joy Fairy.

This is your mission: Go forth and laugh 100 times or more every day, and help others to laugh that often as well. Well, at least laugh more than 17 times a day!

At The Joy Project, we try to help people in their mission to be joy fairies by **manufacturing** *magic wands* that light up and make a magic "brrriiinngg" noise. They are very popular and can make teenagers invisible, partners laugh, misery disappear and all manner of other fun things!

Use one at work to create magic but watch it carefully - everyone will want to use it! You can go further and buy some wings or even a fairy outfit, or just sprinkle fairy dust about - who knows - you may have the best day of your life!

LAUGHTER – THE GREAT CONNECTOR

Comedian and musician Victor Borge said, *"Laughter is the shortest distance between people."* Laughter is the great connector. It connects individuals and groups, overcomes arguments and difficulties and helps us lighten up.

I feel the spiritual realms connect *with* people *through* laughter and connect *us to each other* in the same way. Laughing *with* someone because we *consciously* try to see the funny side of the drama in which we find ourselves can transform everything. *Laughter is an alchemical process* - it can transmute pain and negative emotions into joy. Laughing *at* someone is unkind and causes pain.

Think of the most popular people you know; most of them are the life and soul of the party. What does that mean? It means *they are great connectors*. They have the ability to engage, entertain, tell stories, help others laugh and make them feel joyful.

Many women tell me the reason they have a long and successful relationship is because *"he makes me laugh - even after all these years!"* The ability to make someone laugh is a blessing and keeps us connected and we can all do it!

Dale Irvin, a wonderful speaker and friend of mine, has the most infectious laugh I have ever heard! I suggested he make a recording of his laugh so we can listen to it on the way to work, home or to appointments to put us in a great frame of mind.

Do you have a friend with an infectious laugh who would enjoy you recording them? Have a group of friends over one night for a laughter party - and record the results! Or tickle and play with your toddlers and capture their precious laughter. That sound would fill your heart, lift your spirit and make you laugh anytime!

Laughter is wonderful for your heart and soul, great for your body, connects you with others, puts things in perspective, releases stuck stuff, and heals! *We are blessed with the capacity to laugh so we should exercise that gift.* The spiritual realms are playful. We need to be as well!

Voltaire said, *"God is a comedian playing to an audience too afraid to laugh."* Why let fear destroy one of the most precious gifts humans have? Be brave! *If you look silly, who cares? The spiritual part of you and your body love it when you laugh.*

LAUGHTER JOY-ERCISE 1: PRACTICE SMILING AND LIGHTENING UP!

"Everyone smiles in the same language!"
Anonymous

Stop Taking Yourself So Seriously!

Today, your focus is to *smile all day – mouth and eyes.* Smile when you wake up, in the shower and smile at everyone.

Greet complete strangers with a smile and you'll notice that most of them smile back. Smile at little children. Smile at your neighbors even if you don't like them!

Smiling uses far fewer muscles than frowning, and if I am going to have any wrinkles, I would rather have laughter lines than frown lines!

Remember, smiling with your mouth *and eyes* releases endorphins, so no matter how badly you feel, it's a powerful way to change the physiological makeup of your body. *Smiling is the doorway to lightening up!*

When I arrived in the U.S., I had no idea there would be a cultural gap. I figured we all spoke English and watched the same television programs and were very similar. *Wrong*!

The Australian culture does not allow people to take themselves too seriously! If you think you are very important it's amazing how quickly someone comes up and lets you know just how insignificant you really are! We find it easy to laugh at ourselves, and when we do, life is lighter!

We have a phrase for intense, self important people: *"They are so far up themselves, it's dark!"* Today is the day to smile *and* laugh at yourself! *Catch yourself if you are taking yourself and life too seriously.* Work toward lightening and loosening up.

Be Professional And Still Laugh

Let go of *who* you are *supposed* to be, or *what* position you are in, and *let your playful side emerge.* It is absolutely possible to be professional and have fun!

Just because you are an accountant, a lawyer or a medical professional for example, doesn't mean you can't have fun while you work! In fact, people love to think that they can go to their accountant's office to talk about serious financial matters, and still laugh and enjoy themselves.

It's my belief that if you are truly professional at what you do, you will take your work seriously, but not yourself. I took my work as a physical therapist extremely seriously - and yet we did silly things and had a great time.

I also take my speaking very seriously, but if you saw me on stage, you would know that it looks nothing like serious. But the message and the way I impart it are very carefully crafted, and wrapped in great laughter to create the maximum learning experience and benefit for the audience members. If you are a "professional," this is your day to make your interactions fun, while taking the work seriously!

Do You Know Who I Am?

I read a magazine story some time ago about a man at an airport. As often happens in the U.S., weather had caused the cancellation of a lot of flights. There were long lines at the ticket counters. This man stormed up to the desk, pushing in front of a long line of people, banged his hand down on the desk and shouted, *"I need to fly to Chicago!"*

The airline person said as kindly as she could, *"I am sorry sir, and I will help you as quickly as I can. If you could just stand in line…"* He looked at her, slammed his hand down again and said, *"Do you know who I am?"*

She stopped, motioned for him to wait; picked up her microphone and announced over the loudspeaker, *"Ladies and gentlemen, there is a man at Counter 23 who does not know who he is. If anyone does know who he is, could they please come forward?"*

What a great story! Slow down and realize that the world does not revolve around you. *Stop being offended! Stop thinking everything is about you! Stop taking yourself and things so seriously!* Most people are not out to "offend" us on purpose - in fact, no one *can* "offend" us.

We *take* offence! We *interpret* what they say, *make judgments and assumptions about their intentions*, and then talk ourselves into being offended!

Do you ever wake up and think, *"I want to offend someone today?"*

Most people don't! Save yourself a lot of pain and give people the benefit of the doubt, or at least see the humor in situations instead of taking offense. *Smile. Even if you don't feel like it!* Lighten up. Laugh. Wake up your soul!

LAUGHTER JOY-ERCISE 2: PRACTICE REMEMBERING ALL THE FUNNY TIMES!

> *"Laughter is very powerful medicine. It can lower stress, dissolve anger and unite families in troubled times."*
> Anonymous

This should be a fun day. Take your joy journal and spend 10 minutes writing down all the significant laughter-filled events in your life you can remember.

A favorite memory of mine happened at a New Year's Eve party. I was reading out loud passages from Dave Barry's book, "Dave Barry Turns 40." This is a laugh-out-loud book, and I just knew everyone would love it.

As I was reading, I was laughing so hard that I had tears running down my face and I couldn't keep speaking. I was snorting with laughter! By now of course, the other guests had no idea what I was saying but they were laughing hysterically at me laughing! It was one of the best New Year's Eves ever- *for me!*

I didn't mind being the source of laughter - who cares if you look silly! Remember we are *eradicating our fears* and one of the main ones is humiliation – FOWOT – fear of what others think! When I am laughing and helping others laugh, I am the one doing the internal jogging and waking up my soul and sharing the gift!

My Blond Bullet!

When my gorgeous nephew, Thomas, was a toddler, he used to run towards me with arms outstretched and face glowing with joy. He was blue eyed and blond and I called him my 'blond bullet"! As he did this, I would laugh, and my heart would burst with joy.

Watching my beloved niece and nephew play, laugh and talk gave me endless hours of laughter and joy. Combine all the video footage of your children laughing and playing so you have 20 or 30 minutes of unbridled joy that you can experience over and over again. This makes a wonderful gift for your children when they are older, as well.

In this day of smartphones and Instagram, it is *so easy to create short clips of wonderful moments*. Aim to capture at least one funny moment on video each week!

In Hospitals

When my Mum was in hospital in the last weeks of her life, I arrived from the U.S. with a bag full of my little smiley-face finger puppets (I call them endorphins!). They are bright yellow and have a smiley face on them and little arms stretching out either side. I put them all around her room. I tried to give them to the nurses and doctors.

Sadly, only one doctor and one nurse laughed and took them. The others were not the least bit interested. Maybe they were asleep during the healing and laughter segment in their training!

Luckily, my brother, who is one of the funniest people on earth, arrived and the three of us had an hysterical time playing with them. *If you have a loved one in hospital, surround them with as many laughter inducing things as you can.*

I also had furry toys that would laugh endearingly when thrown against a surface; I brought toys that sang songs; funny hats and magic wands - anything that I thought would help Mama and, as importantly, the medical staff, *smile.*

I wanted her surrounded with joy and laughter when I was not there. Some of my most precious memories of my Mama are of that last week, and the photos I have of her and Simon (my brother) laughing.

The Best Inheritance

Mama had, and still has I am sure, a great sense of humor, and she laughed often. She was never afraid of doing fun, silly things, and her children inherited that wonderful trait. It's a great blessing to be free enough to have fun without being worried about looking silly.

When I was a physical therapist, I used to have joyful times with my patients. We would laugh a lot even when I was encouraging them to do difficult, painful exercises; no matter how sick they were, I would help them laugh. I considered it part of my treatment. I instinctively knew how important it was for them to laugh.

Clowning in hospitals is now an accepted form of therapy in children's wards - pity it isn't in the grownup's ward, since *we need to laugh more than the children!* Today, recall and write down as many funny life moments as you can think of, and tomorrow you'll be making an album in which to keep those memories.

Make sure you *discuss* as many of these moments as you can *at the dinner table tonight* - it should mean you have a fabulous evening!

LAUGHTER JOY-ERCISE 3: PRACTICE FINDING JOY FILLED PHOTOS

"Laughter is the shock absorber that eases the blows of life."
Anonymous

Make Albums

If you have children, I guarantee that you have photos of them in your wallet. Not always to brag with, of course! But so that when you look at them, you feel joy in your heart.

Apart from the photos in your wallet, hopefully you have lots of other "magic moment laughter images" somewhere in your house, on your computer or phone. Today is the day to find them, and put them in physical or online (or Facebook) albums.

Keep one at work, one at home, and carry one with you. Print one photo and frame or laminate it. Look at it every time you want to laugh or smile. Make a collage of your favorite images in a frame. Or load them into a digital frame. Place them on your desk, and in prominent places at home.

The photos we usually display are those in which we are perfectly groomed and carefully choreographed but they don't make us laugh! Instead, find the ones where you may not look perfect, but anyone looking at that photo smiles and is touched by the joy.

If you scrapbook, imagine the fun you will have making a specific family-laughter album! Our first joy tribe was set up by Cynthia in the USA. She created tribes called The JOY bookers! Imagine how much fun they have!

After Losing Someone You Love

When I typed this book, I had many photos of my Mother with my brother and family in various stages of laugher. As therapy after she died, I made collages in large photo frames of her laughing – alone or with others.

She brought joy to many people and I wanted to capture that for others. That way, I too remembered her with laughter and gratitude, and I stopped focusing on my own pain.

Create a laughter album and make that a slide show as your screen saver. Imagine how good you will feel when you are taking a quick break if you see a series of joy-filled photos of you and your family or friends laughing. It will energize you for the rest of the day!

Phones, apps and digital cameras these days are small and easy to carry. Carry one with you everywhere so you can capture those unexpected laughter moments on film. They are treasures. These are moments of souls waking up and dancing. *Every time you look at them, your soul does a little JOY jig!*

Collect Funny Video Clips

If you don't have any photos of your own, do an Internet search for funny pictures or video clips. One of the best videos I've seen is of a panda bear mother and her cub.

The mother is sitting in the corner of a cage noisily chewing on some food. Her teeny little baby panda is lying at her feet sound asleep. Suddenly the teeny baby has a huge sneeze! The mother nearly jumps out of her fur! It is the funniest thing to watch and I keep it on my desktop and watch it every so often just to laugh!

Be creative about all the ways you can surround yourself with triggers for laughter. Maybe you and your family can sit at dinner together tonight and brainstorm ways to do it. Teach them the value of lightening up, laughing a lot and actively seeking reasons to laugh!

LAUGHTER JOY-ERCISE 4: PRACTICE WATCHING FUNNY MOVIES

"A smile starts on the lips, a grin spreads to the eyes, a chuckle comes from the belly; but a good laugh bursts forth from the soul, overflows and bubbles all around"
Carolyn Birmingham.

There will be at least one movie in your life that has made you laugh out loud. Find that movie and watch it tonight if you can. For me, it's "The Pink Panther Strikes Again." No matter how many times I see it, I laugh.

Silly Inspector Clouseau and his classic line, *"Does your durg bite?"* always makes me laugh out loud! (If you have not seen it, I highly recommend it!) Another favorite is, *"There's a Girl in My Soup,"* and *"Hitch"* was really funny. Many people love the *"I Love Lucy"* series. Lucille Ball's facial expressions are hysterical!

Home Movies – The Funniest Of All!

Nothing makes you laugh more than watching you, your children or family members from years before. My sister had all our ancient baby movies that were on film transferred onto DVD.

One of the funniest and most treasured nights of my life was sitting with Mum watching them. We watched the same little segment about 20 times and were snorting with laughter! It was even funnier in reverse!

No one else would have laughed so hard watching this video because it was of me, about two years old, very chubby, in a funny little bikini doing nothing but jumping in and out of a wading pool, but Mama and I had a fabulous time.

Vince and Michelle, the parents of our God children, have an hysterical video of the time Vince proposed! At the end of the movie, the camera is filming the sky and ground because Michelle, who was holding the camera, was laughing so hard she couldn't keep him in the frame. It's all funny - but that's the funniest part! Can you find something like that? Or create one?

If all else fails and you can't find a movie that's funny - what about taping or a funny television show? Or make your own funniest home videos - plan a night where everyone in the family is in front of the camera doing laughable things. This is also very good blackmail material to use with teenagers!

If you can't do any of the above, *play charades*! That's almost like a movie and guaranteed to make you all laugh out loud! There are many movies and roads to laughter. Your mission today is to find one for you and your family.

LAUGHTER JOY-ERCISE 5:
PRACTICE LAUGHING OUT LOUD AND
HELPING OTHERS LAUGH

"Mirth is God's medicine. Everybody ought to bathe in it."
Henry Ward Beecher

Today's mission is just to *laugh out loud and to help others laugh.* Laugh when you wake up; on the way to work; at work; in stores; on the way home; on public transport - wherever you are, laugh out loud at least once! Watch how others around you smile with you! It doesn't even have to be real - you can fake it, it still works!

One of the things I often have audiences do is to laugh hysterically. On demand! When I introduce the idea, everyone groans. But then they start, and what begins as fake becomes genuine.

All I can say is that watching a room full of thousands of people laughing out loud is alchemical! Laughing changes the audience, the group dynamics, and often transforms the way they look at life and themselves.

The only reason people grumble about the exercise is because they feel silly and are concerned about *"what others will think"* - which means they are frightened other people will judge them as silly! There's that old FOWOT thing!

But as Hafiz says, God loves it when you laugh! And so does your Divine self!

Laugh With – Not At!

To help others laugh, it's important to laugh *with* them or *at* yourself, but not *at other people.* This is obvious, but some people need reminding! Laughing *at* others shuts *your* soul down - and extinguishes *their* spirit.

Helping others laugh can transform their perspective on the world; you can make a difference in someone's life today just by helping them find something at which to laugh.

But I Am Not Funny!

If you are thinking, *"I am not a funny person,"* you don't have to be! You can ask questions that elicit laughter from the person. Consider asking them about the funniest memory they have, or have them tell you stories about their children's most classic lines.

No parent/aunt/uncle/godparent escapes without some fabulous little tales about toddlers, who do something that is so funny you have to walk into another room and burst into laughter! Or ask them about the funniest movie they have seen or funniest book they have read. You don't have to tell jokes or be the "life and soul of the party" to help others laugh!

Today you could also try spending time with the funniest people you know. There are always people you can talk to that make you laugh or with whom you laugh - call them on the phone and bring joy to their life today! *Treasure the Joy Fairies at work!* They are angels.

It doesn't matter what you do to create laughter today as long as it is respectful. Just laugh!

Find Funny Things On The Web

If you can't think of anything to help others laugh, Google the funniest Youtube clips. Children and animals are always a wonderful source of laughter! The following was one of those anonymous emails sent around the world. If you are the author, please let me know so I can acknowledge you!

JACK (age 3) was watching his Mom breast-feeding his new baby sister. After a while he asked, *"Mom why do you have two? Is one for hot and one for cold?"*

JAMES (age 4) was listening to a Bible story. His dad read: *"The man named Lot was warned to take his wife and flee out of the city but his wife looked back and was turned to salt."* Concerned, James asked, *"What happened to the flea?"* (SO CUTE!)

And this one is a classic! *"Dear Lord,"* the minister began, with arms extended toward heaven and a rapturous look on his upturned face. *"Without you, we are but dust..."* He would have continued, but at that moment, a 4-year-old girl leaned over to her mother and asked quite loudly, *"Mom, what is butt dust?"*

Go forth, laugh and make someone else laugh today.

LAUGHTER JOY-ERCISE 6:
PRACTICE MAKING A LAUGHTER JOURNAL

"What soap is to the body, laughter is to the soul."
Yiddish Proverb

Read Funny Books

If you don't have any of his books yet, buy one of Dave Barry's today. I think he is one of the funniest men on earth. Remember my New Year Eve story? I especially enjoyed *"Dave Barry Turns 40,"* but if you are under 40, perhaps another book would work for you.

The original A.A. Milne version of *"Winnie The Pooh!"* is a favorite. I remember when I was a little girl of about 5, I would make Mum sit on my bed each night and read it repeatedly. (You know how little children do that!)

I loved the section on catching a "heffalump." I used to laugh and laugh, and she would laugh and it was the most magical of times! What a gift for your children to *find a book they love you to read that makes them laugh.* Do you have any like that? You will both benefit.

Sadly, our God children don't think the heffalump story is as funny as I did, but I still made them listen to it while I laughed! But then they laughed because I was laughing. So it still works! They think I am a dork, but I am quite proud of that. Reading books that make you laugh is wonderful – we learn, grow, develop *and* are filled with endorphins!

Create Your Own Funny Book

Maybe you can compile all the funny stories that make you laugh into one document and create your own "funny, laugh-out-loud" book! Or write your own funny material? At least *you* would find it funny.

Keep a fun journal or laughter journal - write down things that happen to you every day or each week that made you laugh or you found funny. Put photos in it or drawings of things you saw - be creative! Imagine how much Fun you would have reading that every few months.

How great would it be if your family created a family fun album, on which you all worked once a week or more? I think that would be a fabulous activity for everyone and teach children wonderful lessons, while creating great memories.

Whatever material or book you find that makes you laugh, read it today and keep it handy. Commit yourself to reading more humorous books and finding funny books for your children. If cartoon books make you laugh, read those. I love reading Bill Cosby's books, as well. His sense of humor is spectacular and appeals to almost everyone. Whatever works for you - find some funny things to read, or write... and laugh out loud!

LAUGHTER JOY-ERCISE 7: PRACTICE TRANSFORMING TOUGH MEMORIES WITH LAUGHTER

Laughter will transform memories. It can rewire your brain – literally! This is going to sound a bit odd but it works! If you can tell a story of something difficult in your life while keeping a smile on your face as you tell it, something magical seems to happen to the chemicals linked with that memory.

As we smile and tell the story, we might initially find it difficult. We need to ask the friend who is listening to remind us to keep smiling as we tell the story, and that often makes everyone laugh. (This works best with medium-sized memories, not the giant traumas of life.)

I believe part of the body reprograms the memory, and the pain is somehow transformed. Try it! I have done this several times and with others as well - and it really does work.

Look for the humor in difficult memories. This may take some work, but if you can find something funny about what happened or how you reacted, the pain of the memory may diminish or disappear. In your mind, scroll through events that still bring pain to your life and see if you can find some humor in them - especially embarrassing moments!

My Most Embarrassing Moment!

This is one of my most, if not the most, embarrassing memories: You may remember it from an earlier chapter – but it's a great example!

I was 21. I had just finished college and was very naïve. I moved away from home into a house with four other people about my own age or a little older. They were doctors, teachers or lawyers and all appeared to me to be very sophisticated.

They teased me mercilessly - especially about boyfriends - and often had many good laughs at my expense! I had a crush on the psychiatrist in our little household. He didn't know how I felt, but I believed the world was full of good and kind people, and so I told the other female in the group, a teacher!

One day I came home from work and she and the lawyer rushed up to me and said, *"John (the psychiatrist, name changed!) wanted us to give you this."* I unwrapped the cheapest, nastiest friendship ring I had ever seen! A normal adult at this stage would have laughed and seen right through the plot - but not naive me!

The whole saga would take too long to tell, but I was worried about offending, and hopeful that the psychiatrist might have some interest, so I played right into my roommates hands! This torture lasted several hours, with all members of the household playing along, weaving this yarn.

It took me about a month to laugh hysterically at the thought of what went on, but I still went bright red at the thought of it! Today I don't go red at all! The pain of embarrassment was transformed in my memory banks with that laughter.

Change Your Perspective

Use this important technique on some of your present tough life situations. Search, dig and delve to find something funny about what is or was going on.

In your mind, "stand outside" or "step back" from the situation and *observe yourself,* the situation or others. From this perspective, we can often see something funny about what is going on.

Remember, stuff happens and there is *always some lesson* for us to learn and something we can laugh at − even if it's to laugh at ourselves!

Joy Secret #10

Love

*"Love is patient, love is kind. It does not envy, it does not boast, it is not proud.
It is not rude, it is not self-seeking. It is not easily angered,
it keeps no record of wrongs.
Love does not delight in evil, but rejoices with the truth.
It always protects, always trusts, always hopes, always perseveres. Love never fails."*
I Corinthians 13:4-8

YOUR SEVEN MINUTES

- When you think of love, do you think of romantic love? Love from your family? Loving yourself?
- Whom do you love? Who loves you? Do you feel loved?
- Who *unconditionally* loves you?
- Who *unconditionally accepts* you? Do you?
- How do you behave when you feel loved? Think of a time when you first "fell in love". How did you feel about yourself at that time?
- Would you call yourself a loving person?
- How do you behave when *you* are being loving - what gestures or words do you use? How do you feel?
- Do you believe you are lovable, worth loving or worthy of love? No matter what parents do, if a toddler doesn't *perceive* they are loved, they don't feel lovable. Our parents try hard to love us unconditionally – but it's a rare quality to master!
- When you feel love for someone, where do you feel it in your body?
- Can you receive love from others?
- Can you recall a time in life when you "glowed" you were so loved? Or have you seen others glowing with the light of love?
- How does someone look when they are loved? Or loving?
- Find the different types of love in your life, and reflect on them.

Not feeling worthy of being loved, lovable or good enough is one of the greatest unconscious human fears – especially in western cultures.

It remains a hidden driver of our behavior sabotaging relationships and success. *Remember, the most important thing in life is how you feel about yourself* – learn how you truly love yourself during this chapter!

AMANDA'S TAKE: LOVE IS ALCHEMICAL

Love Yourself First - Warts And All

Unconditional love is alchemical; it transmutes. It comes from a deep understanding of the true nature of life – how *we are all one with no separation.* With that *divine consciousness,* everything changes at the *"speed of love"!*

To many, love means romantic love - that stuff of intimate relationships. *Unconditional* love is so much more! *The flow of love is a force that can save the world.* It holds the world together. It cushions us and nurtures us. We are love. *All* of us. Sadly, few of us know, feel or believe that.

The most important thing in life is how well you accept and love yourself *because it underpins all your behaviors.* In our hearts we can all access love for ourselves, and others: it's where we understand our true essence and connect with God, Divine Love, Oneness or Source. No matter what religion or belief system you explore - *they all have love as the core.*

Unfortunately, our fears, egos, personalities and wounds create protective barriers or veils around our heart, blocking the flow of love. Some people have never known love and don't know how to be loving, lovable or loved.

Our task this week is *to remove the barriers so we access our true, lovable selves:* To open our hearts to Divine love, feel it and share it, which creates the flow that allows more comes into our lives. Your true self is the astonishing light Hafiz mentions in Secret #4 – Reverence. When you finally see who you *really* are, it's so beautiful and bright you'll probably need dark glasses!

There is a little poem that may help you remember you *are* full of light – meant to shine out into the world. I am sorry I can't find the source so tell me if you know!

"I wish I was a glowworm,
A glowworm's never moody!
It's hard to be unhappy
When the sun shines out your booty!"

LOVE COMES IN ALL SORTS OF SHAPES AND SIZES.

Love comes in all sorts of "disguises". It manifests in gratitude; appreciation; hope; reverence; forgiveness; generosity; kindness; laughter; compassion; empathy; blessings; mercy; grace; play or in just giving people your time. Whenever you are engaged in those activities, you are receiving, feeling and giving love – you are in the flow.

Love is continuously poured out of the heavens into our hearts, the organs of true love. *Our work is to feel loved and to transmit love to others in our thoughts actions and words.* The more we give away, the more love pours in - it is a never-ending flow. Never hoard or keep love to yourself - it blocks the divine stream and makes your heart shrivel!

Shine Your Light

When we're full of real love, we're like a magnet to others! When we're conscious of, and listen to, our heart's inspiration we are always guided truthfully. One of the ways we can love ourselves, and others, is to fill our hearts with unconditional love and light, and then *shine that light* on everyone we meet.

Have you seen those religious paintings and icons that are of Christ, Mary or an angel, and their heart is lit up and has a beam of light radiating forth? Imagine you are doing that with every person you meet.

Before I speak, I pray for my heart and the room to be filled with love so that people are given what they need. Then I imagine a stream of golden white light filled with love coming from my heart, filling the room. Try it before you judge it!

You can do this with a person or people in front of you. You can even do it by *imagining* them in front of you, and surrounding them with the "love light".

Love is everywhere - *we just need to wake up, see it, feel it, tap into it, and live in - and from - the flow.* Life changes when we are consciously in the flow. Our job is to keep the stream of love flowing *to* us, and *through* us to the world, by filling everything we do with love.

HOW TO TAP INTO LOVE

Everything you have read in this book so far connects you to the love that surrounds you! Be grateful; drop to your heart; talk with your higher self, Angels or God; pray; listen; ask for forgiveness; have joyful, hope-full expectations; wait patiently with faith; be compassionate; do loving acts; forgive everyone and give love - especially to yourself!

This leads you to being joyful, kind, positive, non judgmental, generous, able to see the Divine spark in everyone you meet and adept at using your heart as your guide.

Our Spirit is *always* connected to us. We may not always feel connected to our Divine selves, but we have the capacity to become aware of our connection. Sometimes we forget that capacity or struggle with it, most often during tough times.

Once we understand the powerful results of true prayer, we realize that it's always best to begin *anything* with true prayer - which is connection to the Divine. True praying/ connection happens deep within our hearts, with real faith, appreciation, feeling, humility and reverence.

It Is Done

When you have finished your request or praying, believe *"it is done"*, *feel* as if what you asked for has happened already. The New American Bible indicates this in a letter from James 1:3-5: *"For you know that testing of your faith produces perseverance. …. But if any of you lacks wisdom, he should ask of God who gives to all generously and ungrudgingly and he will be given it. But he should ask in faith, not doubting. For the one who doubts is like a wave on the seas, that is driven and tossed about by the wind."*

And again in Chapter 4, verse 3: *"You do not possess because you do not ask. You ask, but do not receive, because you ask wrongly to spend it on your passions",* rather than asking for the *highest good of all.*

If your requests seem unanswered, your faith and belief may need to be stronger; or you may be doubting; or what you were asking for was not the best thing for you, the world or another or it may not be the right timing.

Asking with clarity, for God's will or for what is yours by Divine right, or for what is in the highest good of all in every situation is essential! *Whether you ask in prayer, or ask the Universe, Infinite Spirit or your Higher Selves clearly for what you want, it takes practice, faith and consciousness.*

When we pray only for ourselves, our own pleasures or something we want but don't need, it won't work. When we request things that will be of benefit *to others and* us; that will help us in some way to do good; or bring love into the world and make a positive change, our prayers are answered - *in Divine timing!*

Our Gifts Are For Serving Others

Any gift from the spiritual realms is a gift to you for others. Many people think life is just about our own satisfaction or spiritual growth, but it's not. *We are here to be of service* - to make this world a different place; to contribute what only we can do or think, whether it is to parent, scrub floors, arrange flowers, create something, or build and sell things.

Each person has to do what their heart leads them to do, and to love doing it. We don't all have same gifts. *Take time to feel what gifts you have in your heart - feel* what you are moved to do, what you have a passion for, what you love to do. Then ask if you were right with what you felt!

Using our gifts allows love to flow through us to others. This sounds simple and it is! It's not so easy sometimes, but it is simple. What are your gifts?

GIVE LOVE – IN MANY WAYS

If you did nothing else other than give yourself and others more love and serve others, your life would change – *at the speed of love!* That is, incredibly fast!

Give in everything, but especially give love and thanks. Give away what you no longer use - or better, *give away some of the things that are useful or mean a lot to you!* Give to people who have less than you and more than you. Give of your time as well as yourself. Be generous with your love; there is plenty to go around.

I believe I have prospered and grown in my business and life because I give all I can. If I can't give out loud, then I give in silence. I hold people in my heart if I am unable to give at an earthly level. It has taken me years to really grasp that giving love by holding someone in my heart is the best way and I should always start there!

When I am not operating from love, my spirit becomes "mean" – judgmental, unkind, impatient etc.! As soon as I am aware of it, I stop and if I can't change how I feel, I put people in my heart, hold them there and ask God to help me - and them.

Stop being frightened that if you give something up, there will be less for you. Life does not work that way. *Your fears* do. Have faith and stay in your heart – in the flow of giving and receiving love.

ROMANTIC LOVE
– FALLING IN LOVE WITH WHOM?

"There is an immense difference between love and desire." 1
Claire Blatchford

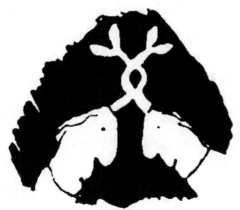

I have been "in love" many times – I like to think as preparation for this chapter! I have learned that when we "fall" in love with another, we see ourselves as we truly are. *We "fall" in love with ourselves!*

The other person initially sees us as the astonishing being of light that we are, they reflect that to us, and we fall in love with our true selves - our "I AM"! We see ourselves as God sees us. We feel light, wonderful, joyful, loving and loved. Our spirit expands; we're more generous, giving and gracious with everyone. We look fabulous and our eyes sparkle.

Oh No - The Warts!

Because we are human – our amazing light has a few flaws I call warts! *At some stage, this special person sees our warts.* And then *we* see our warts! We're not perfect any more!

Our newly found self love falters. We remember all the "bad stuff", and instead of seeing ourselves as who we really are, we allow the criticizer back in! *Then we "fall" out of love - with ourselves.* We do the same for our partners, by the way! They "fall" in love with us because *through us, they fall in love with who they really are.*

If only we could live believing and remembering the image of ourselves as they first saw us - *that is the real us anyway* – our soul and spirit – not our personality or ego (the warts)!

Can you remember how lovable you were and how wonderful you felt when you "fell" in love? Learning to love ourselves, warts and all, and seeing the perfection of our imperfections makes us "love radiators".

It allows us to accept and love someone else, warts and all.

Warts can be contagious – so accept them but don't catch them!

OUR SPIRITUAL TEACHERS

"For one human being to love another: that is perhaps the most difficult of our tasks; the ultimate, the last test and proof, the work for which all other work is but preparation."
Rainer Maria Rilke

Our intimate partners, life challenges and relatives are a gift to help us grow spiritually.

Everyone is our teacher, but we can grow more (and often more painfully) with those closest to us!

These relationships and our growth involve sacrifice of the ego or "compromise" -

cornerstones of love. When we *sacrifice* our selfish wants or ego for another, constantly *look out* for them, try to see things as *they* see them, be *supportive* and *serve them* with a spirit of love, we grow.

When you *choose* to compromise (i.e. grow and develop), you *agree* to do something that is not your first choice and you *must* do it with the right spirit – willingly and preferably joyfully! Doing it with a spirit of resentment, anger or resignation is worse than not doing it at all – for everyone.

SELF-LESS-NESS

Intimate relationships offer us a great opportunity to become less selfish. The next time you are in the middle of a huge argument and you are ready to scream at your partner, stop, and in a state of awe and wonder, *appreciate them as your spiritual teacher*! Feel incredibly *grateful* that they are putting themselves through all this pain so you can learn!

Then look at yourself and your behavior to find the lesson you are supposed to be learning. Ask yourself *"what is it in me that is causing me to react this way?"* This question helps you focus on the real source of this fight!

Making the effort to grow together spiritually can lead to a love that is much deeper and more fulfilling than romantic love. It is calmer, gentler, more harmonious, safer, more profound, satisfying, and nurtures your hearts. It requires maturity and consciousness and is called growing up!

Less Sex – Danger or Opportunity?

Many relationships falter when the warts are seen. There is less sex *but take this as a sign of the need for real heart to heart connection* – for growing up, and doing the work of learning to love and accept *yourself just as you are; and unconditionally accepting your partner just as they are* – and *still* loving them. It takes consistent work, but everything good takes work. Persist - it's really worth the effort.

The Gift From Children

If you want a steep lesson in becoming selfless - have children! One of the hardest lessons in my life was being *unable* to have my own children, although I have been blessed with nieces, nephews and Godchildren I adore.

I can't imagine loving my own children more, so I can feel, by proxy, some of the lessons a parent learns, but I have to rely on my Higher Self to help me be selfless.

If you are a parent, silently bless your child for the some-times excruciating lessons they bring! Whatever you do, strive to do it with pure, *unconditional* love - from your heart.

Loving yourself is the best gift you can give your children! It models healthy self esteem for them and stops neediness, codependence and dysfunctional love.

OUR REAL MOTIVATION – FEAR OR LOVE?

Unless we are very alert, we can be easily fooled that the motivation for our actions is love - when really it's selfish. Be vigilant – wake up to anything you do that is influenced by greed, manipulation, insecurity, envy, jealousy, resentment, frustration, revenge, anger or fear and don't do it!

We have to *wake up* and become conscious of our motives, as they are most often created by *unconscious* fears. *We live lives of habits and patterns ruled unconsciously by fears.* The need for *more* (of everything) and *control* issues often surface *when our inner child feels unsafe* – even if the *adult* you now are really *is* safe.

Greed and control separate, constrict, and harden our hearts and arise from selfishness. They bring a desire for power and cause suffering. Greed can be disguised as wanting or using power and control, being selfish, needy or demanding! *Love connects, expands, softens and lightens us. It brings peace and joy.*

Make a sign for your home that asks, *"Have I created safety for myself today?"* Talk with your children about greed, power and control, but also teach them about *feeling safe, setting boundaries, loving themselves, selfless love, sharing, appreciating time together and non-materialistic values.*

Talking openly and honestly about these aspects of life is a vital part of becoming a joyful adult, and helps us (and them) be conscious of what is motivating or driving us. Stay awake and alert: *Understand* your fears and *eradicate* them so they stop affecting your capacity to love.

UNCONDITIONAL LOVE

As far as I know, God, Christ and Buddha could constantly give unconditional love and very few humans ever have. We may have experienced moments of unconditional love, but rarely is it constant!

People may love us despite our warts; they may love us, *and* our warts; some may truly unconditionally love us, in which case you are genuinely blessed! Pure unconditional love is rare. It's a choice.

We can *choose* to love and *totally accept* a person, warts and all – or not. Unconditionally loving and accepting our selves, and others, brings that capacity out in them.

Everyone is worth loving! *Truly loving ourselves and others unconditionally is our life purpose.*

I can't imagine how pure Divine love is. It's constant, forgiving and always wants the best for us. It pours grace and compassion over us, helps, accepts and supports us, and wants nothing back. That is unconditional love. And it's why so few humans master it in one lifetime!

I feel love for my husband. I feel it for my family and friends, especially my mother. I have not mastered true, unconditional love, but I'm aiming for unconditional acceptance as a first step - *accepting people totally for who they are, right now, without judging or wanting to change anything about them.* And accepting that everything is perfect, just as it is, right now.

Loving unconditionally doesn't mean you let others do anything they like to you, or walk all over you – *boundaries need to exist.* It *does* mean you see them for the astonishing beings of light they really are – and you *hold that belief* for them – so they can grow into it.

You may not like their behavior, words or actions at times, but you love them – their spirits – *who* they *really* are. You want only the best for them – even if it's not the easiest for you. You want to help and support them on their journey – not to take over, control or take responsibility for it.

Sometimes that means letting go of your "stuff", or letting them go! Use this information as a trigger for ongoing inner exploration – learn to unconditionally accept and love yourself; find your own astonishing light and shine it on others!

LOVE YOURSELF

> *"You, yourself, as much as anybody in the entire universe, deserve your love and affection."*
> *Buddha*

Claire Blatchford's wonderful books - *"Becoming - A Call to Love;" "Turning"* and *"Friend of My Heart"* - really help us understand love.

Deaf from early childhood, she developed her inner listening capacity and discovered an "inner friend". The friend in her books is Christ. Even if you don't believe in Christ, they are worth reading. In *"Friend of my Heart"* she says *"My own interpretation is that, through the discovery that I am loved by him, I came to love myself"….* He tells her: *"You must love yourself, then all else will fall into place."*

Being In Love – With Whom?

Remember that falling in love with another is part of the process of falling in love with our true selves. Our beloved loves us and sees us as the best we can be. We *can* be like that! We *are* like that in God's eyes. The difference is that Infinite Love *knows our potential and is loving and patient with us, while we strive (or not!) to reach that potential!*

Most of us have had at least one experience of being "in love" and every aspect of our lives was better. We gave more love to others, everything seemed easier, life was smoother, stress bothered us less, we were more relaxed, peaceful, more fulfilled and *much* more joyful!

We realized who we really were (love) and what we were truly capable of (love). When we are "in love" with another (but really ourselves), we are filled with joy, astonishing light and true love. The layers of self-doubt disappear as that other person helps us believe we are special.

We are totally connected to real love and this person, and we feel safe and fulfilled. Consequently, our fears dissipate. We have faith that our hopeful expectations will eventuate. We are generous, open, accepting, compassionate and patient.

This is the state of self-love. Cherish it! If we rely on another human for it, we are then dependent on *their* capacity to love themselves, *rather than thriving in the flow of unconditional love.*

Stepping Into Love

The gift from the person who loves us is a chance to experience what it is like *to know and love our true selves.* They are mirrors reflecting to us who we really are, and what *we can be!*

They teach us we are lovable *and* worthy of being loved, despite the warts that emerge after we are out of the romantic phase of love. There is a difference between blindly "falling in" love and consciously "stepping into" love. Either way, it feels great - we are in a giant vat of love! We're surrounded, supported, nourished by it and connected to everything.

If the process is unconscious, someone can pluck us out of the vat *before* we are even conscious of the fact that we have been in a vat! We suddenly feel abandoned, desolate, alone and empty; and self-doubt, a major enemy of self-love, creeps in.

The fears that we are not lovable; not good enough; there is something wrong with us (they often tell us that too!); that we have baggage (who doesn't?) and many other *emotional judgments convince us that we really are unlovable.*

Self-love and self-doubt both exist in the heart. Your heart has to choose which one to follow! If we don't know how we ended up in, or out of, the vat of love, we can't consciously find our way back, and feel lost and miserable.

We can consciously decide to live in, and sustain, a state of reverence and love. In fact, the "growing up" I talked of earlier is about *becoming more conscious in the relationship,* and choosing to love *yourself and* the other person.

What's Your Story?

Do you *really feel* lovable? Do you feel worthy of being loved - especially by yourself? Do you believe you are good enough? Do you allow your judgments, thoughts and fears to convince you that you are unworthy, no good, ugly and flawed in so many ways that no one would want you?

Challenge these stories. They are most likely based on false beliefs from the past – often from the comments of others. If there is some truth to them, then do something about changing! If there is no truth when you filter those beliefs or fears through your heart, change your stories.

If everybody acted from their true, lovable heart selves, we would treat ourselves, and everyone else, with love and reverence. We are all connected – no matter how it appears!

Look into the mirror, look deeply into your eyes, and see through to your heart and say *"Namaste"* to your spirit. *Listen for the gentle reply from your divine self.* If you are single, this all still applies to you! Even if you have never had an intimate relationship with anyone, you have had wonderful friendships where people see you as you really are, and you can use that as a starting place.

Often people who are *single and happy* are very discerning, and good at loving themselves anyway! *Self-love starts with you - you don't need anyone else.*

LOVE AND LIKE

I have learned that you can love someone but not like them very much! When I am at my spiritual best and in my heart, I can do this very well. I am practicing sending love to people I don't particularly like - or more accurately, whose actions, motives or intentions I don't like.

Occasionally we meet someone and instantly gel, or the opposite happens. We sense a person's spirit and it doesn't gel with us in which case, it may be wise to them avoid them if possible! We are built to detect negative chemistry, electricity and magnetism.

When we say, *"I don't like so and so,"* we may be feeling mismatched chemistry, or we may really be saying we don't like their morals or values, which are reflected in the way they behave or how they treat others. Be aware of how your own judgments and "stuff" influence you! Think to yourself *"I don't like the way they are treating me right now,"* which is *very* different from "I don't like *you*."

How To Deal With Someone You Don't Like

If there is a person you don' t like - go to your heart and find love for them, or just put them in your heart and surround them with love. You don't have to like them or like what they do *or be around them*.

If what they are doing is abusive, violent or harmful, remove yourself physically from the offending person, "place" them into your heart, sincerely surround them with love, and move on. Or away!

If you must be around that person, do the "putting them into your heart and surrounding them with God's light and love" exercise. You will be amazed at how they seem different!

This works only if you do it sincerely, gently, with love and *have no attachment to any outcome*.

Holding them in your heart and allowing the alchemical magic of love to work on you and them is a magical exercise! When you do this, either you change, they change, or *everything* changes because love is present.

LOVE JOY-ERCISE 1:
PRACTICE WEARING GOD GLASSES!

"Thou shalt love the Lord thy God with all thy heart, and with all thy soul, and with all thy might. This is the first and greatest commandment."
Matthew 22: 37,38

Love and honor The Divinity in you first - and the rest will follow! It's your daily task for the rest of your life. Fill yourself with love and gratitude for Divine Love, your Inside God, the spiritual realms, and all that is done for you.

One of the best ways to do this is to see the spiritual spark in every person we meet and treat them with patience, understanding, kindness and love. What if we put on "God Glasses"? We would see the world through Divine eyes. Wouldn't that be awesome?

If we were wearing "God Glasses", we could *really* see people as they truly are, with no judgment. We would sense, know and feel their astonishing light and beauty. We would see past all the superficial attributes most of us normally focus on - and we would interact with love and encouragement.

Encouragement is not always positive or nurturing! It can be confronting, challenging and maybe even disciplining! *Setting boundaries is a form of encouragement and important for children* – and grown ups - *to feel safe!*

Divine Time

Each day, allocate some time to be connected to God; to spirit; to your inner Divinity. Better still, *live* the whole day aware and connected. *Stay connected* and seek wisdom and guidance before you do anything major, or minor!

Then, *ask what you can do to help* God or the spiritual realms! We pray when we need help, change, or guidance. Or we pray when we are desperate and need a miracle, and when that miracle arrives, we go back to life as usual. That's not very reverent, grateful or loving. Our memories are short!

We need to do our part by patiently waiting for spiritual timing, holding onto faith and being joyfully expectant that *"it is done"* - with the highest good of all in mind; and by being a blessing to others every day.

Being joyfully expectant of answers and having patience and faith demonstrates our love in a different way. Keep on asking and listening. Do what you feel you are being guided to do.

Loving Yourself

Loving yourself is a direct way to love others – we all have that Divine spark in us. If we treat ourselves badly, it's the same as treating everyone badly.

Any parent seeing a child unhappy, or harming themselves, feels tremendous pain. So do the spiritual realms when they see us treating ourselves badly. Like parents, the Divine knows the gifts, grace and blessings we have been given. *How sad when we live unaware of them.*

Do Your Work

There is a story about a man who was drowning in the ocean. He asked God to help him. Soon after, a ship came sailing by and the sailors called out, *"We can save you."* The drowning man responded, *"No thanks - God has said he is going to save me. I'll wait."*

Then a submarine surfaced near him and sent out a rescue party. The man replied in the same way. Finally, as he was growing very tired, a helicopter flew over and lowered a man to pluck him out of the ocean, only to receive the same *"No thanks"* from the nearly drowned man.

Finally, the man did drown and when he reached heaven, he said angrily to God, *"Where were you? I was faithful and waited."* God replied, *"I sent you a ship, a submarine and a helicopter. What more could I do?"*

We are all offered help, but we also have to do our work, our *part*! We have to ask, look for, and recognize, the angels sent in all disguises; to wait patiently with joyful expectations for the best outcome; to actively listen for inspiration about what we need to do.

Life isn't just handed to us on a platter - *we have a responsibility as well*. There are the times when we are freely blessed with grace, but I suspect we receive more grace when we have tried hard to do what we are meant to be doing.

Prayers

Say your prayers *with* feeling, *from* your heart *and believe they are answered already*. Take a deep breath before you start and center yourself in your heart. Kneeling helps sometimes as well!

Repeating prayers that you know by heart and doing them without thought is better than nothing - but I suspect a *heartfelt prayer that is like a gentle and humble conversation with God* would be more effective! Be

loving in your speech and reverent in all that you say. Show true respect and humility.

No matter what we feel is going on, how bad things are, or what mess we find ourselves in, *trust* that you, with Divine help or guidance, can somehow make good out of the mess or situation. *Look* for the blessing. *Have faith* in the goodness, kindness, grace and love of the highest spiritual realms. - and your Higher Self.

Try to *really feel* that love in your heart. Feel *connected and open* so you can be inspired and comforted. *Allow* yourself to be close to those trying to help you. If you are angry with them, try to see a bigger picture; be humble; be reverent; thank them for all they have done for you. Our vision is often very limited.

Be grateful - very, very grateful, we can never comprehend how much we have been given. Be honest, open and completely in your heart. Pray from your heart. Send your Angels zoots. I bet they love zoots! Mum does!

LOVE JOY-ERCISE 2: PRACTICE BEING A LOVE RAY-DIATOR!

> *"Today, greet every person inwardly as if they were wearing this sign on their forehead, "God lives here."*
> Mary Forte

Be conscious of the Spiritual spark living in every person and thing. Feel a sense of wonder and humility as you speak to others. You may just find that the whole world is happy today and full of wonderful people, and *you* feel much more joyful. Doesn't that sound great!

Imagine that you have a stream of golden, white love light coming from the sun into the top of your head. It travels down to your heart, swirls around in the most magnificent patterns, fills up your heart, and then radiates out to surround you and others.

Do this when you wake up, before you go to bed, before (or in) meetings, at dinner, lunch, with "challenging" people, or wherever you are. Practice it everywhere. If you are driving, keep your eyes open! It only takes a few seconds to do if your intentions are pure. And it is easy once you have practiced it. This makes you a "love ray-diator!"

This is another sign you could create for your house - *"Be a love ray-diator!"* Instead of giving children ray guns of the laser variety, we could give them love ray guns! *We have a love ray gun!* Shaped like a heart, our magic wands, when you pressed radiate light and make a wonderful noise! (www.amandagore.com)

Only Kind And Loving Words

Listen to what you say to yourself all day today. If your words are not *loving or kind* (to yourself or others), immediately replace them with loving or at least neutral words.

Let nothing un-loving – verbally or non verbally - come out of you today. No rolling of the eyeballs or sighing, no snickering, sneering, slumping, shaking your head or closing your eyes in "quiet despair!" No thinking, *"Here we go again"* or *"I knew this would happen!"*

For your family, try especially hard today. Do nothing but love them, think positively and "ray" Divine light over them! *Keep them all in your heart - it's big enough!* Shower and surround them with light and love all day, and speak only lovingly to them.

Encourage them and nurture them with your words, non-verbals and thoughts. *Focus on the good points* of people around you. Continually remind yourself of the positive not the negative – it really is a *conscious choice* we make.

It's just a bad pattern and habit to focus long and hard on all the negative points, and forget all the good points. *You can break that habit if you want to.*

Think only loving thoughts; see the I AM in everyone; catch and stop any judgment; listen very carefully to what you say to yourself; read nothing but inspiring, positive material; watch only uplifting television programs and above all, bathe yourself and your family in your love.

Today, there will be no sarcasm, or *preconceived expectations* of difficulty or disappointment *based on the past. Be present.* Let go of that old stuff. It's a big day! If you can do just a few of these things, it will be a great day!

See the sign on everyone's forehead – *"God Lives Here"*. Treat them as if you were talking to an Angelic being.

LOVE JOY-ERCISE 3:
PRACTICE LOVING ACTIONS

> *"Love many things, for therein lies the true strength,*
> *and whosoever loves much performs much, and can accomplish much,*
> *and what is done in love is done well."*
> Vincent Van Gogh

A Critical Question

I often ask audiences, *"Where do we learn to give love?"* You should see the blank looks in response! We learn to give love from our parents, and our parents may have struggled to show it in a way we could sense or feel.

When we begin relationships, we don't ever discuss this - we just assume we know how to show someone love, and we do - *the way our family showed us.*

But the person we're trying to love came from a completely different family and *was shown love in different ways.* Early in a relationship, this difference doesn't matter - but later on, it can lead to misunderstanding as we both *think* we are being loving to the other, *but it's not recognized.*

To prevent this scenario, remember this wonderful question, *"What do I do that makes you feel that I love you?"* You might be greeted with a blank stare! But repeat the question and wait for the answer, which might amaze you! It's astonishing how little things we do unconsciously – or better, consciously - make others feel truly loved.

Once you ask this question and receive your answer, *you are obliged to do what they ask!* If you are not prepared to do that, then don't ask the question. Do what your family members tell you *with joy and reverence.* If you do it begrudgingly, resentfully or tell yourself, *"I can't believe I am doing this!"*- it's *not* love.

Ask your children as well - it is a fabulous way to teach them about love and loving, and for you to learn what makes *them* feel loved. You may be surprised at the answers! Have them ask you the same question!

How To Help

Remember, loving is all about *giving* - you are *freely* giving something that you know makes them feel loved. *It's the spirit in which you do it!*

Anybody you help is receiving your love. Find people to help today, but ask them if they would like your help first! That's one of my learning challenges - *to wait for people to ask me for help before I do it!* I struggle a lot with that so I know it's a major lesson.

I really do believe there are times when we can give gifts in the form of help without being asked - like doing something that really needs to be done for our parents, friends or partner if they have not had time to do it or are hesitant to ask. We could take out the garbage for an elderly neighbor, mow their lawn or shovel their snow.

I mentioned earlier that, in retrospect, this was a tough lesson I learned with Mama. How I wish now that I had sat with her and loved her instead of running around "helping" her by doing the shopping, cleaning, cooking and other stuff.

We help more sometimes by just sitting with someone and surrounding them with love, and engaging and laughing with them. I wish I had. Learn from me, and go straight out and call or visit your elderly parent or parents, talk with them and tell them what is going on in your life. Or just sit, be with them and love them.

Invite them to talk about their favorite things; listen to the same old stories with love and interest (this is *really* loving!); be present with them; cry with them; laugh with them; *share your life* with them - talk to them and let them feel they are a part of your life - an important part!

Be present when you are there - *you are not giving them heart time if your mind is somewhere else.* Your heart and mind need to be with them completely for you to really actively love them.

Affection and hugging are not the only powerful ways to show love! Any kind of tenderness or loving gesture or touch - even a loving look - can change someone's day. Sending zoots is another great way to give love!

Volunteering is way of acting out love; so is mentoring and teaching. Anytime we serve another it's love in action. True joy comes from serving. Call a friend who is having a tough time. Call or visit someone you have not spoken to for a while and say, *"Hello, I am thinking of you."*

Leave a little love note under the pillow for your children or partner; smile at strangers; be thoughtful - think about what others would like or what would make them happy; write a letter telling someone how special they are to you and mail it to them; spread little heart confetti around someone's desk!

There are hundreds of little loving actions you can do every day. Be creative. Do something loving today!

LOVE JOY-ERCISE 4: PRACTICE LOVING YOUR LIFE

> *"I am not sure exactly what heaven will be like,*
> *but I do know that when we die and it comes time for God to judge us,*
> *He will NOT ask,*
> *'How many good things have you done in your life?'*
> *Rather He will ask,*
> *'How much LOVE did you put into what you did?'"*
> Mother Teresa

Do you love your life? Really love it? When someone asks, "How are you?" can you answer with an enthusiastic, *"I love my life!"* If not - today is the day to start.

So many people grumble and moan about what they have to do, how horrible their job is, and how hard life is. *Consider the alternative!* Imagine how much you would love this life of yours if you were told you only had three months to live!

If you are the sort of person who would not change a thing in your life with this news, be thankful. Most people would make changes and they would often be significant changes.

Most certainly they would start to *savor all the moments* - no matter how challenging! Or they would let go of grudges, issues of control or irritations - realizing that's the "small stuff". They would stop wasting precious time being angry or annoyed.

They would concentrate more on loving and spending time with people they love and on the really important things in life - *which of course are not things*!

Your life has made you what and who you are. When people want to change the past, I wonder if they don't like themselves. You are the person you are *because* you went through those things. Blaming the past is like driving with a huge rear vision mirror in front of you! You see only what has passed - not *the present* or what possibilities lie ahead.

Somewhere there will be one, or many, points where *you* made a decision, or a choice, to move in the direction of this life you are currently living. If *you* got you here, then *you* can get you out of here!

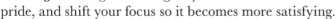

If you hate your job and can't find purpose and meaning in what you are doing, then leave! If you can't leave, then make it your mission to *find* a purpose or some meaning and to be an outstanding employee, no matter what your job entails. Just doing that will give you a sense of pride, and shift your focus so it becomes more satisfying.

Find all the good parts of the job and *focus on the blessings the job gives you* - such as financial security or medical insurance or interaction with great people. Our jobs fill the majority of our lifetime, so make sure you *choose* to enjoy yours and experience a sense of fulfillment from it.

If you grumble and hate every minute of what you do each day, not only do you become an energy sucker and alienate everyone, but *you* ruin *your* chances of enjoyment, promotion or recognition. You also give nothing or contribute little, and deep down, you feel badly about yourself. Aim to be the best you can be no matter what you are doing.

What about loving your life *even* if it needs changing? *Find* something to love about it - and *focus on that part* until the changes are in place. Love your current life, as it is sure to be giving you great lessons. Be grateful for it. *Look for the divine gifts it bears.*

If you have decided you want a new life, or want to modify your current one, *be patient*. It may be that you still have to learn some lessons while in this job or relationship before you can move on.

What you think you want may not always be what you actually need. Spiritual wisdom knows the right time for everything. Maybe they're waiting for you to make the most of what you have, *before* you are given an alternative! In other words, *love what you have*. It may need changing, but focus on the good things about your life as you arrange for the changes to occur. Stop looking in the rear view mirror. Do your work. Learn your lessons. Love your life.

LOVE JOY-ERCISE 5:
PRACTICE GIVING EVERYONE TA DA'S!

"The little unremembered acts of kindness and love
are the best parts of a person's life."
William Wordsworth

This is another day to make others feel great! Isn't life
wonderful? Your mission is to see all the silent TA-DA's today.

People want to feel special, accepted, recognized and acknowledged
for *who* they are, *just as they are.* These are primary motivating forces in
life, both at work and at home.

Why do young teens join gangs, or people have affairs? Why do some
children blossom and excel at school and in life, when *just one teacher*
takes an interest in them? If just *one* person at work cares about,
or takes an interest in us and what we are doing, why do we find
ourselves performing better and trying harder?
All these things happen because of recognition and acknowledgement
of *who* we are, as much as what we have done. *It's a powerful form of*
motivation and one of the ways we "wrap" others in love.

Look For The TA- DAs

After one of my presentations, a man named Roger from Wisconsin
shared with me a story about visiting his sister, who had a 4-year-old
son.

This nephew asked Uncle Roger to come and watch his gymnastics
competition. The little boy was walking on a balance beam, which
was about an inch off the ground, as he was only 4! He jumped off
the end in triumph and threw his hands up in the air and shouted
"TA-DA!" Isn't that wonderful?

Of course all the adults clapped and cheered. All toddlers love doing
anything that generates attention and acknowledgement, so they are
all masters of doing TA-DAs!

Writing one of my monthly email newsletters on this topic, I realized
that we all love doing TA-DAs until about age eight, when it becomes
"un-cool" to do them out loud! But I believe we all keep doing silent
TA-DAs on the inside. We are closet TA-DAists!

Every time we do something of which we are proud or pleased,
inside we are jumping up and shouting TA-DA! The trouble is, most

people don't see these silent TA-DAs and we feel de-motivated or disappointed. Seeing silent TA- DAs is the single most motivating thing we can do.

We need to *consciously* look for people's silent TA-DAs, listen for them and say, *"I think that deserves a TA-DA!"*

Watch their faces glow and spirits shine when you do notice, because you just gave some love, and inspired them to go out and be even better.

This is a brilliant management, leadership or parenting tip! See and acknowledge others TA-DAs. *Give yourself TA-DAs!* Today, recognize TA-DAs in at least three people.

Be on the lookout for those moments when they are telling you something that could deserve a TA-DA! - it may be very small, so listen and watch carefully. Say, as often as you can, *"I think that deserves a TA-DA!"* and enjoy the response.

Look for opportunities to make someone feel special. Make a generous comment about someone's children - they are always opportunities for TA-DAs!

A TA-DA Culture

Create a TA-DA culture at your workplace. Have TA-DA awards. Let people nominate the person of the month who deserves a TA-DA! Talk about TA-DAs at staff meetings.

Create opportunities for people to be given TA-DAs!

Give people *sincere* compliments. Tell them they are looking great (and mean it!); or that they have done a wonderful job; or tell them something you sincerely appreciate about them or what they do for you, others or their work. Comment on a quality you admire in them. There are a thousand ways of making someone feel special. Give yourself a TA-DA for doing all this!

LOVE JOY-ERCISE 6:
PRACTICE LOVING YOURSELF

> *"Your task is not to seek for love, but merely to seek and find all the barriers within yourself that you have built against it."*
>
> *Rumi*

Wake up and walk straight to the mirror today and say *"Namaste"* to yourself! Today is the day you find your incredible I AM spirit!

Re-read the section on loving yourself above and go through today seeing yourself *from your heart's perspective*, and not your judgment's. No negative or destructive self-talk today! Not one word - only goodness, kindness, compassion, and tenderness with yourself. Give yourself a break - even if no one else does!

Acknowledge and compliment yourself on a job well done. *TA-DA yourself!* Allow yourself to make mistakes without berating or judging yourself. Understand you're doing your best and if you could do it better - you would. In other words, *give yourself grace*. Be the person that is in your true heart.

Follow your heart's knowings - they are not emotions or feelings but knowings. Your criticizer gives you all the facts, reasons, judgments and nasty stuff. Your true heart only gives you wisdom, love and truth. *Ask your heart today what you need to do to find self-love, and what barriers you need to remove.* Listen carefully and then do it.

Love your body even if it is not in perfect shape - whose is? Treat it well today. Take time to truly nourish it with lovingly prepared food, instead of shoving processed fast food in, as quickly and unconsciously as you can.

Make Your Eyes Sparkle!

See if you can *make your own eyes sparkle* with inspiration, motivation or enthusiasm today! Find ways to give yourself joy. Do all the things an unconditionally loving parent would do for you! Even if you didn't have loving parents, you will have seen how other loving parents behave, so treat yourself like that today - be patient, kind, caring, nurturing, understanding, compassionate and hug yourself!

What or who inspires you? Spend time with them or read about them today. *What motivates you?* Spend some time doing that today as well. Pursue your passion in some way and notice how you feel. If you don't have a passion, find one! Begin the search now.

Be enthusiastic, even if you are generally not an enthusiastic person. It's fun and a way to express an exuberant side of your personality! Even if you surprise people and they say, *"What have you done with the old (insert your name here)?",* laugh and say, *"This is who is inside the old me!"*

Love yourself enough to *be real and authentic* in front of others - be who you really are, and if they don't like it, bad luck for them! When we find the seed of I AM inside us and allow that to shine forth, *it is the real us* and we are incredibly loving *and lovable.* Go ahead - love yourself, be the real you, and watch your world change!

LOVE JOY-ERCISE 7: PRACTICE HOLDING PEOPLE IN YOUR HEART

> *"Today, see if you can stretch your heart and expand your love so that it touches not only those to whom you can give it easily, but also to those who need it so much."* [2]
> *Daphne Rose Kingma*

The heart rules all the other organs and functions of the body. Most people think that the brain is the most important organ for life but they are wrong! Once the heart stops, life stops. People can be brain dead and still alive - you may know someone like that!

Make sure you are not one of them! Be conscious of the power and beauty of your heart today. The alchemical capacities of the heart are to love, heal, forgive, and change *everything.*

We tap into this alchemy when we hold people in our hearts. Think of someone with whom you would like a better relationship, or someone who is causing you a lot of grief or pain in your life. Create an image of them or sense their qualities and "place" them inside your heart.

A Reminder On How To Drop To Your Heart

Sit quietly and imagine there is a chute going from the top of your head to the inside of your heart - like a laundry or water chute.

Place this person into the top of the chute and gently slide them down to the interior of your heart - which is very spacious and beautiful!

Allow them to be there for a moment or so. If it feels really good - keep them there as long as you like. While you hold that person in your heart, all the love and light that lives in the heart caresses them and gives them whatever they need.

You have no intention *other than being a blessing* and keeping them in your heart, so it can work its magic. *This is true service.* Notice how you feel while you are doing this. There's usually a sense of peace that settles on you as your heart works on you, as well!

If you want to, after you have done this, you can imagine your heart kind of turning inside out and ray-ing the love out. As you gently ray these light forces out, the person floats out in front of you on those rays and you can "see" them in front of you surrounded by a beautiful light.

The first time I did this at a Sacred Service class, the light was a gorgeous pink and then after that, it was golden, white or both! This might sound very "New Age" and cosmic, but I promise it's not.

I learned how to do this heart work with Robert and Cheryl Sardello and I have actually seen, felt, heard and experienced profound changes in both myself, and others doing this exercise. I just need to remind myself to do it more often. Like all humans, I am so busy trying to do things to improve circumstances, *I forget the most powerful thing to do is hold others in my heart!*

If I have a business meeting, I do this before the meeting and I do it before I speak, always. *You can hold a lot of people in your heart!* Make a commitment today that you will remember to put people in your heart before you do anything else! Every day, from now on. It will be awesome!

---- Joy Secret #11 ----

Cheerful Enthusiasm

YOUR SEVEN MINUTES

"A cheerful spirit is one of the most valuable gifts ever bestowed upon humanity by a kind Creator. It will sustain the soul in the darkest and most dreary places of this world. It will hold in check the demons of despair, and stifle the power of discouragement and hopelessness."
James H. Aughey

- Are you a cheerful person?
- Are you an enthusiastic person?
- Are you passionate about something that you whole-heartedly believe in?
- Are you optimistic?
- Do you feel your life has purpose and meaning?
- If not, why not? You are not allowed to blame anybody or any thing! This is the time to take responsibility for your life *as it is* right now.

What is it in you that has blocked any of the above?

Beliefs? Thoughts? Fears? Expectations? Living in the past? Judgments? Other things? Make a few notes about what might be affecting you and your enthusiasm and what you can do about it.

Ask your heart if there is anything you are not conscious of that is blocking your joy – and listen carefully! It will probably be a knowing or a sense of something - and then you might have to search further! It's worth being enthusiastic about the work as the joy it brings is awesome!

AMANDA'S TAKE:
IT'S ALWAYS SUNNY ABOVE THE CLOUDS

> *"If you are not getting as much from life as you want to,*
> *then examine the state of your enthusiasm."*
> *Norman Vincent Peale*

"It's always sunny above the clouds" is the name of a newsletter I wrote after a plane ride. We took off from a dark and gloomy airport, burst through the cloud barrier (notice the words), and found magnificent, cloudless blue skies with sunshine that streamed into the windows of the plane.

It dawned on me that *every* time I have left a cloudy, stormy place on the ground, *it's always sunny above the clouds!*

Think of the number of times we speak of people with a "sunny" disposition. Everyone knows that means they are cheerful and joyful, no matter what happens.

Why Sunny Matters!

The sun is very important for cheerfulness - more than we know or remember. There's even a medical condition called SAD - Seasonal Affective Disorder – describing what happens to people's moods during months of limited sunlight.

Apart from it's many other life giving benefits, we now know how important the sun is for good Vitamin D levels, which are critical for every function in our bodies and very important for preventing cancer.

The Inca and other ancient cultures understood the value of the sun so much they actually worshipped it. The Bible tells us to *be like the sun, shining in people's lives*, bringing warmth and goodness.

Spend time in the sun day and thank it – *truly feel* appreciation - for beaming all that life, warmth, light and life into your body and spirit. Without the sun, there would be no life on earth.

Living our first winter in Vermont sure taught me the value of the *warmth* in sunlight! A few days of rain, mist, cold, snow and cloud leave most people feeling gloomy - just like the weather. As soon as the sun, its warmth and light emerge again, our spirits soar. *Be a sun for others!*

A "Sunny" Disposition

Imagine what life would be like if we all aimed to have a sunny disposition, *to be cheerful no matter what clouds were about*, remembering that clouds also give life giving rain and shade; and to be filled with gratitude, seeking the inner and outer gifts of the clouds *and* the sun.

The clouds can represent the trials and tribulations - or *learning opportunities* - in life. Once we move past them, break or burst through them - we find the sun again. It's a great way to look at our life struggles - as cloud cover that only *temporarily* blocks the sun, *knowing* the sun is always there, *even if we can't see it.*

Welcome The Clouds!

"The Bridge Over the River,"[1] is a great book written by the sister of a young soldier named Sigwart, who was killed in World War 1. The sister believed she was able to communicate with her brother after his death.

Sigwart gives many great words of advice from the heavenly realms that have resonated with me. For example, he says we should *"bear all discomforts cheerfully,"* because *"our spirit welcomes upsets because it knows they are for its benefit".*

By welcoming and working through our "clouds" or discomforts - learning our lessons, strengthening our will and soul, we can grow and develop into more joyful, spiritual human beings. *Our challenge is to see the clouds as the gifts they really are!*

WHAT IS REALLY CAUSING YOUR GLOOM?

When "clouds" are present in our life, we can feel unhappy, gloomy, sad, burdened, heavy and hopeless. It can seem like a fog and life is dark or dreary and murky no matter where we look. Our ability to see clearly or understand everything that is *really* going on - the whole picture - is limited.

Gloom comes mostly from unclear thinking, when we give in to negative emotions or self talk, and our perceptions are skewed, inaccurate or just plain wrong! The gloom I am talking about is not clinical depression or any other physiological or medical condition.

Gloom is the opposite of feeling enthusiastic, energetic, sunny, alive and joyful. This whole book is dedicated to eliminating gloom and giving us more control over, and insight into, our moods. As you work your way through the exercises, you will find many help you soar through the clouds to God's sunshine above.

What About Storms, Not Just Clouds?

Storms can be huge, swirling, scary, tumultuous thunderstorms that suddenly appear out of nowhere; or they can be heavy solid, consistent rain or snow that sets in for days; or maybe tornados or hurricanes. *No matter what type of storm we face, the sun returns.*

We, or our circumstances, may be changed, or we may have to recover from damage sustained during the storm, but if we are resilient, if we choose to be cheerful and optimistic, and to think (with a joyful heart) that things will improve, we move forward and reclaim our joy more quickly.

Jeni

A young woman I know suffered through a monster storm. She was a perfectly healthy 32-year-old in a new marriage, but she was not feeling well and was excited because she thought she was pregnant.

A local physician diagnosed her with the flu. Several days later, she collapsed and was rushed to hospital with septicemia - her whole body was poisoned. For seven weeks, she was in intensive care, with a wonderful supportive family around her praying. People thought only a miracle would save her.

And a miracle did happen - she lived, but the damage that had ravaged her body meant she had to have both legs and hands amputated. She, her family and doctors were all very excited and enthusiastic *because they were able to save her wrists.* Makes you think differently, doesn't it?

Continuing on her journey to come off the respirator and start using a badly traumatized body that had not moved for seven weeks, she had to work extremely hard. Her physical therapist said she had never seen anyone so enthusiastic or cheerful about her exercises - all of which involved a lot of pain.

Victim Or Lesson – Your Choice!

People who suffer major trauma like this are in danger of adopting a "victim" mentality. They cannot move past their injuries or stop thinking, *"Poor me, why me, this is unfair, life is not worth living,"* even after a significant time of healing.

This can lead them to feeling trapped – and they are - in self-centeredness, depression, anger, and fear. But not Jen! She defied death and now she is using her sunny, cheerful spirit as a beacon for others - she accepted, learned and grew and is *giving to* others instead of wallowing in depression.

The first time she went out of the hospital was to a McDonalds with her Dad. People stared at her but her only concern was how was the experience affecting her Dad!

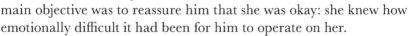

When she went to visit the surgeon who had to do the amputations, her main objective was to reassure him that she was okay: she knew how emotionally difficult it had been for him to operate on her.

She is a truly incredible, compassionate spirit - *she* was the one without hands and feet, and all she did was care for others, and reassure them that everything was great.

The thought of life without feet and hands would be a big challenge for me but not Jen. She is brave, strong and most importantly - *optimistic*. Everyone who knows her and meets her is in awe of her *enthusiastic spirit* and her *will* to move on and start her new life, which I might add, includes children, writing and speaking, and running her own foundation for children with disabilities.

Jen epitomizes another Sigwart saying: *"Tread smilingly on the most difficult paths; in your will lies the strength of fulfillment. Never let thoughts of doubt arise in you. These are great obstacles."* Neither doubt, fear, nor any other obstacle will stop Jen's will *choosing* to be cheerfully enthusiastic!

Reframing

Here is another example of the power of her spirit and determination. I had sent an email asking about her health to Jen's best friend (and one of mine), Somer. Her reply highlights Jen's inspirational spirit:

"She is doing well and unbelievably content. She had physical therapy last night while I was there and they worked on making a tool so she could turn pages in a magazine. I asked if that made her sad or feel dependent.

She enthusiastically replied that it was quite the opposite; it made her feel liberated and independent. That was a huge lesson for me - almost like the glass half-full thing, but putting myself in her shoes, it truly showed me what kind of person I was and how I look at things."

Somer is an inspiration as well. She has battled her own obstacle-filled journey with grace and cheerfulness. Life does not come without obstacles - they are an important part of the journey. *The spirit in which we deal with these obstacles makes all the difference in our lives.*

Learning about Jen's amazing spirit has helped me put whatever I thought were challenges into perspective. Whenever you are feeling grumpy or gloomy, recall her story and use her spirit as a beacon for yours. It's calling you to find the sunshine *behind* something currently worrying you.

Reframing a challenge helps us to see it differently - as a growth opportunity, and a blessing - yes, *a blessing! Find the gifts in the obstacles you face.*

How you face your obstacles determines whether you find the gift or not. Jen not only found her gifts but she is showering others with them. Sigwart said *"The greatness of a human being depends on how much he carries the sun in himself."* [2] Jen and Somer are truly great. Somer is called Somer Sunshine for a reason!

THE ORIGIN OF ENTHUSIASM

*"Years may wrinkle the skin, but
to give up enthusiasm wrinkles the soul."*
Samuel Ullman

The original Greek root of the word "enthusiasm" is "en-theos." *En* meaning in or see; and *theos* meaning God. Enthusiasm means *"having the God within or seeing the God within."*

Enthusiastic people are filled with light, life and love. They are motivated, energetic, passionate, inspired or in love, and always have wonderful, bright, vital, sparkling eyes! It makes them very attractive to everyone. Watch a 4 year olds face when they are telling you a story! *It's the magic of a spirit being or coming alive* that makes our eyes sparkle!

That's your mission, should you choose to accept it! *Put a sparkle into the eyes of every single person you meet!* Share your light with others. Spread your enthusiasm.

If you don't believe you have light within you - your mission is to search for it, or ask for help finding it. It *is* there! The key is to find your God within, your higher self or the Divine inside and around you, and *let that unblock you* so the light will shine into and through you!

Spend time with people like Jen and Somer; *serve others* and you will find your light; help others; focus on what you learn in this book and your light will brighten inside you. *When we are connected to the Divine in our hearts, we are filled with enthusiasm yet feel peaceful, joyful, excited and exciting all at the same time! It's fabulous!*

A PASSION FOR BEING ENTHUSIASTIC

> *"The real secret of success is enthusiasm."*
> Walter Chrysler

How alive do you feel right now? What sorts of things make you feel alive? What gives your life meaning? What purpose do you have for this lifetime or at this time in your life? What makes you feel passionate? These are all critical questions for building joyful enthusiasm.

Having a passion for something makes it easier to be enthusiastic, but I believe we are meant to be enthusiastic about everything, not just what we have a passion for! Why not *be passionate about being enthusiastic, connecting with your spirit and being full of light and life?* Or be passionate and enthusiastic about being alive? It's a choice!

No matter what your life is like now, there is always the opportunity to change. Neuroscience teaches us that we can re-hardwire our brains – and we know love can change our hearts.

There is always a chance to grow, develop and be free of old beliefs; to learn; to be forgiven; to forgive; to stop old patterns; to lighten up; to rethink and reframe. *While you are alive there is still time to learn your lessons, to change!*

Develop your will forces and courage, and embrace whatever it is you have to do to en-JOY your life. Clear your thinking, find your true heart and live from it, see the bigger spiritual picture - there are so many exciting possibilities! I am enthusiastic just typing this!

What Are You Teaching Your Children?

I will never forget a woman I loved being around. She was the most vibrant and enthusiastic person. She told me that when she was growing up, *her mother would put enthusiasm into everything.* She would say in a really excited voice, *"Let's do the washing up!"* and this little girl would say in an equally enthusiastic voice, *"OKAY!"*

And then they would both embark with gusto on washing up. My friend now does this with her children and it's a great lesson. Children model (or absorb) what they see, hear and feel. What are you teaching your children?

My wonderful mother must have done that for me, as I never tackle anything half-heartedly! I don't drag myself out to do stuff I have to do. I may not always be as cheerful as I could be, but I am enthusiastic to have it all done, so I am more focused, efficient and achieve more.

I notice that when I am with my Godchildren, my spirit is fired with enthusiasm and I love it! Isabella would say to me, *"Let's play!"* and I would respond, like the 7-year-old she was, *"Great! What will we play?"* And soon we are both rolling in excitement, enthusiasm and laughter!

Small children cry; tell stories; laugh; play; sing and dance with the greatest enthusiasm - they are naturally full of life. I hang out in a friend's kindergarten just to engage with those bright eyed, excited, enthusiastic, loving toddlers!

As they grow older their enthusiasm becomes "un-cool." Most teenagers have replaced enthusiasm with disdain, and most adults are too drained to be enthusiastic.

Adults don't *choose* to give themselves time to *renew or restore* their connection with their spiritual origins and their life forces.

Remember *real enthusiasm is felt when we are connected to the Divine inside us.* When we feel it in each of our cells it shines out of us. If we remind ourselves to do everything we do with pure love in our hearts, and remember our spiritual nature then our enthusiasm will make us sparkle. *Feel* your Spirit first. Then do!

Meaning And Purpose In Life – Your Work Or Your Job?

Things that give our lives meaning and purpose will ignite the sparks of joyful enthusiasm inside us. We rarely have a deep sense of fulfillment and satisfaction from just making money or buying material possessions. That may give us some short-term happiness, but nothing deep or sustaining.

For deep, abiding, fulfilling satisfaction, we need to be working with something - at work or on our own time - that *inspires us and gives our life meaning and purpose.* Find your purpose, *seek* or create some meaning in what you do.

What inspired you as a child? What excited you? What did you love to learn about? What did you love to do? What activities make you feel wonderful? Swing dancing, painting, playing a musical instrument, reading, learning, playing tennis, exercising, bike riding, laughing or hiking?

These can make you feel great short-term, but they don't give you abiding fulfillment - unless you can find a way to *combine the activity you love with doing something for the world or others* - some form of serving.

Perhaps you could become a *teacher* of swing or another form of dancing and share the joy of it with others, while helping them become fit at the same time! Or you could teach any of the things that you love to do and help others experience your enthusiasm.

You can even turn tedious tasks into playful activities to generate enthusiasm! Sing as you clean, or make what you are doing into a game and celebrate when you finish.

There is a big difference between a "job" and "work". *Our "work" is what we are meant to be doing* - the work of developing ourselves, serving and loving others and making our own unique contribution to the universe. *What can you do to combine your work with your job?*

How I Fell Into Speaking

I am so blessed that I was led to a path where I really do what I love. I feel I have a strong purpose, and there is great meaning to what I do. It's a calling for me.

Being a speaker combines my work and my job. I had little to do with it, mind you! It was through grace more than anything that I "fell" into speaking! I was a physical therapist consulting in ergonomics. I had coauthored a book, which prompted a meeting planner to invite me to a conference, where inspirational speaker Ron Tacchi was the emcee.

At the end of my presentation, he said, *"You should be a speaker!"* and I answered, *"What's a speaker?"*

He then mentored me into the business, which in itself was a huge blessing, as he was one of the best speakers I have ever heard. I am humbled when I consider how I have been guided through a wonderful career, traveling to many countries, having amazing experiences and meeting incredible people.

I am blessed to feel God makes a difference through me. I love my work, and I work diligently to do what I believe the spiritual realms want me to do.

DO YOUR BEST AND ENTHUSIASM GROWS

If you dislike your job, it is not healthy for you or others with whom you work! Choose to find ways to make the job fun, or to do it better than it has ever been done.

Use your intellect to find ways to make that possible. Challenging yourself is a wonderful way to build enthusiasm and motivation! Make it an *achievable* challenge – one that is *just beyond* your usual grasp.

With this spirit, *your job may become your work.* You will be noticed and your character and enthusiasm will make you attractive for promotions. More importantly, *you will feel better about yourself.*

How Do You Make Yourself And Others Feel?

When you feel great about yourself, you are full of joy, and cheerfully enthusiastic about everything. Because you feel great, *you make everyone else around you feel great.* This is one of the best ways to ensure your success in every field!

Keep practicing all you have learned in this book to keep yourself joyful and enthusiastic - and you will brighten the lives of others while making sure you are successful in every aspect of your life! TA DA!

If your meaning in life comes from other than your job, still do your job the very best you can. Be honest; operate with integrity and loyalty; do the right thing by everyone, including yourself; be cheerful and humble; feel good about yourself. *You will be surprised at how enthusiasm and respect appears and grows in your life when you live this way.*

Consider for a few minutes the times when you have been really enthusiastic in life. What were the circumstances? Can you find any common factors that might give you clues as to the qualities of things that fire you up?

In your conversations, what topics *literally* make you wake up? If you begin a conversation feeling tired and flat, and finish feeling wide awake, excited and cheerful - then you have a big clue!

What are your *values* and what's important in life for you? It's my nature to be curious and I love to learn – it's my No. 1 value and I find if I'm not learning, some part of my spirit shrivels. I can do almost anything, anywhere, *as long as I feel I am learning something.*

Explore your values. See what information they give about you and what gives your life meaning, purpose, and lights your fires of enthusiasm!

We Are Happiest When We Are Serving Others

Everything we do, *everything*, needs to be about serving others. Not being a *servant*, but *serving* them in some way. *We are happiest when we are serving others.*

Whether you are working with customers, your bosses, colleagues, other companies, the community, the world or shareholders, focus on being of service.

Serving others in less fortunate situations reminds us just how blessed we are, and how *joy is not dependent on material possessions.* If we can look at every aspect of our lives as a form of service to others, purpose, meaning and cheerful enthusiasm will flow freely. While we metaphorically "wash the feet of others," we feed *our* hearts and souls as well. It's a win-win.

MIRACLES

If the opportunities to consciously grow and develop don't excite you or make you cheerful, then consider the realm of miracles!

Austrian philosopher and playwright Rudolf Steiner, in a lecture called, *"The Work of the Angel in Our Astral Body,"* says, *"We must get into the habit of being alert… if we do not discover a miracle in our life on a particular day, we have merely lost sight of it."*

He suggests that every night we ask ourselves (and it would be a fun thing to do with someone else, as well) *"What might have happened to me today?"* Then *look for the "mini" miracles,* which is what I call them.

Major miracles happen every day to someone somewhere, but miracles are not usually of that magnitude every day in our lives. However, *mini-miracles do happen* every day.

Imagine you are running out the door to make an appointment, but someone turns up at your house and delays you. This makes you annoyed, stressed and tense and ruins your day. Reflect on this event in the evening.

Who knows if an angel orchestrated the delay? As a result of that delay, you could have avoided a car crash that might have harmed you! Choosing to *look for* miracles in this way transforms your perceptions and life.

If a disappointing interview result or decision at work had been different, perhaps it would have put you in a job you hated and that made you miserable. Missing a plane, which put you into a foul mood for the day could have saved your life. *We never know because we never see the whole picture.*

In other words, before you sleep, look at what you deem "negative" aspects of your life, and *knowing* there is a wise guidance behind them, find the miracles. It will grow your consciousness of this higher wisdom – and it's fun! It makes the end of the day a much more cheerful and miraculous experience!

How To Wake Up Excited!

Someone sent me this recently as a preparation for our "journeys" while we sleep. It's from a Rudolf Steiner lecture, Cosmic and Human Metamorphosis - Lecture 3.

"I am going to sleep; until I wake, my Soul will be in the Spiritual world. There it will meet with the guiding-power of my earth-life, who lives in the Spiritual world, and who soars round and surrounds my head. My Soul will have the meeting with my Genius."

For some, it sounds a bit cosmic, but I think it's an exciting way to create enthusiasm for what *inspiration may come to you in the morning*! Your genius will instruct your soul and who knows how you will wake up or what you will be aware of in the morning! See - it's exciting!

MOODS AND YOU

Who is in charge of your mood? Of course, it's you! Only *you* can be responsible for how you react, and although your feelings can be hurt, *you* can manage your hurt emotions with cheerfulness, activity or by doing something to make yourself feel better.

Remember, *how you feel about yourself* will affect everything else. Everything.

I often have to remind myself that my mood is my choice and I have the resources to change it and be happier or more enthusiastic. I exercise my will and *become* cheerful – most of the time, but if I'm really tired, I find it difficult!

So I warn others if I know it is "that" time of the month, or I don't feel well, or I am very tired and I know I am more likely to be grumpy or difficult. I say, *"This has nothing to do with you, but I am feeling sick right now"*. I take responsibility, warn others, and I try to do the things I need to do so I return to a cheerful and enthusiastic state. Like sleep!

Are you willing to take charge of your moods, how you feel and choose to smile your way through everything? Or at least treat other people well and not make them suffer because you are tired, miserable or angry.

One thing that can help a great deal is to say, "I am *experiencing or feeling* depressed /angry /frustrated right now" - not "I *am* depressed/angry/frustrated."

This is a small change but it has a *profound* effect. If you say, *"I AM depressed."*, you are downloading that negative pattern into all of your cells. You are owning it, becoming it and maintaining it.

What You Can Do To Bust A "Bad Mood"

Connect to your heart. The heart is never in a bad mood!

- Exercise and release endorphins. (Check with a doctor if you don't usually do this, and just move as much as the doctor deems prudent).
- Do some deep breathing exercises.
- Be patient, and ask to become aware of what fear is causing this mood and challenge or eradicate the fear!
- Smile - even a fake smile if you wrinkle around your eyes - your "crows feet" - releases endorphins!
- Watch a comedy movie.
- Listen to what you are saying to yourself and change anything negative or judgmental to positive and kind.
- Learn something new.
- Go somewhere where you can serve someone who is less fortunate than you.
- Think of Jen and stop feeling sorry for yourself – if you are.
- Laugh even if you don't feel like it.
- Read uplifting books, listen to uplifting music or watch uplifting movies
- Call a good friend and talk about good times.
- Look through or create a photo album of happy times.
- Go for a walk in nature. Absorb the wonderful vibrations from the flowers, trees, grass, rocks and water and anything beautiful you find out there!
- Make a gratitude list of all the blessings in your life and those things for which you are grateful. Put on your gratitude glasses.
- Look for the miracles in your day before you go to sleep!

There are zillions ways to let off steam; take responsibility for how you feel and *do something* to find your joy!

ARE YOU A SPIRIT IGNITER OR FOOFER?

I believe that we all have a pilot light inside our hearts - just like a gas stove top. By turning a switch on the gas stove we can *ignite* that flame or *extinguish* it.

Every one of us has a choice with people - we can ignite their inner flame or light, or blow it out with a single breath. We can make another person's day, or extinguish their spirit with a word, smile, look or gesture. There are two types of people - "spirit igniters" or "spirit foofers"!

The "foofers" blow out that pilot light the way we would blow out a candle. Most of us have had moments where *we* have "foofed" out someone's spirit – or someone has "foofed" ours! This book shows you how to be an igniter, and never be a "foofer" again!

Spirit igniters have eyes that sparkle with excitement, enthusiasm and joy, which they radiate over everyone they encounter, in turn lighting other spirits and making them sparkle!

"Spirit foofers" can blow out your spirit with one nasty glance or cutting word! Haven't you met someone or worked with a person like that? Someone who looks at you, or speaks to you in such a tone that your spirit immediately retreats? A person whose spirit has shriveled has eyes that are lifeless, not sparkling, twinkling or smiling.

Make it a goal to ignite someone's spirit each day. If it's your habit to behave as a spirit "foofer" – stop it! *Now*! *Observe* yourself, laugh at yourself, *change* and apologize - I am sure you didn't really mean to do it!

Celebrate

Another way to keep enthusiasm alive is to celebrate!

Celebrate major life events and little ones. Celebrate that you have your health, loved ones, a car, or a roof over your head - or not! Celebrate the sunrise or the sunset; celebrate the onset of spring, or any other season; celebrate that you lost a pound! Celebrate by yourself and with others!

Doing a little celebration dance – a JOY jig - or sing a song which works just as well as large expensive events! I know this sounds silly, but we all need to find small ways to celebrate that touch our hearts and change our physiology.

Give someone a TA-DA! Tell them they deserve a TA-DA and watch their spirits sparkle! Give *yourself* a TA-DA and do it in front of the mirror! Smile at yourself and say, *"Well done!"*

Celebrate just by feeling good and *enjoying that feeling.* Or celebrate by slowing down for a few minutes, just sitting and enjoying a view or quiet moment.

Find small and meaningful ways to celebrate more frequently, so we *focus* on life being a series of mini-celebrations rather than a series of disappointments, struggles or difficulties!

This helps us maintain a cheerful attitude in the face of everything that comes out way. It also teaches our children resilience and how to focus on and *celebrate what's right in the world* and not what's wrong everywhere!

SMILE – WITH JOY!

There is a Tibetan saying *"When you smile at life, half the smile is for your face; the other half is for someone else's!"* Isn't that true?

What happens to our face when a baby or toddler smiles at us? We smile back! Even if a grownup smiles at us, our natural tendency is to smile back. *It's neurological* – our smiles and eye contact are triggering mirror neurons in both our brains!

How sad it is that it often gives us a surprise or shock when we look up and someone is smiling at us. What has happened to make us so disconnected from everyone that we're uncomfortable if someone gives us a sincere and genuine smile from the heart?

Many of us immediately wonder what that person is smiling at, or worse, *why* they are smiling at us. In fact, it may be just that someone had a happy thought and their face automatically showed it with a smile, and you were blessed enough to be one of the recipients.

Is That A Real Smile?

There are a lot of different smiles out there! When you smile, if you don't involve your eyes i.e. the "crows feet" muscles around the eyes, then not only is it interpreted as an insincere smile – but it also causes cardiovascular distress in you! *We need to be authentic* – or our hearts pick it up and they have little distress attacks! Seriously.

Some people make a smile look like a grimace! Or they smile and their eyes don't smile, so it doesn't feel like a genuine smile – and isn't! Think of all the different types of smiles you have experienced - and given!

The best smile for me is the smile that radiates out of someone's cheerful heart - and especially a smile from a young child. Their eyes sparkle and their whole face is full of joy. Those smiles make your spirit shine so brightly others will need sunglasses!

Smiles cost nothing and give a great deal more than we can quantify - both to ourselves, and to others. We actually release endorphins (the body's natural happy drugs) with a large grin.

We can release them any time we like by laughing or smiling *sincerely*. Put a giant grin on your face, feel the smile in your heart, make your eyes smile as well, and you will be releasing endorphins. Share your smiles today!

CHEERFUL ENTHUSIASM JOY-ERCISE 1: PRACTICE LOOKING FOR THE MIRACLES

> *"It's faith in something and enthusiasm for something that makes a life worth living."*
> Oliver Wendell Holmes

Today your mission is to *find* miracles wherever you look! The easiest place to see miracles is in nature. Engineers tell us the bumblebee can't fly according to the laws of aerodynamics - but it does.

Think about plants that burst (literally) into life after being buried by snow for six months; or the way the sun comes up every day and the oceans flow; the way small plants find a crack, take root and grow in the concrete jungles of our cities. Nature is full of daily miraculous events.

And so are people. The miracles of caring, creativity, kindness, compassion and resilience happen every minute somewhere. So does the miracle of healing, not to mention the miracles that love produces every day.

Watch programs on television that are about miracles. Avoid violent, cruel, anger-filled shows that shrink your heart. Instead *record programs about joy, angels and miracles* to uplift your soul and remind you that miracles do happen every day.

Put on your *miracle glasses* today! See everything through those glasses, and before you go to sleep every night, review your day to search for the hidden work of your angels.

Examine anything that caused you frustration, delayed you, or upset you, and try to imagine how it was a gift. You may be surprised. I know that since I started doing this, I no longer see airport delays or cancellations as a frustrating inconvenience.

I am grateful for the work of my angels who know more than I do, and are making sure that *I am where I need to be.* Who knows? I might meet someone important for my life on the next plane, or I may have missed an accident or a worse delay somewhere else.

Our Guardian Angels help and guide us all the time. We need to learn to listen carefully, hear them, heed their advice and *appreciate* them!

What we comprehend is so limited compared to the wisdom of the spiritual worlds. Be open. Listen carefully. Be grateful.

Miracles do happen every day. Expect them, look for and rejoice in them!

CHEERFUL ENTHUSIASM JOY-ERCISE 2: PRACTICE CHOOSING A GOOD MOOD

> *"The best way to cheer yourself up is to cheer someone else up."*
> Mark Twain

Have you ever noticed how good it feels to make someone else laugh - or to cheer them up? Today is the day you can develop your capacity to keep yourself joyful and spread that joy.

No matter how you feel, how you woke up, or what happens to you, your mission today is to *choose* to stay cheerful and *share* that mood!

Sustain that attitude of cheerfulness all day. Let nothing change it for more than a few moments. Find the will forces to make sure that you maintain the state at all times. As my Qi Gong teacher tells us to believe *"every day is a good day; every place is a good place; every thing is a good thing."*

If someone asks you to do something you don't want to do, cheerfully take the task on! *Find* a way to feel good about every thing that you do today and sustain the mood all day long, until the moment your head hits the pillow. At that moment, review the day and see how much better it flowed - and what miracles occurred.

Cheerfulness Adjustment Moment

Have you ever seen a sign outside a pub or bar that says "attitude-adjustment hour"? Perhaps each hour today needs to include a cheerfulness-adjustment moment? Be aware and keep track of what emotions creep in, and whenever the feeling of cheerfulness fades, immediately have a cheerfulness-adjustment moment!

Think of all the reasons for being cheerful in your life, and if you can't think of any, *just choose* to be cheerful and see how your life changes! If all else fails, watch *First World Problems* on YouTube and put all your problems into perspective!

Choose to be someone who will see the cup half full and not complain that it is half empty. Did you know that optimists live longer than pessimists, and cynical people may be harming their hearts? People who are angry, cynical, stressed, and distrustful have more inflammation in their bodies than others, and this leads to increased risks for cardiovascular disease.

So now there are even more reasons to choose to be cheerful! You'll live longer, and more importantly, *everyone will want you to!*

CHEERFUL ENTHUSIASM JOY-ERCISE 3: PRACTICE FACING DIFFICULTIES WITH CHEERFUL ENTHUSIASM

"How do you go from where you are to where you want to be?
I think you have to have an enthusiasm for life."
Jim Valvano

Today's journey is to face every difficulty with cheerfulness and enthusiasm *for the spiritual growth experience it is!* When something goes wrong - instead of groaning, sighing, and thinking, *"Here we go again!"*, say to yourself, *"Goodie!"* or something like that!

And then say, *"I wonder what I am meant to be learning here?"* Then proceed to *look enthusiastically* for that *lesson and understanding*.

The pessimist saw a large pile of horse manure and was immediately disgusted. He muttered, *"I knew I wasn't going to find anything good"* and walked off unhappy. The little optimist ran down the stairs, saw the manure and excitedly and enthusiastically started diving through it. When his parents asked him what he was doing, he said, *"With all this horse manure, there has to be a horse somewhere!"*

These two *chose* completely different responses to the same situation. We all have that choice - we can choose how to respond (and not react) to all situations. *It may not be easy but we can do it!* Practicing that discipline is a great way to develop our will forces.

We can say this prayer to the spiritual realms every night, just before we go to sleep to keep us on the right path: *"I pray that I did everything you wanted me to do today. If I didn't, give me the strength that I might do it tomorrow."*

Perhaps each night you work on cheerful enthusiasm (or anything else), you could include: *"Tomorrow I shall have reached my goal of facing every difficulty with cheerful enthusiasm."* You might be amazed at how many less difficulties you encounter! *Thinking with your heart changes your life.*

CHEERFUL ENTHUSIASM JOY-ERCISE 4: PRACTICE PASSIONATE ENTHUSIASM!

"I consider my ability to arouse enthusiasm among men the greatest asset I possess. The way to develop the best that is in a man is by appreciation and encouragement."
Charles M. Schwab

Your goal for today is to be passionate and enthusiastic about *everything* you do - even if it is just washing dishes! *Appreciate* and *encourage* other people with that same gusto.

If you have a million little things to do, try to make each one, no matter how mundane, fun! Mary, my great friend, taught me that. She even tries to make her children's homework fun. It's much easier to be enthusiastic about something you enjoy doing, so whatever you do, *find a way to make it fun*.

Remember the story I told you earlier about Dianne, my friend in Australia? In 2007, she was diagnosed with a tumor on her pituitary gland and was losing her vision and her speech. As you can imagine, it was a very stressful time. She called me and despite her circumstances, Dianne was still able to laugh.

She had and still has the most optimistic and cheerful attitude - and passionately embraced all the natural therapies with such enthusiasm and gusto that her condition vastly improved, and she amazed her doctors with her progress.

She did a tremendous amount of work to heal herself. A devout Christian, she had complete faith that she would be healed, but she didn't passively wait for it to occur. She remained cheerful and diligently and passionately did her part of the healing. It worked!

If you are struggling to be enthusiastic and cheerful because you have a tough day ahead or a day full of "chores," *find gratitude in your heart*, and be enthusiastic that you are healthy enough to do the chores or tackle the day!

And if you do have a medical or other condition that is filling you with fear, *breathe deeply*. Challenge your thinking and handle it like Dianne or Jeni did. Research, find the right people to help you, take charge of your health, and enthusiastically do what you can to assist your body, Spirit or God in the healing process. Be passionate about keeping your heart full of faith and hope.

We are told in the Bible five times to "be of good cheer" in the face of *all adversity. It does not say be of good cheer only during the good times!* Spirit is always *with* you. It's *in* you. Find peace in that.

Have courage knowing *you are not alone*. And even if you don't believe in the Bible, it's still great advice. You can be disappointed and walk away from the pile of manure - or you can passionately look for the gift hidden in it! Your choice! Your will forces! Your life!

CHEERFUL ENTHUSIASM JOY-ERCISE 5: PRACTICE SMILING AND MAKING SPIRITS SPARKLE!

> *"Enthusiasm is contagious; start an epidemic."*
> *Anonymous*

Today, wake up and immediately smile - include your eyes! Before you climb out of bed, know that you are not alone, spiritually. The Divine is with you! Smile and say, *"Good morning!"* to those realms and also to everyone person you meet!

Smile with your heart *and eyes* - not just your face. Smile at your family over breakfast and when they ask you why, tell them, *"I have just decided to be cheerful today because I can!"* If you have chosen to smile from your heart at everyone today, you have chosen to be a spirit igniter! You will be spreading light, love and joy wherever you go.

If you see a stranger on the street and smile, watch them smile back. If they don't, send them love, for they may not be used to people smiling at them, or they may not know how to receive a gift with grace, because most people don't give love or joy freely.

Receive smiles from others today - especially babies and toddlers - and then smile back with both your face and your heart. It's a joyous exchange. Have you ever walked into a house and had a child's eyes light up as he or she sees you? Or seen them run toward you shouting your name with excited, enthusiastic, unbridled joy?

I am blessed because my nephew and niece, Thomas and Clelia, did this to me when they were toddlers. Each time it happened, I thought my heart would burst with joy. I can't begin to explain the incredible feeling, but *I can recall it anytime I like and smile!* If you have never had this happen - rent a child as quickly as possible! This is a feeling everyone should have at least once.

Imagine helping others feel that level of joy from the way you greet them! Today is your chance. Go forth and make people's spirits sparkle! *Become a human sparkler!*

CHEERFUL ENTHUSIASM JOY-ERCISE 6: PRACTICE BELIEVING THINGS WILL IMPROVE

"We act as though comfort and luxury were the chief requirements of life, when all that we need to make us really happy is something to be enthusiastic about."
Charles Kingsley

Remember, *it's always sunny above the clouds!* So no matter what challenges you face today or what problems you have, *today is the day to feel the joy in your heart.* Have absolute faith and believe that things will improve - maybe not in your preferred time frame, but in God's - which I'm sure will bring better results!

Who knows what a mess we would be in if we had always been given everything we thought we wanted, *exactly when we wanted it*! With the benefit of hindsight - how many of those things you wished for, if they had been granted, would have gone on to be a problem?

How many times have you had a lover that you thought you couldn't live without, or some relationship that devastated you when it ended? Or maybe it was a job interview you didn't win or business you *believed* you wanted fell through?

Although you were disappointed at the time or even devastated, when you look back now, you realize it was the best thing that happened to you!

For me, one of those situations was when I was 45, losing all the money I had worked so hard to accumulate! I was left with half a million dollars worth of debt. I must say, had I known about cheerful enthusiasm at that time, my will forces would have been a lot stronger by now!

But in retrospect, this experience was one of the best things that ever happened to me. Not only did I finally understand in every cell of my body that *money did not* bring security, but it also took me to the U.S.A.

Without being in that gracious and generous country, I would not have regained financial stability as quickly, nor found the spiritual path I am meant to be on - with incredible, amazing teachers who have blessed me, and continue to bless me.

Today is another day to *reflect on how your life's "disasters" turned into blessings* - or at least on how something good came out of something horrible or not so good. The spiritual realms have a way of doing that! They don't create the horrible events, but *they can work to turn them into good.* Remember, there is *always* sunshine above the clouds. *Know* that. *Believe* it with every cell in your body. *Do* your work. *Wait patiently* while doing your work, with a joyful heart full of *certainty* and *faith* that the clouds will pass, and the sun will shine again.

CHEERFUL ENTHUSIASM JOY-ERCISE 7: PRACTICE FINDING YOUR WORK

> *"When a person applies enthusiasm to his job, the job will itself become alive with exciting new possibilities."*
> *Norman Vincent Peale*

Your job is your job, but *it can also be your work,* depending on how you look at it and do it. Your *work* is manna for your soul. It fulfills you and satisfies you, and it usually involves serving others. Go to your job and make it your work. This is your practice today.

Everyone in *every* job serves others in some way - the boss, colleagues, customers, clients, the country or the community. It does not matter how lowly you feel your job is, you are *part* of a serving team. *Teams only function well when all parts do their best at work with and serve all the others.*

Author and inventor Buckminster Fuller said, *"The whole is greater than the sum of the parts."* That means that when we all connect and contribute to the team, the results are much better. Ambitious, selfish people who ignore, harm or cut down others for their own personal goals may realize apparent short-term success, but their success will probably not last, and they won't be happy, fulfilled or satisfied. They won't be honored because they're not honoring others.

People who think, *"My pie will be smaller if you have some of it!"* don't understand the laws of life! Giving more, helping more, and serving more can only bring you more - although that should not be your motivation, of course!

Your motivation is to serve others and when you focus on that, you may be surprised at how joy, contentment, fulfillment, satisfaction and financial rewards appear in your life. It just magically flows in while you are focused on others and *doing what you are meant to be doing*.

If you know in your heart that the job you are in is not for you, complete your tasks and do the job the best you can while you look for your *real* work. This will make your job less arduous and may miraculously lead you to your real work.

Never grumble again about your job! For starters, you have one - millions don't. Be grateful!

You also have the choice to make your job enjoyable, even if it is making beds in a motel, and there is a football team in the room making suggestive comments about you! Yes - this happened to me! Although it was not the most pleasant experience at the time, I smiled and laughed as I told them I would come back later - when they had gone!

The more you grumble and complain, the less people want to be around you and the more you gather other grumbling, complaining spirit "foofers". You are creating your own special set of storm clouds and carrying them with you wherever you go. You're not contributing to the team - in fact, you may be aiding in destroying it.

Never underestimate the power of one spirit "foofer" on a whole organization. If that is you, stop it today! Stop any negative thoughts about your job. Enthusiastically find good things instead; become a spirit igniter; serve others the best you can, and *find your work*. It may be right under your nose!

Be a spirit igniter!

--- **Joy Secret #12** ---

Equanimity (Inner Peace)

"Be still and know that I AM."
Psalm 46:10

YOUR SEVEN MINUTES

- What does equanimity mean to you?
- Are you thinking *"I can't even spell it, let alone know what it is!"*
- Is your nervous system almost always on red alert?
- Do you panic, feel stressed or worry a lot?
- Are you fearful most of the time?
- Do you see life as a series of crises? If so, why?
- Is it challenging for you to let go of "stuff" that has happened to you?
- Do you take time each day to seek God's peace?

What creates a deep sense of peace or calm in you - not a passive state, but one in which you are aware and alert, yet relaxed and feel really alive?

Have you ever felt a state of inner peace and contentment? Explore that memory, and identify the aspects that brought you peace.

AMANDA'S TAKE:

> *"Peace comes from within. Do not seek it without."*
> Gautama Buddha

> *"Peace is not submissive nor passive. On the contrary,*
> *peace is an overwhelming force which comes from within us,*
> *disrespectful of everything around us, a firm coalition*
> *of spirit and soul standing against all the unrest that abounds."*
> C. JoyBell C.

What Is Equanimity? It's More Than Inner Peace!

It's a state of inner peace, wisdom, awareness, contentment, courage, love, enthusiasm, connection and joy! And more!

Equanimity is that state of composure which the Bible speaks of as *"the peace that passeth understanding"*. It refers to a feeling of *deep calm in even the most adverse situation*, and it usually *comes from Divine inspiration and grace*.

In a state of equanimity, we are totally at peace, content, connected to perfect love, composed, and always seem to know the right thing to do. We are aware of the whole picture and can put ourselves into another person's shoes yet hold firm to what needs to be done, or boundaries set, at the same time.

Many see equanimity as a Divine gift and it can be seen clearly at times of crisis when composure seems to "descend" on a person. If you can work towards feeling deep inner peace and live within it most of the time, your life will be joyful beyond measure!

I love this excerpt from a Hafiz poem so beautifully translated by Daniel Ladinsky in *"Love Poems From God"*.

"PERFECT EQUANIMITY"

Look how a mirror

will reflect with perfect equanimity

all actions before it

There is no act in this world

that will ever cause the mirror to look away.

There is no act in this world

that will ever make the mirror

Say "no."

The mirror, like perfect love, will just keep giving

Of itself to all before it.

How did the mirror get like that, so polite,

so grand, so compassionate?

It watched God.

Yes, the mirror remembers the Beloved looking into itself

as the Beloved shaped existence's heart

and the mirror's Soul." [1]

Many definitions I've encountered describe equanimity mostly as a state of mind. *But it's more than that!* The heart and soul aspect I really found useful was from Robert Sardello, in his wonderful book, *"The Power of Soul: Living the Twelve Virtues"*.

"Suppression of an emotion can outwardly look like equanimity. Equanimity does not look flat, for it is not an absence. The person of equanimity bears a countenance of buoyancy, accompanied with an inner light that shines from the soul, lighting the eyes expressed as an engaged interest in all that one encounters."

Another interesting definition came from a talk given by a Buddhist teacher named Gil Fronsdal, who kindly gave me permission to reproduce it here. "The English word 'equanimity' translates two separate Pali words used by the Buddha. Each represents a different aspect of equanimity.

'Upekkha,' meaning 'to look over,' refers to the equanimity that arises from the power of observation, the ability to see without being caught by what we see....to see with patience. We might understand this as 'seeing with understanding.' The second word often translated as equanimity is 'tatramajjhattata,' meaning 'to stand in the middle of all this.'"

So I imagine we are in a state equanimity when we are in a balanced place, and can clearly see from a higher perspective, and really understand what is going on at all levels - to be involved, and at the same time observing.

When the concept of equanimity came to me as one of the secrets for joy, I thought, *"What do I know about equanimity!"* It's something I have always wanted and never seem to achieve!

Bubbling Serenity!

One of my few memories as a young girl was a desire to be serene. (If you knew me, you would be laughing out loud at this!) In my 20s I decided that what I really wanted to be was "bubbling or excited serene" - so that I was not boring! You are probably laughing louder now!

I suspect the inspiration that came to me about being "bubbling serene" was to show me that *we can feel peace, and be alive, interested, enthusiastic, active and dynamically participating in what we are meant to be doing in life.* Simultaneously we can sense the bigger, spiritual picture of what is *really* going on – and know that all will be well no matter how it looks now.

Years later, when I was a convener of a conference on ergonomics, I was driving one of our speakers around Sydney. He asked me, *"What is the one thing you want most in life?"*

To my complete surprise, out of my mouth fell the words *"inner peace."* Honestly, I looked around and thought, *"Who said that?"* I didn't really think about it much after that. It was just part of me that submerged back into the chaos of daily life - until...I started writing this book.

And then I did a lot of thinking, meditation and reflection on equanimity! I realized that what came out of my mouth that day was a true desire; a reminder for me to pay attention to how I could develop inner peace – my bubbling serenity!

The Peace Manifesto

When we can really can sense the bigger spiritual world around us, and remember that

- An infinite wisdom is in charge of everything
- most things happen for a reason
- and we always have more help than we can imagine, we find and keep our inner peace.

Our free will (what we think we want!) can interfere with our divine plan – so staying connected and recognizing the divine design for our lives is essential.

Equanimity is a good word to describe the state of:

- Being conscious of how everything interacts
- Being connected
- Always aware of the bigger picture and
- *Knowing* everything is perfect just as it is - no matter what happens! Consequently, you feel true, deep inner peace.

I am pretty sure equanimity was the last chapter in this book because it's the culmination and combination of all the secrets!

ENEMIES OF EQUANIMITY OR INNER PEACE

ENEMY #1:

Not Letting Go

Not letting go of past hurts and wounds, old stuff, expectations, our own outcomes, judgment, selfishness, greed, desperation and neediness can destroy our peace!

Not letting go can leave us feeling fearful, like victims, unforgiving, resentful, angry, needing to be right and controlling everything! Most of us need to let go of at least one thing. You know what you must let go of so you can be free to move on. Make the choice to do it now.

A Fun Way Of Letting Go: Drop Your Potatoes!

Imagine you have a sack of potatoes on one side of you and an empty sack on the other. You are going to pull out a potato for every person who has ever offended you, wounded you, upset you, harmed you, or "done" anything wrong to you - in your eyes.

Write their name on the potato and place it in the empty sack. Continue doing that until you have covered every single person. Then start on the situations in life that were "unfair", or whatever it is that you judged should not have happened. Write on a potato for each one of them.

When you have finished, pick up the newly filled sack of potatoes and carry that with you *everywhere* you go, *everyday*, for the rest of your life. Take it to bed, work, church, parties, social events, the bathroom, to sporting or community events - *everywhere* you go.

After six weeks, what will those potatoes be like? They will be turning to liquid, moldy, filled with fungus, smell nasty and just generally be horrible. Yet that is similar to what you are carrying around inside you!

All those hurts, resentments, anger, fears and patterns of the past sit inside you and rot away your soul. *You must drop your potatoes!* Forgive and move on. Those potatoes are taking up the space that light, hope and joy are meant to occupy! Do you really want moldy potatoes instead of light, hope and joy? It's your choice!

Life is full of lessons to *learn, unlearn and relearn*, (It's like FARC, UN-FARC and RE-FARC!) and the future is too full of exciting possibilities for us to waste our time focusing on those rotten potatoes. Carefully examine your thoughts. They can keep the old potatoes like negative stuff, destructive emotions and unhealthy patterns alive. *All of them come from the past and destroy the present.*

Your heart is wiser and wastes no time on the bitterness and disappointments generated by feeling a victim, having expectations, or selfish desires.

Instead of just hanging onto potatoes, we need to seek spiritual help, and *take responsibility* for ourselves and for what we have *created*. Find all the judgments, selfishness, greed, neediness, fears and anything else you are hanging onto from the past and let them go.

It will free you up, make you lighter, and allow you to see, or sense, the wonderful things that may be coming towards you from the future.

ENEMY #2:

Indifference – Letting Go Too Much, Giving Up

If you let go so much that you become indifferent, or just don't care for yourself, others or the effect you have on them, there is no "brotherly love" or connection to the whole. There is just self-centeredness and isolation.

To be indifferent is to "go to sleep" and separate ourselves. Separation is the opposite of equanimity. It robs us of equanimity. With indifference, we withdraw from the spiritual realms, people, life, and disconnect from the lessons available to us.

Indifference can be felt in many ways – maybe as numbness or as passive-aggressiveness and we allow those feelings to dominate our behavior. *"WhatEVER!"* is a disrespectful expression that's too common! The *tone of voice* in which it is usually expressed is derogatory, and often accompanied by someone walking away disconnecting, leaving everyone frustrated and hurt or angry.

There's no life force behind the words. The person has given up, separated, withdrawn or retreated into numbness. Indifference can kill your soul! *Everything you do, say and think has an impact on someone else, and the world.* You are not an island!

You Always Affect Others

You are, whether you accept it or not, intricately connected to everyone else and to the spiritual realms, so be considerate and conscious of your connections. Be aware of others around you. You are affecting them and they are affecting you.

A simple example of this can be seen in planes. Have you ever been trying to board when the plane is running late?

The flight attendants are constantly asking people to allow others to pass by, and yet, there are always those unconscious, indifferent souls who spend five minutes organizing themselves, while there are 200 people lined up behind them, waiting.

That person holding up all the others is not in a state of equanimity! They may be calm, but they are *unaware* of the distress or frustration they are causing. They are indifferent, and either don't care, or are unconscious of the inconvenience they are causing others.

Equanimity Is Very Active And Dynamic

Equanimity does not mean finding peace by being indifferent, separated, calm, bland or flat-lining all emotions! It is a very *active* state.

We can feel our emotions, but hopefully balance them with an *understanding* of the bigger scheme of things, which brings a sense of peace. *A sense of calm comes from knowing all is as it should be.*

From that state of wisdom, we feel brotherly love and compassion, and view things as they *really* are - not as we *perceive* them to be. We may feel very strongly about something, but we are conscious of not imposing our ideas on others. We allow them the freedom to make their own decisions and choices, *no matter how hard that is to watch.*

If we cling to the idea that others must do something because we think it is best for them, *we are taking their free will away,* and imposing ours on them. It is frustrating and disappointing for everyone.

So rather than becoming indifferent to (or separated from) what others do as a way to avoid our *own* disappointment, we need to accept that *they* are responsible for their own lives, directions and outcomes.

We maintain our relationship with them, and are still involved, but perhaps more in a supportive role, with patience and grace, *allowing them* to be in control of their journey.

ENEMY # 3:

Worrying And Rushing

Being caught in worry, anxiety, stress, fear and rushing is another way to destroy equanimity through separation. *These states all arise from our thoughts or judgments*, and would not appear if we remained connected to our Spirit and other people's hearts.

Rushing

In a blinding flash of the obvious I realized that one of the major things that disturbed my peace was rushing. Rushing is not the same as moving quickly! We can achieve a lot during the day by moving quickly *without* rushing or *feeling* rushed.

The minute I start to rush, I disconnect and focus solely on the panic rapidly rising in me that I will not be ready on time, or be at the place I need to be, or make an appointment on time - or whatever it might be.

Realizing that rushing was an issue for me was a great learning experience. Since then, I have made sure that I am organized, and the likelihood of last-minute changes or rushing is minimal. Life is much smoother and more pleasant.

I now try to catch myself as soon as the state of rushing sneaks up on me, I breathe and stop it! I change what I am saying to myself. I drop to my heart, relax, and find that the old adage, *"more haste, less speed"* is really true! What does rushing do to you?

Worry

There's a difference between worry and concern. When we worry, we either *can't* do anything about the situation, or *don't* do anything about it. We allow our thoughts to run round and round, creating *a cycle of stress and distress.*

Concern is knowing there's a problem, taking care of it, or doing what we can do, and *letting it go*; or just being conscious that the problem is there and *not worrying*. Concern isn't distressing, and it makes us aware and sensibly cautious. *Worry* is counter-productive and disturbs equanimity.

Did you know that Olympic and elite athletes spend about three hours a day mentally rehearsing? They not only train physically, they also mentally train by meditating and repeatedly imagining themselves performing perfectly.

They shoot perfect baskets or hurdle brilliantly or make perfect maneuvers time after time in their minds. As they do this, micro muscle movements occur and they unconsciously train their bodies physically to make perfect moves. *Vividly imagining what they want to have happen* - with sound, movement and feeling - facilitates their success.

Think about worry for a moment - what is it? Worry is vividly imagining what you *don't want to have happen* - usually in Technicolor, with surround sound! It's accompanied with all the feelings, horror and fears that you would have if the thing you're worrying about were *actually* happening*!*

If we know that vividly imagining what you *do* want to have happen *makes that significantly more likely to occur*, why would we think that vividly imagining what we *don't* want to have happen is different? Worry, in my opinion, is not only useless and a waste of time, but it may well be harmful!

Listen To What You Say To Yourself

It's very useful to be aware of what you say to yourself and have a series of optimistic thoughts to replace the stress creating thoughts of worry. Make a list of things you would rather program into your imagination and repeat or replay them often. This is yet another excellent example of FARC-ing! (To rewire your brain - Focus, Attention and awareness, Repetition and Celebration!)

If you are worried about exams, tests, interviews or a meeting, do the work you are supposed to do, and prepare appropriately instead of trapping yourself in negative, worrying thoughts and inaction.

Repeat (this takes an act of will) preferred sentences like, *"I am well-prepared."; "I have done the work. I will be breathing and calm."; "I am full of trust and faith that if I am meant to be in this job, I will."* or the many other statements you could make relevant to your situation.

Believe what you are saying - so make sure they are the truth! It's simple and easy to choose to make positive statements but very few people are aware of the destructive "criticizer" thoughts they need to replace.

Move to your heart where the wisdom lives. Your heart will guide you, banish worry, tell you what you need to do at that time, settle you down, put things in perspective, and bring equanimity.

ENEMY #4:

Stress

Sometimes we have to push ourselves to do things - which we can *perceive* as stressful.

But if we push ourselves and achieve a lot, we usually feel good at the end of the day. It may have been exhausting, but we feel we were productive. Allowing feelings or thoughts of stress to take over can paralyze us and we don't do anything.

If someone says, *"Don't stress about that"*, it doesn't mean, *"Don't do anything"!* Instead, it probably means *do something but stop stressing about it.* Remember, stress is a fact of life; it doesn't have to be a way of life!

The interesting thing about stress is that there can be situations that create physical stress, such as extreme cold, heat or poor health, but we rarely mean that when we say *"stress."* It's more common to use the word stress when we mean anxiety or tension. We say we are "stressed" when we are anxious, fearful, or out of balance - a *psychological* state that causes a *physiological* reaction.

In terms of psychology, there are no events, people or things that stress us! It's what we tell ourselves or imagine about the event that occurred, that creates the stress.

Stress comes from our perceptions, beliefs and expectations.

For example, imagine four women sitting in a house on a hill. They see a thunderstorm approaching. One woman loves thunderstorms and she is excited and can't wait for it to arrive. Her body releases *pleasurable* hormones and chemicals. Another woman is indifferent to thunderstorms, and her body chemistry stays the same.

The third woman is terrified of thunderstorms because one frightened her when she was a little girl. When she sees the storm, she panics and is filled with anxiety and fear. Her body is swarming with nasty stress hormones that make her feel terrible.

The fourth woman is concerned by the thunderstorm, assesses the potential danger and takes certain precautions and prepares wisely. She does what needs to be done and might push herself to do it, but all without stress.

Such different responses and outcomes from exactly the same event!

Can you see how the Neanderthal part of our brain can control us if we are not conscious of what is going on? AMMY (The Amygdala in our brains) takes over and we lose touch with reality. Instead, what we perceive, say to ourselves, and expect to happen, rules us.

If we perceive a storm as dangerous and scary, it will be for us! Others may see it as God putting on a fireworks display! If it really is a dangerous storm, a cautious, prudent person will review the situation, prepare, and deal with it.

Monitor your perceptions and thoughts - challenge those that cause stress or inaction. When we *allow* stress to rule our lives, we have little chance of finding equanimity.

ENEMY #5:

Extreme Emotions

There is a huge difference between negative emotions and intuition or "gut feelings". Reflect for a minute on the difference between an acute emotion like panic (which I usually feel in my chest) and a gut feeling.

Acute panic "*attacks*" us! Before we know it, we have stopped breathing, narrowed our focus and can only see our own perceived or real "danger" - we are totally unaware of anything else.

On the other hand, a "gut feeling" is more a quiet voice warning us that something somewhere is not right (or something *is* right!). *A gut feeling creates an awareness, or a conscious state in us,* putting us on alert, so we're not blindsided and can take appropriate action.

Wild Horses!

Extreme emotional states make it difficult to feel or find equanimity. While I was meditating on this chapter, this powerful image came to me: Negative emotions are like horses that gallop in, unseen or unnoticed by us, and somehow, these horses put us on their backs and ride away at high speed!

We are miles down the road, completely focused on hanging onto the wildly galloping horse, before we even know we are on a horse let alone, where we are! When we're in the state of equanimity, we see the "horse" and feel the emotion, but we *choose not to be swept up and carried away* - on the "galloping horse"!

We recognize *we have a choice.* We can be conscious of what is really happening and make wiser decisions. If we are in a position to *observe* what is happening, rather than unknowingly being carried away with the "horses of emotion," then we can take a deep breath, and "step outside" ourselves.

Observe, review the situation for what it really is, and then step back in, and participate in an appropriate way that brings peace, harmony or balance.

It's probably a fun exercise to start talking about the "horses of emotion" in your family - make it a routine dinner table discussion! *"Were you carried away by a horse of emotion today?"* You might be surprised at how many "teaching moments" emerge.

ENEMY #6:

Reacting Or Feeling?

Feelings are those inner "knowings" or "gut feelings" we have all had at some time in our lives. That sense of "I just *knew* it!". And we most likely did!

The heart is far more powerful than most of us imagine. *It is the source of our knowing.* If we learn to place our attention in our hearts and stay there for a while *before* our "horse of reaction" sends us off into negative emotions. If we see with the "eyes" of our heart, then every aspect of our lives would change.

The heart can be (if we are conscious) the balance point between our emotions and everything else that is happening - both in the cosmos and the rest of our world! It can give us insights, wisdom and guide us (with gut feelings) so we will *respond rather than react.*

Listen carefully for the guidance from our hearts and those gut feelings. They can be easily missed in the chaos of daily life - and certainly when that emotional horse is about to, or has, run away with us!

ENEMY #7:

Doubt And Fear

> *"Doubt makes the mountain which faith can move."*
> *Proverbs*

The English word doubt is derived from the Latin word duo, meaning two. Double originated from the same word as doubt. To doubt means to be double-minded. It can be useful or harmful. There's a big difference between the *pattern* of doubting everything and recognizing doubt as an *intermittent* warning sign.

If we are in the habit of never believing anything we hear or see, we are doomed to a life of rigidity, ignorance, fear, denial and suspicion.

If we unquestioningly believe everything we hear or learn, we are in danger of being led astray by doctrines that are false and potentially harmful, or overwhelmed by all the opposing conditions and information we discover.

And if we sit in the middle and never have the courage to make a choice, we are doomed to a life of indecision and procrastination! Imagine a line with doubt at one end and its opposite, certainty, at the other; the pivot point in the middle would be *faith* that comes through *the wisdom of the heart*.

Doubt is a part of life, and I believe it's often *an invitation to explore further,* rather than continuing on a particular path. *Certainty about everything blocks learning, as much as disbelieving everything does.* Neither provides the balanced view of wisdom.

I, and many friends of mine, have gone through our greatest growth periods after doubt crept - or swept - into our lives! The doubts may have been about our purpose in life, or the wisdom of a relationship or some choice we had made. They may have been about our chosen career or some other major life activity.

When we have a gut feeling that something is wrong - perhaps it's a sign *we don't have enough information for clear thinking*. Our guts cannot digest and make sense of what is going on. *Perceive doubts as an invitation to seek more information*, instead of ignoring, being paralyzed by or sneering at them.

The information you uncover through your heart will guide you to the right path, and may help you grow and develop as a spiritual human being. If you just stew in doubt, and walk around thinking and feeling, *"I don't know!"; "What if it isn't?"*, or *"What if it is?"*, you don't use your hearts wisdom, your will forces or courage to act on the *signal* doubt gives you.

This is a major cause for procrastination - rightly so in some cases. Action without adequate information may lead to unwise choices. But often our gut feelings are trying to warn us about something we are contemplating doing or being involved in, whether that's a relationship, a business venture or a life change. *The way we "hear" that warning is doubt.*

Many famous business leaders say they made their best decisions by *"following my gut feeling."*

How many times have you felt uneasy, doubtful, or uncertain about making a commitment to someone - personally or in business? If we ignore that warning, and try to rationalize or intellectualize the decision, we don't feel peace, *even though* the facts seem logical and sensible.

Your insides are screaming out at you, *"Don't do this!"* with the "language" of doubt! Remember my story of my first marriage? I knew I was doing the wrong thing. I *knew* it. But I didn't have the courage to stop the ceremony. I had doubts well before that day but didn't act on them.

Can you recall doing something you just knew was the wrong thing to do, yet you continued and it turned out a disaster? That can be the consequence of doubt ignored or unexplored! *When in doubt - ask questions!*

Faith And Trust

Doubt that denies, rejects or blocks belief or faith in the spiritual realms, the wisdom of nature and/or God, *in my opinion*, also blocks joy. Trust, faith, hearing our inner wisdom and living spiritually aware and connected are essential for equanimity.

We can have composure on our own, but true equanimity, the *deep peace that passes all understanding*, comes from connection to God, the spiritual realms and our higher selves.

Brenda, our wonderful next-door neighbor in Vermont, told me a story that epitomizes deep spiritual equanimity. Two of her nephews were riding snowmobiles on her father's property. They had a head-on crash in which one of them was critically injured.

He was not breathing when found, had skull and facial fractures, a compound fractured femur, and his right leg was almost severed above the knee. While waiting for the medical helicopter, Brenda was extremely upset and was comforting the sisters of one of the boys. In her words, while standing there, she heard God's voice say very clearly, *"Both boys are going to be fine."*

Immediately she was filled with an incredible sense of peace, and *knew* they would recover. She didn't know how it would happen, because the injuries were so bad, but *she had absolute faith it would happen.*

In intensive care, the family was told that because of the severity of his injuries and the time he would be in intensive care, he would develop infections, pneumonia and blood clots. *None of those things happened.* He had an extraordinary, rapid recovery and amazed everyone.

Instead of taking a year to be back to normal activities, it took four months! *That's the power of God in action – miracles* - He makes good out of terrible things, and Brenda's faith and trust helped.

Fear- The Opposite Of Faith And Joy

Fear (the opposite of faith) disrupts everything and prevents inner peace. If Brenda, a qualified nurse, had chosen to fear what was going to happen based on her past experiences in hospitals, her faith would have wavered. Instead, she chose to believe what she was told, even though she knew the injuries were life-threatening. Her faith sustained her family.

The choices we make - to bring the past into the present, to anticipate a repeat of a terrible pattern or expect something worse, or to listen to and believe the wisdom of the spiritual worlds will govern our fears and lives. Pay attention and follow the guidance you are given through listening, praying and holding faith – like Brenda did – and feel the calm.

We don't like change, even though it's constant and keeps our brains alert. We fear change because we don't know what will happen and we don't like uncertainty. *There is an infinite wisdom that does know.*

If we surrender to, receive and believe divine wisdom, it will guide us in divine timing to the deep peace of equanimity. Fear of uncertainty is just a fear of the future. What's the point? It's the future – we'll never know it in advance!

Fear hinders or overrides faith and the development of our capacity for equanimity. Fear paralyzes us and stops our life forces flowing. *Faith overcomes fear* - but we have to consciously hold that faith. Make a choice. Will you operate today from fear, or from faith and trust?

Meditation For Courage

Here is a meditation from Rudolf Steiner that may help you actually *feel* the presence of equanimity and understand it a bit better.

"We must eradicate from the soul all fear and terror of what comes towards us from the future;

We must look forward with absolute equanimity to whatever comes, and we must think only that whatever comes is given to us by a world direction full of wisdom.

It is part of what we must learn during this age, namely to act out of pure trust in the ever present help of the spiritual world; truly nothing else will do if our courage is not to fail us.

Therefore let us discipline our will and let us seek the awakening from within ourselves, every morning and every evening." 2

ENEMY #8:

The Cycles

Another friend of mine became paralyzed with fear when she started doubting her chosen career. She was in a great job, the company loved what she did, and she was very successful, yet she was plagued by doubts about whether she wanted to be a lawyer.

That expanded into doubt and negative emotions about who she was, what the company thought of her, and what she wanted to do with her life.

Her gut sent her signals that she was not meant to be in that profession – through gut feelings felt as doubt. But instead of exploring that and all the consequences with equanimity (i.e. through her heart), her doubts and fear took control!

She was comparing herself negatively with what she *perceived* to be more experienced, professional peers, and others in her personal life. This led to a cycle of negative thoughts, but not action. *Comparisons destroy contentment!* She found herself depressed, anxious and unhappy. *Doubt is your signal to take action* – to go on a journey of inner exploration.

We can be conscious of doubt and then freeze with fear, *rather than exploring the cause or source* of the doubt. Of course, when this is happening to *us*, it's not at all obvious!

We just feel stuck, worried, depressed, anxious or stressed.

We don't even realize that we have tapes playing the same negative, fear-inspiring junk over and over! *We have to stop the cycle!* Recent research even shows these negative loops in our brain circuitry. The loops *actually give our brains a serotonin reward* if we repeat the negative behavior, so we really need to *consciously* act with our will – use will power - to stop the cycles.

Awareness, breathing and exercise are critical to help us break those loops. As well as *stopping the negative thought cycle* and tapping into our hearts. Be conscious that a "horse" of fear and anxiety has run away with you. See the "horse" for what it is, and make conscious decisions to stop, breathe and listen to your hearts guidance.

Confusion takes over when we are not in the flow of listening to our hearts, often because we are not doing what we are supposed to, or we don't have enough information.

Do Something!

The minute you are aware that you're trapped within your negative self-talk cycle (when you have given into fear, depression or anxiety) - you must *do something!*

Go for a run, or exercise until you are so absorbed that you can't think any more (after checking with a doctor!). Listen to uplifting music or read uplifting books or meditate. Do some housework, or best of all, *volunteer* or *be of service.*

When we help others consciously, serving them, we often feel better because it takes our minds off ourselves. It puts our needs in proper perspective. When you are in your heart, being of service, you may find some truth about what is going on will emerge. You'll have a sense of equanimity gently flow through you - often without even knowing it.

Serve others enthusiastically!

At the end of the time of serving others, your soul is lighter. A miracle has happened! You feel at peace, more joyful and have a sense of what will help your situation. Remember, miracles happen in the heart all the time!

I believe everyone needs to work in some form of service to others for at least a few days every year! Our world would transform. If you go home consumed by all your own problems or if you don't feel joyful for the blessings in your life, including all the struggles, doubts, difficulties, then spend more time in service!

Working in hospitals helped me learn that lesson early in my career. It was a real blessing and helped me develop empathy.

Once we realize there are messages from our hearts and guts and we listen for them, we need to *act* on them. Have the courage to explore the questions that are arising from that doubt, and have *more courage* to accept the answers. *Doubt can be a doorway to inner peace and wisdom – step through that doorway!*

ENEMY #9:

Selfishness

> *"The great danger for family life, in the midst of any society*
> *whose idols are pleasure, comfort and independence,*
> *lies in the fact that people close their hearts and become selfish."*
> *Pope John Paul II*

Extremely selfish people have a sense of themselves *only*; or worse, they have a very good sense of others yet manipulate the situation to achieve their own goals. Selfishness leads to separation - either from others or the spiritual realms.

On the other hand, people who believe they are unimportant and don't matter, are *separated from themselves,* and therefore separated from their Spirit and others.

To find the balance, we need to develop *a true sense of ourselves, and a sense of community* - to recognize that we are always an integral part of a community, of the whole. *We are individuals and* part of the whole at the same time. Losing sight of either one of those blocks our capacity for equanimity.

The critical factor here is *disregard for others*, or disregard for *yourself.* To have regard for someone means to *respect or honor them*, or see them with your heart. Selfishness or extreme self*less*ness are all about dishonoring, disrespecting and closing our hearts "eyes and ears."

Brotherly Love – We Are All One

"The firm basis of all spiritual power is equanimity, quietude is a very positive state; an active peace, contagious, powerful, which controls and calms, which puts everything in order, organizes…. True quietude is a very great force, a very great strength. Calmness belongs to the strong." [3]
Sri Arubindo and the Mother

I woke up one morning with the thought that equanimity results in brotherly love. I had no idea what that meant! So I started investigating. Did you know that the Greek word for brotherly love is Philadelphia and it's mentioned in Revelations in the Bible? I didn't!

John tells us in the Bible (John 4:12 4) that if we love one another, God abides in us and His love is perfected. *How we physically and emotionally treat others is basically how we are choosing to treat God/our own divinity/ our higher selves.* What are you choosing?

Brotherly love (I was not told "sisterly love" so am using the term "brotherly" as a generic one!) is demonstrated when we are conscious enough to see the *true* spiritual being in everyone we meet - our "brothers" - and that we really *are* all one – bothers and sisters. It's a pretty big concept!

I can only imagine that if we make even teeny little steps in the direction of unconditional or brotherly love, we will be doing very well in our spiritual growth!

Any movement away from judgment, and towards truly seeing others in their magnificence, realizing that we all have a Divine spark inside us, brings us closer to equanimity and *real* brotherly love.

HOW TO FIND EQUANIMITY?

My friend Kathy is my model for equanimity and "brotherly" – or sisterly - love! She is very, wise, calm, patient, optimistic and encouraging; she is highly conscious, intuitive, spiritual, kind and sees the potential in all people – and *holds* it for them.

She *nourishes* the unfolding of that potential - *in the other person's time frame!* She still feels what most of us feel - but the horses of emotion *never* carry her away. Being around Kathy is what I imagine a flower would feel like when it is planted in fertile soil - she is like the fertile soil, rain and sunshine that allows the flower to blossom.

And at the same time Kathy takes good care of, and makes some time for, herself. She rarely rushes and is never is a state of stressed chaos, despite having a million things to do. There is a sense of grounded-ness with her and just having her in the room makes me feel calm and peaceful!

Do you know anyone like that? Hang around them - a lot! Kathy is our role model in this section. I have listed what we need to do, and then how Kathy applies that in everyday life. Pattern your lives in a similar manner and your life will flow with equanimity and joy.

Use Your Gifts

Aim to live in a state of *true understanding, consciousness and awareness.* Our work as humans is to develop and grow spiritually, to be actively using our gifts to fulfill our purpose in life and to do what we are meant to be doing - while still contributing positively to others. That contribution might be to accept and support others in what they do, or to love them *despite* what they do or think.

Take some time now to identify, and use, the gifts you have been given. If you don't know, ask your best friends (who love and accept you) what they think your spiritual gifts are.

What Would Kathy Do?

Kathy's accurate insights and perceptions of her own gifts, allows her to sense the difficulties others face in their lives.

One of her gifts is the ability to gently offer – in perfect timing - subtle suggestions to share an alternative approach or thought, for us to look at it - if we choose. Her suggestions shine a light on what we could be doing - but she is truly not attached to us following her suggestion!

Mary, another mentor, is also brilliant at that! I, on the other hand, am very good at offering advice and trying to fix your life! You don't even have to ask for it! It's one of my special talents that requires changing!

If we see a need and try to help or fix things *without* being asked, it can be detrimental for others and /or our relationship. Instead we need to listen for, or recognize requests for assistance - direct or subtle.

Our opinions and advice are generally not what people want to hear, even if they are great ideas! The way I offer them is not so much of an invitation, as a strong suggestion! And yes, I have asked Kathy and Mary to coach me! I am also learning offer help *with no attachment* - and *only* when I am asked in some way!

Instead of feeling excited because I believe I know what will work for someone else and expecting them to do it, I am working at letting

go and giving freely, *when asked*. No strings! And on fixing *only* me, and doing what *I* am meant to be doing, or being.

We are all works in progress – but it took me a long time to realize I am in charge *only* of my own progress - *not* every one else's!

OBSERVE, DON'T JUDGE

Judging others is an entrenched pattern in most of us! We must avoid judging others, or breaking our relationship with them if *they* don't do what *we* think is right for them, or what we want them to do. *To love someone without judgment, takes acceptance, constant consciousness and observation of our thoughts.* We are supposed to love them no matter what they do or *don't do*.

I can recall many situations in my life where everything would have been transformed if I had the courage, capacity and will to love with *brotherly* love; to treat the other as a special, wise spiritual being; to stay connected and to allow their own wisdom to unfold instead of pushing *my fix* on them!

What Would Kathy Do?

Kathy's favorite saying is, *"Observe - don't judge."* She would observe, wait patiently for a feeling to unfold, "drop" to her heart, sense what it tells her to do, and then she would respond - not react!

I, on the other hand, am often quick to process (not necessarily accurate but quick!); sum things up; decide on a course of action and immediately embark on it. Only afterwards do I sometimes see the chaos I caused, and drama I created!

If I had been seeing though my heart like Kathy, I would have avoided a great deal of stress - for me and everyone else! Imagine what it would be like *if we had compassion and patience for everyone, and could give them grace, or at the very least understanding, rather than judgment.*

SEE YOURSELF AS YOU REALLY ARE

If we can see and accept ourselves as we truly are, then we allow those around us the freedom to be who they really are, and brotherly love or a sense of oneness emerges.

Larry Byram, founder of *Higher Alignment* suggests that once we can see ourselves clearly, we can stop projecting onto everyone else, and see them as they really are!

What would life be like if we felt safe, secure and loved as ourselves! If we *really* understood who we are, we could free ourselves to focus on helping others see their own beauty. Larry also says, *"When we know our own goodness, we allow others to connect with theirs."*

Who do you know, love and totally accept despite all that you know about them? How do you treat them? Can you treat others more like this? *Will you?* Who truly knows you, loves you and totally accepts you?

What Would Kathy Do?

Kathy would create a situation in which a person feels great about him - or herself. She already sees herself very clearly, knows herself well and feels good about what she sees! From that place of equanimity, she can find the real beauty in others, *even if they can't see it themselves, and she can be gracious with them, because she can give herself grace.*

Are you a "projector"? Do you routinely project your stuff onto others? *Or do others feel good about themselves around you? Do* you bring out the best in others? *Do you help others to see the "astonishing light" that is inside them?*

Now is a great time to start accepting yourself. From that place, accepting others is easy!

John Gottman, an expert on relationships who runs the "love lab" at Washington State University, says that the *"paradox of relationships is that people change when they feel accepted for who they are."* I would add to that, when they *feel loved* for who they are, *despite* their behaviors and beliefs.

FILTER EVERYTHING THROUGH A PURE HEART

If we filtered everything through the wisdom of our hearts before we acted or spoke, our lives would be transformed. *The heart is the seat of equanimity.*

How do we filter everything? It's pretty simple: Make a conscious effort *to place your attention, an issue or people into your heart and hold them there* until you "hear" from your heart what to do, or not do. You may have unconsciously already experienced the *seemingly insignificant but very powerful work* of holding people in your heart, allowing the heart to work it's magic! It's not always easy, but it is very simple!

Our hearts are the connection – the portal - between the spiritual worlds and us. The wisdom of the spiritual worlds can be perceived and understood by our hearts, so our *pure* heart will always receive the right answer! When we make judgments, we have answers as well, but rarely the right ones!

Our job is to listen to and trust our heart for information about what is going on, what we need to do, and *wait* for it to tell us how we can behave or contribute. Interestingly, that behavior may be to cheerfully wait, with a good attitude, patience and equanimity, and feel confident that something good will emerge!

What Would Kathy Do?

As soon as Kathy hears something that is likely to, or starts to trigger a reaction, she uses the "drop to your heart technique!" I have been doing this consciously since the Sacred Service class, but to catch yourself in time, just before you are about to react, takes dedication and attention!

It involves "hovering" above the situation for a fraction of a second, seeing what is going on, stopping, breathing, taking the issue to your heart, listening carefully for guidance and then responding - all in a couple of seconds! When I can do it, it works very well!

The process of dropping to my heart only takes a second, and after a few more seconds in the heart, everything takes on a different perspective.... *but it does take consciousness and discipline to do it. It's much easier to explode!*

We have to stay very aware of our instant reactions and once we notice them, use our will forces to say, *"Stop! Drop to my heart and wait."* And we need to *breathe* as we do it. A lot! Try this next time you are about to snap back at someone; you might be surprised at how well things work out.

HAVE FAITH, TRUST AND COURAGE

Believe, and have faith that something full of love and wisdom, bigger than we can imagine, has a plan for us spanning a far longer period than we can comprehend. This plan can bring us more joy than we can imagine. We just need to *be receptive* and allow it!

What if we woke up every morning and said, *"I will. I will to do Thy will,"* and listened for what that was. Then had the desire, courage, capacity and will to hold fast to that faith, trust and inspiration. How different life would be if we could see the whole picture and not just our tiny little lives!

Have you ever reached a point where you exhausted yourself trying to fix everything for everyone and could do no more; or you spent days

caught in negative thoughts going round and round, and finally gave up! And sure enough, when you let go, and allowed that infinite love and wisdom to step in and handle everything, it all worked out!

How many times have you limped through a life crisis, wondering why it is happening to you and feeling sorry for yourself, only to have insight several months or years later as to what was really going on? Suddenly, in a "blinding flash of insight", you suddenly understood why that happened!

Be courageous and know that we generally have no clue of what is really going on, but things happen for a reason! If we tune in and pay attention, and accept that what is happening has a purpose, we may see glimpses of the phenomenal wisdom that is all around us, always.

In the Bible, wisdom is called Sophia. Let her guide you. Have faith that wisdom will work things out for the best. Listen for what you are guided to do, and do it!

What Would Kathy Do?

Kathy finds a lot of things *"interesting"!* Instead of an immediate panic reaction, she says to herself,

"Interesting. I wonder what is really going on here? What's this really about? What is trying to emerge, arrive or unfold?"

Robert Sardello also has a wonderful way of reframing everything as "interesting"! Just that single change can transform any situation, especially a potentially explosive one! It instantly transports you into a curious observer position.

I have actually taught something similar for many years with this example: How many times has something happened, or a phone call has come in with bad news, and your immediate, visceral response is, *"Oh, no!"*

As soon as we shout out loud or silently *"Oh, no!"*, a panic message is sent out to all our glands, and we immediately release all sorts of stress chemicals that destroy any physiological calm we may have had.

If we instead think to ourselves, *"Oh, that's interesting."* or *"Okay, this is going to be an adventure!"*, or *"Hmmmm, I wonder what is really going on here!"* a completely different reaction occurs in the body. There is no flood of adrenalin or cortisol, and *we can calmly continue with curiosity as an interested observer!* An added plus is that we keep breathing!

Kathy also uses the phrase, *"Oh, well…it will all work out."* That type of response also creates a very different state in our bodies - one of serenity as opposed to immediate fear or panic about what may or may not happen.

It takes will *forces* (our part – we all have free will) and blessings (God's part!) to behave in these ways, and will power and blessings to maintain a *cheerful sense of certainty* that things will actually work out. *Many of the activities in this book are a new form of exercise for our wills.*

We have different exercises for different muscle groups, and in the same way, we need different exercises to target specific aspects of our will not already developed. To build will forces requires discipline.

It takes commitment, effort and courage to hold onto faith, be in our hearts, be cheerful, optimistic and hopeful at times of stress or difficulty - in other words, to be in a state of equanimity - but it's worth it!

With faith, trust, courage and blessings, take life as it comes. Say, *"Oh, that's interesting! or "This is an adventure or mystery. I wonder what is really going on here? What is trying to emerge? What is the wisdom behind this? What is the big picture? What is my role?"*

Or simply repeat, *"It will all work out,"* instead of screaming in panic and running headlong into drama! Easy!

LIVE IN HARMONY WITH THE RHYTHMS OF NATURE

When we feel well, care for ourselves and have reserves of love and energy from which we can draw to give to others, we are more joyful.

If we live life in harmony with the rhythms of nature that surround us, and create rhythms in our own lives that ground us, returning us to our heart center - we develop the capacity of equanimity.

Rhythms or rituals can be something simple like having dinner together as a family; little rituals of connection such as greeting each other with special kisses and hugs; taking walks in nature regularly; having weekly special baths; cleaning your face in a special way that nourishes you; reading inspirational material daily; or praying or meditating in a *regular* pattern.

The earth and every aspect of our human bodies are affected by the rhythms and cycles of the planets, cosmos, nature and seasons, to name only a few. Think of all the systems in nature that have rhythms and cycles – tides, sunrises, sunsets, the seasons, mating in animals, plants and their life cycles - *everything in nature has a rhythm!*

And we are part of that whole - our own bodies have cycles - women have menstrual cycles, men have hormonal cycles too; we even have circadian rhythms which create optimal times of the day when our remedies or drugs will work more effectively amongst other things.

I could go on for pages! The point is that we are governed and surrounded by rhythms, and *if* we are in tune with them, and create rituals to flow in harmony with nature's rhythms, we can be joyful, energized, composed and life is easier.

What Would Kathy Do?

Kathy has her own inner state of rhythm. Tuned in and very sensitive to her surroundings, she is acutely aware of the importance of rhythms and rituals. She meditates daily and regularly *makes time to do restorative and renewing activities.*

Create your own routines and be conscious of nature's rhythms around you. Be active, dynamic and renew yourself in spring; enjoy the warmth of summer; shed the old in autumn; contract and build life forces in winter - only to blossom and bloom again in spring!

TAKE RESPONSIBILITY AND LIVE WITH INTEGRITY

Imagine what life would be like if we all *truly* accepted responsibility for our own actions and behaviors; for the state of our lives; for our choices and decisions; and we allowed other adults the freedom to make their own choices, *without judgment* from us.

If we continued to love others *even though* they made choices with which we did not agree, or condone. We may not approve or like what happened, but we could maintain our relationship with them. We would all be a lot more joyful!

To operate with this responsibility requires great maturity, equanimity and a much higher understanding of what really goes on in our world - *knowing that what we actually perceive is just a tiny fraction of what there is to see.*

Very few people *really* take responsibility for themselves, their actions and lives. They *blame* their parents, circumstances, teachers, siblings, the state, the government, and even the weather. You name it, they blame it! *Stop all blame now!*

Blame, defensiveness and equanimity *cannot* co-exist. If you are blaming others or being defensive - look long and carefully at what you *perceive* to be going on. Do you really think others intended to do – or actually did - *what you think or tell yourself* they did? Be aware of what is going on *inside you.*

Did they *want* to harm you? Was it *really* an attack on you? Did they know what they were doing? Did they destroy something for you *on purpose*? If they did, it's an opportunity for forgiveness! If not, it's a great chance for self understanding and insight, which will change your perception and what you habitually say to yourself.

And then look longer and more carefully at yourself! Did you do *everything* that you could possibly have done, with courage, integrity and honesty, to create a different scenario? If you did the best you could, given your level of skills and knowledge, you can hold your head up high, so to speak, and there is no need for blame.

You know you did your best, and you can, with composure, face what you need to face. If there was something more you could have done, learn from your mistakes, change your perception, understand, take responsibility and move on.

What Would Kathy Do?

If you tell Kathy something in confidence, you know that no one - no one - will ever hear it from her. Not even her husband! Her integrity is impeccable. How is your integrity?

Kathy is also a master at knowing what her responsibility is and taking action on it, and *knowing clearly when responsibility lies with others.* In that case, she lets them be responsible! And she stays in harmony, no matter what they do.

Gossip is not a responsible, compassionate, worthy or useful way to spend time. Do you take responsibility for what comes out of your mouth? No one else can be blamed for that! *Making the decision to think only kind or positive thoughts is your responsibility!* If you can walk around knowing that you have thought or said nothing detrimental, harmful, unkind or negative, your path to equanimity will be faster.

Take some time to recognize *patterns* of blaming, defensiveness or reacting that have been created in your past. As you do this, you may be given different insights, which will allow you to change the patterns of behavior.

Do you do the "right" thing - even when no one is looking?
Do you put grocery carts away even if they are not yours?
Do you pick up clothes that fall to the floor in a store?
Do you avoid parking in disabled car spaces?
Do you always put money in parking meters?
Do you keep your commitments?

I am pretty good at doing all those things - although I've been much better since I met my husband. (I never did park in handicapped spots, though!)

Our lives would be without guilt, defensiveness or fear of blame and accusations if we always did the responsible, *kind* or right thing; if we lived with integrity, stayed connected to our hearts and stayed consciously aware of the larger whole - of which *we are an integral and important part.*

BE RECEPTIVE AND OPEN TO WHAT IS EMERGING

Most of us are unconscious of what is *really* going on around us, within us and the connection between the two; the spiritual currents, the nonverbal messages, the elements of nature or the influence of *everything* in the invisible, quantum soup in which we live.

We are unaware of the grand plans of the spiritual wisdom that is operating. *Be open* to the possibility that in every minute, spiritual elements are involved in forming us, our circumstances and shaping the world around us. *We need to be interested and diligent observers*, and at the same time, *actively involved* in what is going on and making our contribution; to be *receptive and* open.

When we are separate from the whole, totally absorbed with ourselves, defending ourselves, judging, full of fear, living in the past, worrying about the future, or rushing we can't be receptive or peaceful!

We need to be fully present and mindful every minute of our lives. What does that mean? It means we are in our hearts, fully conscious of the other person or people, the environment and situation; free of any self-centered thoughts, worries or emotions about anything else; free of judgments, comparisons or idle chatter, and we are truly "with" whatever is going on.

Haven't you met people who listen to you in a way in which you feel really heard? You feel like they understand and care about you. *You feel good around them.* These are present people. Being present is being receptive. Being mindful is being present with your body, mind and spirit.

When we are present (or receptive), we are open to what is there in the moment; we observe with interest *all* levels of communication and activity going on; we look to see what might be unfolding and what might *really* be emerging.

We are interacting with others - but there is a part of us that is aware of the bigger picture and greater activity. *Our perception and understanding are enhanced.*

What Would Kathy Do?

All of the above! She has an incredible capacity for being present, patient, open, receptive, and observant - at all levels. You would swear she is totally involved in her every conversation and she is - and at the same time, she is aware and conscious of the greater spiritual activity that is going on. She really understands. *Really!*

Kathy is so present that she can sense when the other person is not.

When she is saying something important that she really wants the other person to hear - and she has done this with me - she will hold their arms gently and look directly into their eyes.

She then repeats herself, making sure that the listener *really heard, absorbed, and received the meaning* and impact of the words she used! It's very powerful. Of course, this has to be done with love and wisdom! We can't just grab someone and shout, *"Listen to me - this is important!"*

Really effective communication involves looking directly into the eyes of the person we are speaking with; being sure we have their attention, love in our hearts, and then speak directly from our hearts to theirs - via their eyes!

Kathy actively *looks for what is emerging* in a conversation - and deals with that core issue. You must have the intention of being receptive and open to anything that unfolds, *actively seeking to understand the other person,* and having the courage to trust that you will be able to tap into your heart, and deal with whatever happens.

It's also important to be *discerning* about what you are being receptive to, and act on your *inspired* intuition! A pure heart will only allow beneficial information in. It's very important to filter what we sense through a pure heart and if doubt arises, your heart is probably saying, *"Check this out further!"*

BE CONTENT AND CHOOSE YOUR FEELINGS

Have you ever been truly content and serene? I can only remember one moment in my life - I am sure there were more but I can only remember this one - of true contentment, absolute serenity, and I suspect, equanimity. I was babysitting my adored Thomas and Clelia when they were about five and three.

It was bath time and while my nephew kept splashing, I had Clelia in my lap bundled up in a towel. I sat on the side of the bath, and a silence surrounded us. Clelia stopped squirming and my little nephew even stopped splashing, as time seemed to stop.

Believe Everything Is Just As It Should Be

In that moment, every cell in my body knew - just knew - that everything was as it should be. *All in the world was perfect, and I felt absolute peace and contentment.* It was a fabulous experience. It lasted about 20 seconds and years at the same time! And soon we were back to splashing and laughing and running about - but I know *we all felt it*.

In my thinking, serenity and contentment go hand in hand. Are you content with your "lot" right now? And if not, *what is blocking your contentment?* Hint: it's usually what you are *saying to yourself, comparisons* and the way you are *choosing to see the world*.

What can you do about it? If it's a *person* disrupting your peace, then are you allowing someone else to influence your emotions and state? Ultimately – *only you control how you react* – or respond - *to your emotions and people!*

Contrary to most psychological thinking and the children's song, *"Sticks and stones will hurt my bones, but names can never hurt me,"* I believe people can emotionally hurt us – *it's up to us whether we allow it to damage us, or not*. When people are emotionally or verbally abusive, cruel, alcohol affected, manipulative or just moody, they do hurt our emotional body. Physical violence hurts both physical and emotional bodies.

When anyone "hits" us in our emotional body, we can literally feel it. To deal with the pain, we have the capacity to *forgive* and move on, or do something about it. We can tell them what they did made us angry or upset. If that was their intention, we need to set boundaries and ask them not do it again.

If it was unintentional, we can communicate that it hurt, ask them to be more careful in the future and set boundaries. If there is nothing we can do, we can pray for grace, wisdom to know what to do and the strength to forgive and move on.

We are in control of whether we hang onto this hurt and pain in our emotional bodies, and allow it to affect the rest of our lives - or not. *We can* remove the cellular memories but it takes work!

Remember - many events are not emotionally stressful, but what we *tell ourselves about them* makes them either stressful or not. It's like the thunderstorm approaching the house. So who is in control of your emotions? Long-term, and short-term..........you! You might think, "This situation is making me crazy," but really, it is your *interpretation and reaction* that is driving you nuts!

Take responsibility for your emotions and state of mind. Then take action to *do something different:* Remove yourself, change what you say to yourself about it, or go to your heart to seek help.

Examine why you are emotional and see if you can resolve what is causing it - *find the root of your discontent*. It will probably be a fear, habit, pattern or something you have been hanging onto, not something outside you!

Control, Desire And Comparisons – FOMO!

One of the biggest enemies of equanimity is when we compare our lives with others. A nurse called it FOMO! Fear Of Missing Out! How true is that.

Materialism is rampant and most people seem to want more of everything - *more* money, fame, power, control, possessions, clothes, and so on. What happened to the simple life, where we were not consumed by material desires?

Isn't it interesting how the word *"consumerism"* is so common these days? In the simple life, we had only one television (GASP!); or we had only one phone, computer, one car or maybe two modest cars. Being overtaken by desires always leads to imbalance, misery and often to financial hardship.

What We *Really* Want

We all yearn for connection to something greater than us. We may not realize this spiritual yearning, but deep inside our hearts, we yearn for that connection. It manifests as a sense of, *"There must be something more than this to life,"* or *"Is this all there is?"*

This yearning is often misinterpreted as a *desire for some "thing" or person*, so we try to accumulate as much as we can - money, power, fame, sex, stuff and relationships.

hug the load..

Loneliness is at epidemic levels in the Western world and we believe that loneliness and isolation cause disease. One recent poll reported that 4 in 10 Americans admit to frequent feelings of "intense loneliness". When life was simpler, we recognized our desire was for a *connection*, spiritually, with ourselves, and our families.

We spent more time with our families and connected more with them. We used to be more involved in our communities and loneliness was not as common as it is now. We had more communication *face to face* and our children did not stare at tiny little screens, texting or shooting or competing while disconnecting completely from anyone around them.

We weren't addicted to computers and television. Our attention spans were longer than a gnat on speed! We had fewer people living alone and more multigenerational families. We grew our own food, cooked more meals, and had fresh instead of processed foods every day.

Meals were a connection time - not a series of staged, micro waved meals eaten on the run. We were, in short, physically, emotionally and spiritually healthier and more content with our circumstances - more joyful!

We didn't always want more or bigger or better - all of which come from comparing what we have with what others have. Even if it is happiness or joy! *Once we have compared, then we complain, because we perceive someone has what we want!* Remember – *we do not see reality* – we *perceive and judge.* We never really know how life is for someone else – it's only what we imagine!

Stop comparing and complaining, and start making changes that will bring you joy: Take responsibility, pray, accept what you have, be grateful for it, make the best of it, and do the best you can. Be sincerely happy for others, reconnect with God, yourself and others, and you will be on your way to contentment and joy.

What Would Kathy Do?

I don't know that I have ever heard my friend Kathy complain. In all the time I have known her, she has never complained about anything. She might mention things with which she is dissatisfied, but in the same breath, she talks about what she is doing about it.

Her life hasn't been especially easy and it is not perfect yet, but she is content with what she has and does. She has worked very hard for a long time, and now is making changes to allow a more relaxed lifestyle. *She is active in creating her contentment.*

She makes the best of, and *searches for the best* in, every situation, no matter what it is. I have never heard Kathy compare herself with anyone either! I remember my Mama telling me when I was small, *"Comparisons are odious, darling!"*

Of course I had to ask her what that meant - but the phrase certainly stuck! Free yourself from comparisons, coveting, complaining and find contentment and serenity! This poem, *"The, Paradoxical, Commandments"* is from *"Anyway"* by Dr. Kent M. Keith.

I thought it was a great way to finish a section on how to find equanimity and he graciously gave me permission to use it!

"People are illogical, unreasonable, and self-centered. Love them anyway.

If you do good, people will accuse you of selfish ulterior motives. Do good anyway.

If you are successful, you will win false friends and true enemies. Succeed anyway.

The good you do today will be forgotten tomorrow. Do good anyway.

Honesty and frankness make you vulnerable. Be honest and frank anyway.

The biggest men and women with the biggest ideas, can be shot down by the smallest men and women with the smallest minds. Think big anyway.

People favor underdogs but follow only top dogs. Fight for a few underdogs anyway.

What you spend years building may be destroyed overnight. Build anyway.

People really need help but may attack you if you do help them. Help people anyway.

Give the world the best you have and you'll get kicked in the teeth. Give the world the best you have anyway" [5]

EQUANIMITY JOY-ERCISE 1: PRACTICE CONNECTING TO AND HEARING GOD'S LAUGHTER

> *"Hafiz tells us that the Beloved's nature is pure joy,*
> *the closer we come to him,*
> *the more we are able to hear and feel God's laughter.*
> *The rhythm of his laughter is the music of the dance of life.*
> *That music is the essence of love and it is the radiant core of every song of Hafiz.*
> *I am happy even before I have a reason."* [6]
> *Daniel Ladinsky*

If *God's nature is pure joy - so is yours!* We are all parts of the hologram and have God within us, so today is the day you feel joy "before you have a reason!"

Let laughter flow freely. Pray before you climb out of bed and ask what your mission is for today! Then do it!

Be joyful just because you are (hopefully by now,) more connected to yourself and through your heart, to your Higher Self. Recognize the yearning or longing that has been in your heart for what it truly is - *yearning for connection to your Spirit and the Divine.*

Today – *make that connection.* Look for moments to do that - through children, your family, strangers, nature or service. Create, look for, and find joyful moments all day.

Make others smile, acknowledge them, accept them, laugh, let go and lighten up! Skip, play, dance and sing for no reason. Ignore the judgments of others. Do stuff you love to do!

Be kind, loving, gentle and helpful. Visit friends, hug someone, tell them you love them, and be grateful for everything. Go to bed, grateful for all that happened, and assess if you did your best today. If you could have done better - ask for another chance and help tomorrow. Bathe in Divine support, safety and love as you go to sleep!

EQUANIMITY JOY-ERCISE 2: PRACTICE BEING RESPONSIBLE FOR YOU CIRCUMSTANCES AND FEELINGS – CHOOSE PEACE

"First, keep the peace within yourself,
then you can also bring peace to others."
Thomas A Kempis

Explore your life today. *Be conscious of what you feel,* what you are doing, and your motives. Are you taking responsibility for how you feel, what you do and what you say? Have you given responsibility for yourself or aspects of your life to others? Are you expecting others to make you feel better or good about yourself? You may be disappointed if that is the case!

Are you trying to manipulate a situation or others into doing things differently, or being different to suit your own needs and not theirs? Are you taking responsibility for another's life and conditions without being asked to help? Is it appropriate? Is this your job....really?

For a completely different perspective on why others are behaving as they are, think of a person you dislike intensely and put yourself in his or her shoes for today! Well, for an hour at least anyway! If you do this sincerely, you may have a new way of understanding them, and feel peaceful around them instead of wanting to stab them!

If you are not happy with your job, your relationship, or any aspect of your life, *take charge of your contribution to, and participation in, this* situation, and what you say to yourself about it - your story. Be very responsible with this exploration!

Eliminate comparisons, be generous, be happy for others and share freely. Are you happy with what you have? You might as well be, since it's what you have! And it is what it is!

You may desire more in your life, or a change, but examine your desires. If they are all material - beware! If they are all centered on subjects such as, *"I want more money, a bigger house, a better car, more clothes, more power, more prestige, more things"* - be very careful and explore a little deeper.

If your desires are centered around, *"I want to serve and contribute more and be on purpose, following the divine plan for my life,"* then you are on track! And money will flow to you - the more you give, the more comes towards you. *The more generous you are with your spirit and your possessions, the more contentment you will find.*

If you find yourself rushing, worrying or stressed - *stop, take a breath, drop to your heart,* and stop the negative loop in your mind. Meditate, look at funny photos, breathe, exercise or do something that you know will help you calm down.

Also today be *aware of negative emotions* and any horses of emotion that are galloping around trying to carry you away. If you realize you are on a horse - immediately climb off and take charge of your emotional state! *Whatever mood you are in, you are in control of it.*

Choose to *connect with your spiritual self today* and you will be composed and peaceful in every situation. This could be a joy filled day! Your aim is to feel content and peaceful the whole day.

EQUANIMITY JOY-ERCISE 3: PRACTICE KNOWING THE SPIRITUAL WORLD IS HERE – EVERYWHERE – NOW!

Angels, ancestors, fairies, elemental beings, tree spirits and animal spirits are everywhere. Invite them to speak to you today! *Your mission is to have faith and trust that everything in your life is touched, and orchestrated to some degree, by the Divine.* Be discerning and beware of unfounded, damaging skepticism stealing your receptivity!

Examine from, and with, your heart all that is happening to you; all the dilemmas, difficulties, pain, good things, uncertainties and see if you can find a bigger picture.

Is there a reason this may be happening? Is there a *lesson* you need to be learning that you are currently not appreciating?

There is a higher wisdom and a bigger plan than you can comprehend. You may not understand, but still make sure you are doing what you are supposed to be doing to progress. Ask that higher wisdom if you are on the right path.

If you can't think of anything you are meant to be doing or learning, then *ask for guidance.* It takes an act of will and a lot of practice to go to your heart and *stay there at all times.*

Most of us just wander around, *unconscious* of our stories, fears and judgments. We need to *wake up and remember to stay in our hearts* - or visit them as often as possible. We are in connection with the spiritual worlds - even if we don't know it! *Our hearts are the portals through to the spiritual world.* That's why the heart is so important for us to reconnect with ourselves, God and others.

Be *patient*, as it may take longer for the spiritual world to bring you *what you need than you would like.* Although sometimes it happens suddenly! So talk to your wise helpers, be patient and *look for the inspiration* that is always there for you.

EQUANIMITY JOY-ERCISE 4: BROTHERLY LOVE

Observe; don't judge; love instead. This is your mantra for today. If you find yourself judging, ask, *"Am I perfect yet? Am I at the level where I can judge another?"* and silently ask for that person's forgiveness and send them love.

Know that you are them, and they are you, and we are all holograms of Infinite Spirit. Understand that every action you take, and every word you say today will have an effect on everyone else around you, and probably on the planet as well. Consider that before you act and speak. *Make every action and word kind or loving.*

Next time you are in a group, practice this by being present to the arguments, disagreements and differences, yet stay composed, *accept the members as they are* - send them loving zoots!

When you throw something out of the car window or litter anywhere - you are separating yourself from the world. *Everything you do has an effect* - even what you say to yourself! Make sure that you have only a beneficial effect on everyone and everything today (and every day!)

Try to have some sense of that connection between you and all living things. Look at every plant and flower you pass today and thank it for giving you oxygen! Appreciate the rocks and any nature you may find around you.

It is a little harder in a concrete jungle of rushing, tense bodies, but there are still moments you can feel connected, not with the tension and stress, but *with the deep silence, inner peace and love* that is within every one of us - including ourselves!

Love your "brother". *Everyone and every thing is your "brother"!*

EQUANIMITY JOY-ERCISE 5:
PRACTICE RHYTHMS, RITUALS AND BEING RECEPTIVE

> *"Rhythm is the basis of life, not steady forward progress."*
> The Kabbalah

A big day today! *Step out thi*s morning with the eyes of your heart open! Filter everything that happens to you through your heart and be receptive to what is unfolding in every situation today. Be an involved observer.

Catch yourself doing anything that would block receptivity and learning (like judging, cynicism, fear, rushing, stress, worry) and *drop to your heart to restore your receptivity.* If you notice doubt appearing, *go immediately to your heart and ask questions.*

Explore your feelings further. *Shutting down and judging are not options!* Have a sense that there are lessons for us in everything we are involved in, every day. Look for those lessons.

Be receptive to feelings of peace welling up from beneath your feet, being poured over your head, and filling your heart! *We are always being showered with love and peace but don't recognize it.* Today is the day to start receiving it and feeling it!

Make sure you are respectful of the rhythms of nature and your body. Sleep when it's dark, wake up early, and try to see more sunsets and sunrises - they are both filled with healing energies.

Eat regularly, with consciousness and peace - not in the car, racing to work! Take breaks when you're working. Find a rhythm between intense concentration and creative relaxation, and it will make your work much more effective.

Try to find a park near work or a beautiful view, or some place you can just be and absorb the life forces nature and the sun gives us. *"Be still and know the I AM."*

Spend a little time every day in the sun if you can. Create little rituals that help bring rhythm to your daily life. Have an *unwind ritual* on the way home so there is a separation between work and home. Have a *dinner ritual.* Mediate at the same time each day. Exercise each day.

I am sure you can think of many ways to restore some sense of rhythm that will *reconnect you to yourself* - and the rest of us!

EQUANIMITY JOY-ERCISE 6:
PRACTICE FINDING YOUR PURPOSE AND
DOING THE RIGHT THING

> *"Make your work to be in keeping with your purpose."*
> *Leonardo da Vinci*

Are you fulfilling your purpose in life? Are you making a contribution of which you are proud? Do you have a nagging feeling that there is something that you are meant to be doing and you're not? Are you feeling connected ?

If you don't know what your life purpose is, make it a goal or your intention to find out. Pray about it; discuss it with your family; see vocational guidance people - and search your heart - it will have the answers!

To help you identify your purpose...

- Think of all the things about which you feel strongly, care about a great deal or are passionate.
- What makes you feel this way?
- Why are they important to you?
- Are there things to which you are indifferent, numb, resentful or passively aggressive? What has happened that you feel that way?
- If you don't care about certain things, ask yourself why. Think about why *others* would care about things you are not interested in.

Apart from pursuing your purpose with passion, what can you do to change your level of enthusiasm? Be responsible and if you're aware that you are allowing others to do what you are supposed to be doing, stop! *Take charge of yourself and your life!*

You are not a victim, and you need not be helpless or hopeless. *You are an amazing spiritual being within a human body, and you need to live as that.* Let go of old stuff that is poisoning your spirit - release it and move on.

No blame, no victim, no shame - *just stand up inside and have faith and courage*, and start doing what you are supposed to be doing - or take steps in that direction. Begin your true journey in some way today.

Do the right thing today - be of the highest character, be trustworthy, honorable, and act with integrity, even if no one else is watching or will know about it. *You* will know.

EQUANIMITY JOY-ERCISE 7:
PRACTICE BEING YOUR TRUE SELF AND TRULY KNOW OTHERS

We are all like a single cell in a body – each with an important job and intricately connected to, and affecting, everything else. It's important to understand what sort of cell you are, do your allocated job, and act in harmony with every other cell - whether close to you, or trillions of cells away. Imagine the impact you have on all of them, and the impact every other cell has on you.

Spend this day suspending all opinions, judgments and ideas about other people - and yourself! Try to tap into the real you - the one in your heart that God sees, uncolored by upbringing, parents, siblings and life to date.

Dwell on (or find out) what is important to you; what you really value; what or who really excites you and makes you passionate; what or who drains you; and identify any patterns of behavior that you feel aren't the real you.

Write, *"Who am I?"* at the top of a page, and then describe who you think you are, *not what you do* but who you are. Ask your partner or best friend to do this, as well! *Try to see others today as they really are.*

Look with your true heart and see the person who is your wife, husband or partner - check to see if you are really seeing an ex-partner as you look at them, or projecting other qualities onto them, and treating them as if they were someone else. Think very carefully on this one - *feel* into it. It's often difficult to be aware that you are doing this.

How well do you know your partner? Both of you can write a list of, *"Who do I think my partner is?"* and then compare notes! Do you really know what is important to them? Do you really understand them? With time (and possibly some counseling!), you may discover a whole new person!

Maybe this project will take a little longer than a day! LOL. But today is a great start!

Epilogue

Everything always depends on *the way* in which things are done – not only what we do, but *how* we do it and more importantly, *the spirit in which we do it.* The *activity* and *results* are also important!

Pray for inspiration to do the right things, take action in the right spirit and *allow* the Divine to provide the resources needed to make a great outcome possible.

Our work is to use our gifts and talents to help and serve others where we can.

Life consists of continuously planting seeds, which develop and grow. Plant the right seeds! It's about having the right spirit, asking for the right blessings and doing the right thing!

Do the things in this book and you will be planting all the seeds for joy – they will grow and the spirit of joy will fill your life.

TA DA to you!

TO BOOK AMANDA GORE FOR AN EVENT:

To book for speaking engagements and all other enquiries email
magic@amandagore.com

CONTACT: www.amandagore.com

FOR MAGIC WANDS, ENDORPHINS, GRATITUDE GLASSES AND OTHER JOY GOODIES:

Visit the store on www.amandagore.com or www.thejoyproject.com

LOOK FOR THE APPS
on the websites

The apps extend the book into every day habit changing tools!
There are more coming as well!

FOR THE ONLINE LEARNING PROGRAM:

www.thejoyproject.com

FOR MORE BOOKS BY AMANDA:

The Gift of Gratitude

visit www.amandagore.com

VISIT AMANDA'S YOUTUBE CHANNEL:
amandagoretv

http://www.youtube.com/user/amandagoretv

"Scatter Joy"
Ralph Waldo Emerson

Joy Is An Inside Job ONLINE

Finding Joy in Everyday Life

Based on the book **Joy Is An Inside Job** this 12 part program is a unique opportunity to delve deeply into what makes us joyful and how to build it into every day. It lets you undertake your own research to drive your own learning to a "PhD" in Joy!

Gratitude | Compassion & Grace | Hope | Reverence

Generosity | Forgiveness | Energy & Vitality | Listening

Laughter | Love | Cheerful Enthusiasm | Equanimity - Inner peace

You can do it in your own time and at your own pace but at the end of it, you will have connected with other "Joy Mates" who are studying with you – <u>and</u> you will have embedded the strategies you are studying to rewire your brain for *joy!*

Find out more about the online learning program at
www.thejoyproject.com

www.joyisaninside job.com

A PICTURE VERSION OF SECRET #1 - GRATITUDE

The Gift of Gratitude by Amanda Gore and Lenore Lewis

"The Gift of Gratitude is a treasure!"

"An easy read with a great message"

"One of my favourite books!"

"...could not put it down - made me look at life differently and now starting to see the difference in my everyday life..."

"This book has a message for anyone that reads it."

"I love the way that Amanda just grabs you by the heart."

It is impossible to have a heart full of gratitude and a heart full of misery at the same time! Gratitude is the foundation step for joy... it is a proven anti-depressant, a great way to sleep better and turns relationships around!

This great little book - *The Gift of Gratitude,* is a pictorial version of Secret #1 – the foundation for joy – Gratitude. It's full of simple tips and methods to increase your "gratitude intelligence". It's a perfect gift for friends and family or your team at work... it's easy to read, pretty and actually effective!

Gratitude changes the way you look at the world!

Available with Amanda's other books at:

www.thejoyproject.com,

www.amandagore.com

www.joyisaninsidejob.com

or from Amazon for Kindle

Books to Read

Silence. Robert Sardello

The Power of Soul. Robert Sardello

Freeing The Soul From Fear. Robert Sardello

Love and The Soul. Robert Sardello

I Heard God Laughing – Poems of Hope and Joy. Daniel Ladinsky

The People Pill. Ken Wright

Unlock Your Hormones. Dr. Graeme Williams

Learned Optimism. Martin Seligman

Emotional Intelligence. Daniel Goleman

The Gift – Poems by Hafiz. Daniel Ladinsky

Dangerous Grains. Braly and Hoggan.

Linchpin. Seth Godin

Healing Lyme. Stephen Harrod Buhner

Celiac Disease – the Hidden Epidemic. Green and Jones

Gut and Psychology Syndrome. Dr Natasha McBride

The Brain That Changes Itself. Norman Doidge

Man's Search for Meaning. Victor Frankel

Turning. Claire Blatchford

Becoming. Claire Blatchford

Friend of My Heart. Claire Blatchford

Illusions. Richard Bach

The Bridge Over the River. Sigwart

The Seven Principles for Making Marriage Work. John Gottman

Sweet Deception. Dr Joseph Mercola

Aspartame Disease - An Ignored Epidemic. H.J. Roberts

Molecules of Emotion. Candace Pert

Seven Habits of Highly Effective People. Stephen Covey

Nourishing Traditions. Sally Fallon

The Heart's Code. Paul Pearsall

Dave Barry Turns 40. Dave Barry

Your Brain At Work. David Rock

The German new Medicine. Dr Hamer

Too Soon To Say Goodbye. Art Buchwald

Anatomy of An Illness. Norman Cousins

The Prayer of Jabez. Dr. Bruce Wilkinson

Silence Your Mind. Dr Ramesh Manocha

RESOURCE INFORMATION:

LYME TESTING/RESEARCH/ TREATING:

http://www.australianbiologics.com.au

http://www.cfnmedicine.com

http://lymeandcancerservices.com

http://igenex.com/Website/

http://www.lymedisease.org.au/about-lyme-disease/diagnosis/

http://www.aldf.com

http://www.klinghardtacademy.com/Lyme-Disease/

SCHOOL OF SPIRITUAL PSYCHOLOGY: For wonderful classes and books. www.spiritualschool.org

MICHAEL GRINDER: www.michaelgrinder.com : Excellent books, programs and courses on group dynamics, non verbal communication and leadership.

LARRY BYRAM: www.higheralignment.com: Excellent information about communication and many other aspects of joy.

JOHN GOTTMAN: www.gottman.com: Emeritus Professor of psychology at the University of Washington, and co-founder of The Gottman Institute.

HEARTMATH: www.heartmath.com: Interesting research on the heart; stress management programs; enhanced performance.

BYRON KATIE: www.thework.com

KATHY WARNER: My friend Kathy in the equanimity section – contact me for information about her workshops!

INFORMATION ABOUT FOODS: I found this website that was informative and appeared balanced: www.foodmatters.tv

INFORMATION ON GOOD WATER PRODUCTS AND MAGNESIUM: www.miracleproducts.com.au

FIRST WORLD PROBLEMS: http://www.youtube.com/watch?v=vN2WzQzxuoA

DR. GRAEME WILLIAMS: www.drgraemewilliams.com

DR. SHERRIL SELLMAN: ww.whatwomenmustknow.com

DR. GREG EMERSON: www.drgregemerson.com

DR WAYNE PICKSTONE: www.uniquehealthandwellness.com.au

DR LEIGH ERIN CONNEALY: http://www.cfnmedicine.com

HO'OPONOPONO: www.hooponopono.org/

THE CHEMICAL MAZE APP: http://www.chemicalmaze.com

FREE MEDITATION AUDIO: www.beyondthemind.com

GREAT NATURAL CLEANING PRODUCTS:
www.hara.com.au

Notes

Front Matter

1. From The Bridge Over the River: After-Death Communications of a Young Artist Who Died in World War 1; (Sigwart Botho Phillip August Eulenburg), translated by Joseph Wetzl; Anthroposophic Press, N.Y.)

Secret 1: Gratitude

1. From *Friend of My Heart: Meeting Christ in Everyday Life* by Claire Blatchford (1999) Lindisfare: Hudson, N.Y.
2. From *Worldly Virtues: A Catalogue of Reflections* by J. A. Gaertner (2002). Excerpted with permission of Phanes Press, imprint of Red Wheel/Weiser; www.redwheel weiser.com. To order, call 800.423.7087.
3. Susan L. Taylor, editor of *Essence* magazine and author of *In the Spirit: The Inspirational Writings of Susan L. Taylor.*
4. Rabbi Harold Kushner, author *of When Bad Things Happen to Good People and How Good Do We Have to Be?*
5. Helen Keller, author of *The Light in My Darkness*, published by Chrysalis: West Chester, Penn.
6. Playwright Bertolt Brecht, from the play *Jungle of Cities*, 1924.

Secret 2: Compassion/ Grace

1. From *The Dalai Lama: My Tibet by the Dalai Lama*; the University of California Press, (1990). Used by permission.
2. From *The Asian Journal of Thomas Merton* by Thomas Merton (1975), New York: New Directions.
3. From *The Wisdom Teachings of the Dalai Lama* by Matthew E. Bunson (1997); Used by permission of Dutton, a division of Penguin Group (USA) Inc.

Secret 3: Hope

1. From *A Long Obedience in the Same Direction: Discipleship in an Instant Society* by Eugene H. Peterson. (1998) Downers Grove, IL: InterVarsity Press. Reprinted with permission.

Secret 4: Reverence

1. From *I Heard God Laughing: Poems of Hope and Joy* by Daniel Ladinsky; Penguin. "My Brilliant Image" by Hafiz, translated by Daniel Ladinsky (1996; 2006) Reprinted with permission.
2. Don Coyhis of the Mohican Nation; president and co-founder of White Bison Inc.; www.whitebison.org; 719.548.1000. Reprinted with permission.
3. *From I Heard God Laughing: Poems of Hope and Joy*, Hafiz, translated by Daniel Ladinsky; 1996; 2006, Penguin. Reprinted with permission.

Secret 6: Forgiveness

1. From *"Some Notes on Forgiveness as an Act of Love"* by Robert Sardello; School of Spiritual Psychology E-letter," (Jan. 2002); www.spiritualschool.org

Secret 7: Energy and Vitality

1. From *The Future of Love* by Daphne Rose Kingma; (1999). Berkeley; Main Street Books. Reprinted with permission.
2. Eve Van Cauter, Professor of Medicine, University of Chicago. Reprinted with permission of the Department of Medicine, University of Chicago.
3. Dr. Sanjay R. Patel of Harvard Medical School. Quoted in an article by Rob Stein, Washington Post, October 9, 2005.

Secret 8: Listening

1. From *Practicing the Sacred Art of Listening* by Kay Lindahl; (www.sacredlistening.com) Reprinted with permission.
2. From *I Heard God Laughing: Poems of Hope and Joy* by Daniel Ladinsky; 1996; 2006, Penguin. Reprinted with permission.
3. U.S. State Department spokesman Robert McCloskey during one of his regular noon briefings during the worst days of the Vietnam War, quoted by Marvin Kalb in TV Guide, March 31, 1984.

Secret 9: Laughter

1. From *I Heard God Laughing: Poems of Hope and Joy*, Hafiz, translated by Daniel Ladinsky; 1996; 2006, Penguin. Reprinted with permission.

Secret 10: Love

1. From *Becoming: A Call to Love* by Claire Blatchford; (2004) Lindisfarne; Hudson, N.Y.

2. From *364 Days of Love* by Daphne Rose Kingma, (1992); Conari Press, Berkeley, CA: Reprinted with permission.

Secret 11: Cheerful Enthusiasm

1. From *The Bridge Over the River: After-Death Communications of a Young Artist Who Died in World War 1*; (Sigwart Botho Phillip August Eulenburg), translated by Joseph Wetzl; Anthroposophic Press, N.Y.)

2. Ibid.

Secret 12: Equanimity / Inner Peace

1. Excerpt from the Penguin anthology, *Love Poems from God*, by Daniel Ladinsky (2002). Reprinted with permission.

2. From an unpublished lecture in Bremen, Germany on Dec. 12, 1911, by Rudolf Steiner: *"Death and Immortality in the Light of Spiritual Science."*

3. From *Powers Within: Selections from the Works of Sri Arubindo and the Mother*; compiled by A. S. Dalal; published by Lotus Press.

John 4:12 No one has seen God at any time; if we love one another, God abides in us, and His love is perfected in us. 4:13 By this we know that we abide in Him and He in us, because He has given us His spirit.
John 3:14-17 We know that we have passes out of death into life, because we love the brethren. He who does not love abides in death. Everyone who hates is brother is a murderer; and you know that no murderer has eternal life abiding in him. We know love by this, that He laid down His life for us; and we ought to lay down our lives for the brethren. But whoever has the world's goods, and sees his brother in need and closes his heart against him, how does the love of God abide in him?

4. *Anyway: The Paradoxical Commandments—Finding Personal Meaning in a Crazy World* by Dr. Kent M. Keith and Spencer Johnson; (1968, 2001); Reprinted with permission.

5. *From I Heard God Laughing: Poems of Hope and Joy* by Daniel Ladinsky; 1996; 2006, Penguin. Reprinted with permission.

6. *The Power of Soul: Living the Twelve Virtues* By Robert Sardello Hampton Roads Publishing Company; Jan. 1, 2003. Reprinted with permission.

7. Gil Fronsdal - www.insightmeditationcenter.org

Summary Of
The Exercises

CHAPTER 1: GRATITUDE:

Sunday: Gratitude To God
Monday: Workplace Gratitude:
Tuesday: Home Gratitude
Wednesday: 'The Past' Gratitude
Thursday: Body Gratitude Day
Friday: Nature Gratitude
Saturday: Heart Gratitude

CHAPTER 2: COMPASSION

Sunday: Self Less Ness
Monday: Self Less Ness
Tuesday: Compassion For Your Boss, Colleagues And Customers
Wednesday: Compassion At Home
Thursday: Compassion At Home
Friday: Compassion For Your 'Enemies'
Saturday: Compassion For Yourself

CHAPTER 3: HOPE

Sunday: Hope And Faith
Monday: Find Where Hope Lives In Your Body
Tuesday: Hope For Yourself
Wednesday: Find The Fears; Move To Hope
Thursday: Hopeful Expectations
Friday: Tackle Something Difficult With Hope
Saturday: Difference Between Hop-Ing And Hope-Full

CHAPTER 8: LISTENING

Sunday: Listen To God
Monday: Listen With Your Heart For Feelings – Let People Feel Safe
With You
Tuesday: Why Am I Battering Myself?
Wednesday: Listen To Your Heart
Thursday: Listen With Discernment: Speak Only Good
Friday: Ask Questions
Saturday: Disguises That Words Take On

CHAPTER 9: LAUGHTER

Sunday: Smile And Stop Taking Your Self So Seriously!
Monday: Remember All The Funny Times In Your Life
Tuesday: Find Photos Of As Many Funny Times As You Can
Wednesday: Watch The Movie That Makes You Laugh Out Loud
Thursday: Laugh, And Help Others Laugh.
Friday: Make A Laughter Journal And Read Funny 'Stuff'
Saturday: Turn Around Tough Memories With Laughter

CHAPTER 10: LOVE

Sunday: Love God
Monday: Be A Love Ray-Diator! Think Only Loving Thoughts
Tuesday: Loving Actions
Wednesday: Love Your Life
Thursday: Give Everyone Ta Da's
Friday: Love Yourself
Saturday: Hold People In Your Heart

CHAPTER 11: CHEERFUL ENTHUSIASM

Sunday: Look For The Miracles
Monday: Choose Your Moods
Tuesday: Face All Your Difficulties With Cheerfulness
Wednesday: Be Passionate About Being Enthusiastic
Thursday: Smile All Day – At Everyone!
Friday: Always Think With A Joyful Heart That Things Will Steadily
Improve
Saturday: Find Your Work

CHAPTER 12: EQUANIMITY

Sunday: Peace, Pure Joy And Hear God's Laughter
Monday: Feel Composed And Peaceful In All Situations
Tuesday: Knowing The Spiritual World Is Here, Now
Wednesday: Brotherly Love
Thursday: Rhythms, Rituals And Being Receptive
Friday: Find Your Purpose; Do The Right Thing.
Saturday: See Yourself And Others For Whom You Really Are!

F.A.R.C.

Is my formula for change; for rewiring the brain!
It stands for Focus, Awareness and attention; Repetition and Celebration!

WHO IS AMANDA GORE?

She is the CEO of The Joy Project, a speaker and very blessed person!

Her background in physical therapy, psychology, neurolinguistics, ergonomics, and group dynamics has created a unique platform for her motivational speaking career.

For 25 years Amanda has been inspiring groups worldwide with humor, honesty and her simple, effective philosophies, some of which you can read about in this book!

WHO IS LENORE LEWIS

Lenore Lewis is the inspiration behind this book and The Joy Project.

Amanda's mother co "wrote" this book via "downloads"!

She was an extraordinary, beautiful, courageous, very joyful woman who was loved and admired by many – and IS an incredible spirit!

For more information or to book Amanda to speak visit

www.amandagore.com or www.thejoyproject.com